Community by Design

NEW URBANISM FOR SUBURBS AND SMALL COMMUNITIES

Kenneth B. Hall, Jr.
Gerald A. Porterfield

WITHDRAWN

McGraw-Hill

New York   San Francisco   Washington, D.C.   Auckland   Bogotá
Caracas   Lisbon   London   Madrid   Mexico City   Milan
Montreal   New Delhi   San Juan   Singapore
Sydney   Tokyo   Toronto

Library of Congress Cataloging-in-Publication Data
Hall, Kenneth B.
    Community by design : new urbanism for suburbs and small communities / Kenneth
B. Hall, Jr., Gerald A. Porterfield.
        p. cm.
    Rev. ed. of: A concise guide to community planning / Gerald A. Porterfield, Kenneth B.
Hall, Jr. c1995.
    Includes bibliographical references and index.
    ISBN 0-07-134523-X
    1. City planning—United States. 2. Regional planning—United States. 3. Community
development—United States. I. Porterfield, Gerald A. II. Porterfield, Gerald A. Concise
guide to community planning. III. Title.

HT167.H29   2001
307.1'216'0973—dc21

00-050049

McGraw-Hill

A Division of The McGraw-Hill Companies

Portions of this book appeared in *A Concise Guide to Community Planning* by Gerald A. Porterfield and
Kenneth B. Hall, Jr. (McGraw-Hill, 1995).

    2 3 4 5 6 7 8 9 0 DOC/DOC 0 7 6 5 4 3 2

ISBN 0-07-134523-X

*The sponsoring editor for this book was Wendy Lochner and the production supervisor was
Pamela A. Pelton. It was set in Matt Antique by North Market Street Graphics.*

Printed and bound by R. R. Donnelley & Sons Company.

This book was printed on recycled, acid-free paper
containing a minimum of 50% recycled, de-inked fiber.

McGraw-Hill books are available at special quantity discounts to use as premiums and sales promotions,
or for use in corporate training programs. For more information, please write to the Director of Special
Sales, Professional Publishing, McGraw-Hill, Two Penn Plaza, New York, NY 10121-2298. Or contact
your local bookstore.

Contents

Chapter 5   What Is the Framework of Community?   79

PART 2
Putting It All Together

Chapter 6   Where Would You Rather Live?   121

Preface

Community by Design has evolved from our earlier book, *A Concise Guide to Community Planning*, portions of which have been updated, expanded, and incorporated here. You will find many new graphics and photos plus a number of elements to make this book more reader-friendly: icons to help you quickly identify components that are repeated throughout; Project Profiles (case studies that will reinforce the practicality of our recommendations); an At-a-Glance feature at the beginning of each chapter to give you a preview of what will be covered; and a summary at the end of each chapter to recap its most important points.

The book is separated into two parts. Part 1, Parts of the Puzzle, encompasses Chapters 1 through 5. Here we discuss the various elements that go into community planning, such as how we define it and then what the process is for creating it. Part 2, Put It All Together, contains Chapters 6 through 11, in which we discuss the elements of community and how they can be assembled to make places we would all be proud to call home. It is here in these chapters that we illustrate the way conventional suburban development typically occurs, the problems this creates, and reasonable alternatives, based on principles of traditional neighborhood designs, that have been used through most of our nation's history.

The graphic sketches and photographs are used as tools for understanding the difference between the two approaches rather than as examples of the best and worst way to do things. To further emphasize the comparison, we will present several Project Profiles highlighting the work of several prominent firms in the field of community design to show you that the recommendations we suggest are more than theoretical discussions; they are effective design solutions that deserve your careful consideration. By putting this information at your fingertips, we hope that this text will become a true handbook for anyone who wants to participate in the community design process. The guidelines we provide should help you develop a critical eye not only in recognizing the problems in your own communities, but more important, in recognizing what you can do to change them. Anyone can identify the problems with the way things have been done in the past, but to pursue excellence in problem solving is a more prized calling.

What the Icons Mean

There are three icons used to highlight certain items in the text. This is what they mean:

- The Notes icon represents a particular point that needs to be emphasized. It may be the definition of a word or a special concept you may find helpful at some later date.

- The Magnifying Glass represents something that you may want to look into further. For instance, we may recommend a book to read or a website to check out.

- The Lightbulb signals that an excerpt from the Charter of the Congress of New Urbanism has been inserted. The Congress of New Urbanism is "a broad-based association of public and private sector leaders, community activists, and multidisciplinary professionals who are committed to reestablishing the relationship between the art of building and the making of community through citizen-based participatory planning and design."[1]

Who Should Read This Book?

Let's face it. The reason suburbia exists in its current form is that land development is commodity-driven. Developers buy land cheap, improve it by building houses, shopping centers, or office parks on it, and then sell it. They build for a familiar market; lending institutions finance a product with a reliable rate of return; customers buy what they can afford. Everybody's happy. Except that we are all tiring of the bland architecture, the seas of asphalt, the traffic lights and taillights, the long lines at our favorite big-box retailer.

Granted, the suburbs have allowed families to own homes who may otherwise be priced out of the market in many metropolitan areas. In the Washington, D.C., area for example, the high cost of land and homes has forced many of those who work inside the Beltway to move farther and farther out into the more rural areas of Virginia and Maryland just to afford a reasonably sized home. But, the long commutes and increasing traffic volumes have increased the stress on individuals and families and caused an explosion of growth in many towns and hamlets that have neither the resources nor expertise to cope with these modern-day problems.

Private developers have hired planning professionals such as architects, landscape architects, engineers, and land surveyors to produce plans and specifications to submit to municipal review boards and commissions in order to build tract houses, shopping centers, golf courses, and office parks. The zoning regulations have become so standardized and full of legal language that our communities all look alike. Zoning, like fast-food franchises, has allowed the lowest common denominator to become the norm, all the while segregating us into single-use pods and a tangle of cul-de-sacs. Today, more and more professionals, politicians, and citizens are taking an active role to ensure that their communities are the product of real vision. This book is for them—and for those who are not yet part of the process but who want to know what it's all about. They may want to understand the terms, to be able to talk about it with their friends, or just to understand what all the fuss is about.

Acknowledgments

Creating this book required the help and cooperation of several people. At Hanbury Evans Newill Vlattas: thanks to Beth Bennet for giving me the idea for the icons, to Mike Taylor for creating them, and to Hillary "the graphics queen" Spencer for help in figuring out how the graphics should work for the Project Profiles. Thanks also to Wesley Page from HENV for contributing some great artwork and for the aerial photos of the sea of tile roofs. Special thanks to Joe Kohl at Dover Kohl & Partners, to Rich McLaughlin at the Town Planning Collaborative, and to Carson Looney, Tobey Israel, Beth Bozeman, and Ann Brazda at Looney Ricks Kiss for putting together awesome project packages for the Project Profiles section of the book. Thanks to Shelley Potichia at the Congress for New Urbanism for letting us include portions of the Congress Charter. Thanks to Wendy Lochner, our editor at McGraw-Hill, who believed that *Community by Design* would be a great book and for being patient with us while we got it done. Last but certainly not least, deep gratitude to the Hall family, who wondered if I would ever be finished—specifically to Susan, who served as proofreader and general punctuation czar.

Introduction

It is safe to say that in the latter half of the twentieth century we abandoned the art of community design in America that took nearly 450 years to develop. From the mid-1500s to the mid-1940s, the design concepts that shaped American towns were based on a vision, a preconceived notion of the kind of place that would be the center of community life. Beginning with *The Laws of the Indies,* which guided the Spanish, and *The Ordering of Towns,* which gave us the New England town model, community design has evolved and improved—sometimes as the result of a private citizen's grand idea (e.g., William Penn's plan for the city of Philadelphia), sometimes as the result of government sponsorship (e.g., Greenbelt town movement).

As the nation grew and the industrial revolution brought the huddled masses to these shores, so came the utopian designs of the social reformers. Ebenezer Howard's Garden City concept, the industrialist's new town model, and the romantic suburb designs were embraced and adapted to the Northeast and the Mid-west. The ebb and flow of ideas such as these has always been born of a vision of how the land

The Metropolis has a necessary and fragile relationship to its agrarian hinterland and natural landscapes. The relationship is environmental, economic and cultural. Farmland and nature are as important to the metropolis as the garden is to the house.

Charter of the Congress for New Urbanism

should be shaped and the social order it would create. This visionary pursuit, however, changed after World War II. The postwar period was a time of new optimism about America's future. After all, we had just won the big war and pulled the nation and the rest of the world out of the Great Depression. The economy was booming and Americans were ready for peace and prosperity. During this time it became possible for great numbers of people to move away from the cities toward a less crowded lifestyle at the urban fringe. Many were able to realize their dream of owning a home and a bit of lawn in the suburbs where land was plentiful, cheap, and void of the ecological issues we struggle with today. This movement, coupled with such government-sponsored programs as the Veterans' Administration and Federal Housing Authority's guaranteed home mortgage programs and the expanding interstate highway system, created a high demand for housing and for new communities in which to build them. But the heritage of community design that had reached its zenith prior to the Great Depression was cast aside in favor of the more expedient suburban residential neighborhoods and the strip commercial development that accompanies it.

The demand for low density and privacy resulted in the consumption of large tracts of land at the expense of the environment and the social structure of the community at large. Unfocused planning and laissez-faire attitudes between burgeoning municipalities and land developers resulted in the chaotic situation we now refer to as *sprawl*. The proliferation of the automobile compounded this situation by increasing the distances that could be easily traversed as our society pursued the basic requirements of daily life: employment, food, shelter, and recreation.

The baby boomers born in this era who were responsible for the increase in social consciousness of the 1960s and 1970s have matured and, as today's consumers, are demanding a higher standard of design for the communities in which they live. It is no longer enough to own one's own home; the community in which it is located must have a unique character, a sense of place, and be environmentally responsible. But how can the suburban sprawl of unchecked and undirected development be replaced by development that is not only born of a vision but is economically feasible, marketable, and environmentally and socially responsible? Accommodating growth without losing the sense of community identity we all crave demands more effective design solutions.

To complicate matters further, environmental concerns have reached a fever pitch in public awareness, not only in this

Figure I.1 The result of laissez-faire attitudes.

country but the world over. The debate over whether global warming is actually occurring, what periodic thinning of the ozone layer really means, what the permissible measurement of particulates is for acceptable water and air quality, as well as our own national considerations regarding wetlands, habitat preservation, old-growth forest protection, and metropolitan growth controls will be formidable challenges to designers, planners, and citizens well into the foreseeable future.

In their day, garden cities, new towns, and romantic suburbs were each espoused as exemplary patterns for new growth and development. More recently, planned unit developments (PUDs) were created, attempting to provide a mixed-use community that also preserved open space for public recreation and environmentally sensitive areas and wildlife habitat. But requiring large greenfield sites to accommodate a variety of housing types and commercial activities meant they were usually situated on the periphery of urbanized areas. In addition, the majority of these types of developments provided at best only minimal opportunities for employment. Long commutes

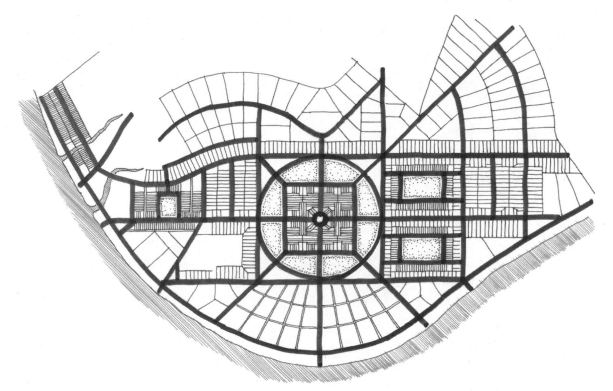

Sketch I.1 Hygeia, Kentucky, 1827.

required residents to endure increasing traffic congestion, and the subsequent abandonment of the residential area during working hours relegated them to bedroom-community status. In effect, they were sprawl.

Today, the concepts embodied in the neotraditionalist villages, otherwise known as *traditional neighborhood developments* (TNDs), represent the design principles that were predominant before World War II. A TND is sized so that most of its residents are within a five-minute walk of its center. The TND center often accommodates places to shop, work, and usually a public square for community gathering and passive recreation. In many TNDs, schools and churches are often found at the center or in close proximity to it. The goal of the TND is to reduce the need for the automobile by centralizing life's necessities within walking distance of housing. The reduced scale of these neighborhoods, reminiscent of the late nineteenth and early twentieth century, addresses the newly kindled desire to escape the gridlock of crowded highways and return to a simpler lifestyle. It seeks to provide the consumer an alternative to typical suburbia by increasing opportunities

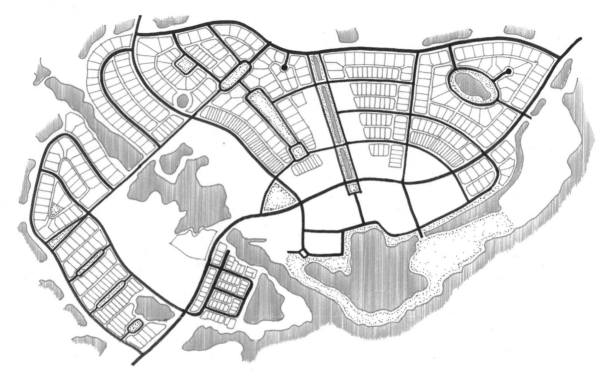

Sketch I.2 Celebration, Florida, 1998.

for interaction between neighbors that epitomizes the concept of community.

As we explore these issues in the coming pages, we intend to provide an efficient and sensitive framework for growth for our existing towns and cities. Continuing down the conventional suburban development road is not an option. Urban planners and public officials must redefine growth parameters, not only in the evolving urban centers of the future, but in the metropolitan centers of today. The continuing struggle between pro-growth and no-growth advocates underlines this need. Sense of place, the heart and soul of community character and identity, can be achieved only through deliberate action in the planning process. True communities do not just occur; they are born of a vision.

Because of the increased awareness of environmental issues and the negative economic ramifications of uncontrolled growth, professional rivalry and political expediency have no place in this process. If we want to effect lasting changes in our towns and cities, it is everyone's responsibility, not just that of the design professionals. And community design is not the domain of a single professional group; it has to be a cooperative effort between the public and private sectors if we really want to start making better places to live.

The rudimentary tools for this task are already in place in the form of an existing system of site plan, subdivision, and zoning regulations. However, this system's flaws lie in the fact that it offers guidelines for solutions that are only minimally acceptable rather than requiring the very best. Indeed, these regulations, in conjunction with the explosion of national commercial chain stores, have in essence created *franchised* cities and towns across America. The essential character of many communities has been lost, making it almost impossible to distinguish one region of the country from another.

If we take positive steps now to establish a framework, we can achieve the changes that are necessary to bring about a stronger sense of community and develop a broader vision than that which is evident in parcel-by-parcel growth. By definition, growth in and of itself is good, as it usually signifies economic vitality and financial health. Where effective master plans for growth are implemented, balanced economic expansion is more apt to be realized, assuring a larger tax base from which the community as a whole benefits. Where no vision for growth exists, sprawl results.

We must be proactive in effecting change, rather than merely reacting to these issues as they emerge. The diversity of housing options, shopping and employment opportunities, recreation and open space, as well as the various forms of transportation, are the building blocks of our communities. In themselves they do not solely embody the image of the community, but in combination they can reflect either balanced, sensitive forethought or an undefined built environment with missed opportunities. It is to this task that we must attend if growth is to be responsible.

Our goal, then, is to provide the reader with an easy-to-comprehend handbook that can be used on a daily basis for an overview of land development issues as well as practical design strategies. Each chapter provides realistic approaches to community design that will take the user step-by-step through the design process. This is not intended to be the last word on the subject, but should be used as a supplement to the many reference works already in publication. The theory, practical applications, and examples provide a format that can be used by anyone—the design professional as a tool for understanding community design or the interested bystander who generally wants to know what it is all about. Although planning policy varies throughout the country, this book will attempt to provide practical design solutions to common problems faced by all.

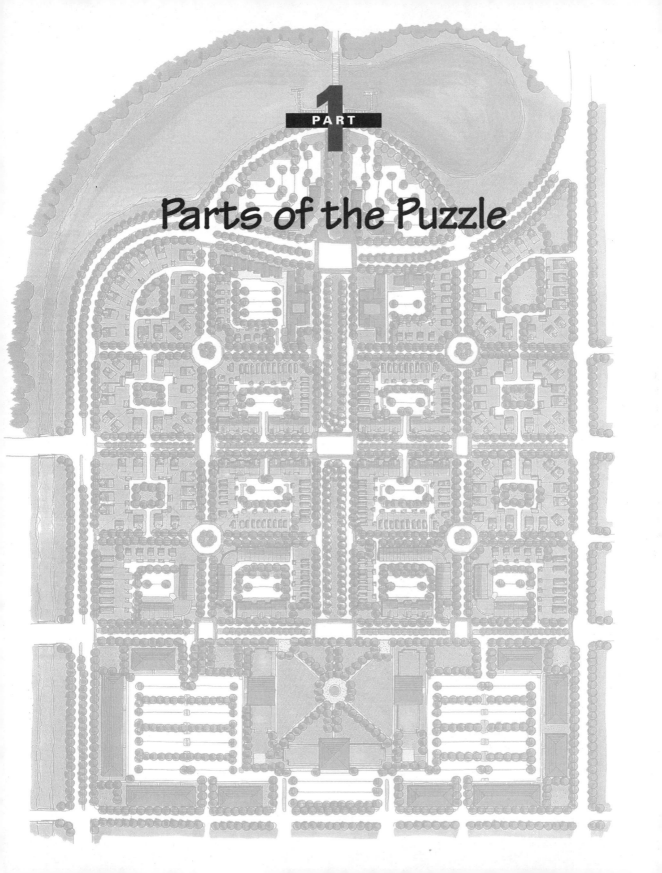

Parts of the Puzzle

What Is Community Design, Anyway?

At a Glance

- ❖ Understanding what community design is all about

- ❖ Looking at the historical patterns in order to understand their relevance for today

- ❖ Defining community in terms we can all understand

- ❖ Recognizing the importance of paths, edges, districts, nodes, and landmarks

- ❖ Identifying the place-making tools of the community designer

Community design is the art of making sustainable living places that both thrive and adapt to people's needs for shelter, livelihood, commerce, recreation, and social order. The nature of community design suggests some predetermined intention rather than haphazard coincidence. But it is more than the adherence to a set of rules for development or a means for implementing the political will of government. It is the merging of what we know about ourselves with what we know about our neighbors when we chose to live in proximity to one another. It is about independence and dependency. It is about architecture and landscape. It is about understanding and building on what we know—the good as well as the bad. It is about creating a better place to live.

In the nation's infancy, communities had to be self-sustaining defensive outposts. This often required people to live in close proximity within a walled enclosure with agricultural fields around the perimeter. We see this form in the Spanish mission towns of the desert Southwest. The design rules for such towns were set out in the Spanish Royal Ordinances known as *The Laws of the Indes,* which described a

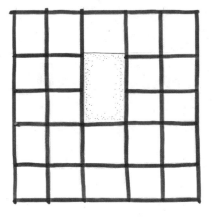

Sketch 1.1 Laws of the Indes Town Plan.

self-sustaining community containing a grid of streets with a rectangular plaza, or commons, at its center. Houses and shops lined opposite sides of the plaza, with the mission church standing at one end and government buildings at the other. The outlying agricultural fields and common pastures provided sustenance and served as the buffer between the town center and the wilderness beyond.[1]

The English settlers of the Northeast had a similar archetype. The medieval *landschaft* (landscape) model with its concentric agricultural fields and common pastures surrounding a group of houses clustered around some type of religious icon or talisman was the antecedent of many of their home villages and hamlets. It is not surprising that the New England town model eventually reflected this heritage. To the Puritans the church meetinghouse was the literal center of community life; the commons, where civic assemblies, militia training, and livestock collection occurred, was adjacent to it along with the town hall, country store, and schoolhouse. Their homes were in loose proximity to the meetinghouse, and all roads were intended to radiate from it.[2]

As colonial towns flourished and the threat of hostile Indian attack abated, so did the predominance of the fortress mentality. When the regular street grid was introduced by William Penn in his design for Philadelphia in 1683, it established a new pattern for town design, one that could easily sustain growth. As the nation flourished and pioneers moved west, the frontier towns were given general form within the Land Ordinance of 1785, which established the uniform size for townships of six square miles.[3] As the nation grew, so did the vision for the design of its towns and cities. New ideas such as the City Beautiful movement were inspired by the 1893 World's Columbian Exposition, and the Garden City movement was inspired by social reformer Ebenezer Howard's 1898 book, *Tomorrow: The Peaceful Path to Real Reform.* From the late nineteenth through the midtwentieth century numerous well-planned towns and suburbs were built based on these and other innovative and place-making concepts. However, during the last

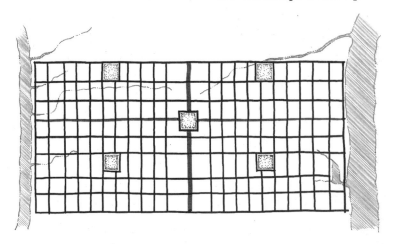

Sketch 1.2 Philadelphia town plan, 1683.

half century the nation has rushed to growth with no clear vision for the product it would produce. The art of city planning was replaced by a preoccupation with parcel plan reviews that focus myopically on the minutiae of detail rather than on how to accommodate growth effectively to make better places for people to live. Town building all but disappeared during this time, with both professionals and average citizens failing to recognize the product of this policy—or perhaps they just became powerless to prevent it within the criteria that had been established. Either way, we must reassess this process and again begin to think of our communities as living organisms that must sustain themselves. We must realize that communities need to adapt and grow because they are guided by a predetermined vision rather than as a result of a set of mandated minimums.

The development and redevelopment of towns and cities should respect historical patterns, precedents, and boundaries.

Charter of the Congress of New Urbanism

Why Design Community?

Communities thrive because they have a reason for being. This reason for being is not something that has been erroneously contrived but rather is a response to some external force or desire from the people who live there. When the reason to exist endures, a community can change and adapt to the societal evolution that inevitably occurs, whether it is the industrial revolution or the information revolution. Regardless of their founders' reasons for creating them, the great places (e.g., cities, communities) of the world have survived because they fulfill the commercial, social, and psychological needs of their citizens. The character and identity for which they are well known have developed as a direct response to their citizens' needs for order and sense of place. The success of these places is due in large part to the trial-and-error method of the forbears of community and city planning as they refined the best components of each place while discarding the unsuccessful, hapless ones that failed to serve their intended purpose. That which remains is more than a testimony to their ingenuity—it reveals the present stage of the place's continuing evolutionary process of development.

Today, technology allows us to change the form of our cities and communities with such speed that the incremental changes which once occurred over the course of centuries now can be completed in only a matter of decades. The patterns of growth that led to the development of cities such as Charleston, South Carolina, or Savannah, Georgia, can be re-created, for good or

Figures 1.1, 1.2, 1.3 **Which pattern of growth has produced a better product?**

ill, in a matter of a few short years, as in Celebration, Florida, or Harbor Town in Memphis, Tennessee. As a case in point, Charleston has survived earthquakes, fires, hurricanes, wars, and economic upheaval, yet it endures as a livable city with much appeal for its citizens and the many tourists who visit it every year. The allure of the historic district, with its crowded streets, shops, and gardens, requires that we take a long look at a method of design that has been abandoned in favor of more modern theories. In fact, a place like Charleston could probably not even be built under one of today's standardized zoning regulations.

The original development of the suburbs as a response to the mass exodus from the crowded conditions of the urban core embodied the principles of Ebenezer Howard's Garden City movement. Howard's optimum living environment consisted of the culture and services of the city combined with the soothing environs of the trees and ponds of the countryside. Modern community planners interpret this ethic in terms of quality-of-life issues, livable space, sense of place, identity, and familiarity.

Contrast this with the development of Tyson's Corner, Virginia, one of the largest metropolitan areas in the United States. Originally a suburb of Washington, D.C., it is now a bustling commercial center for 8 to 10 hours a day, five days a week and is primarily a sterile sequence of uninhabited spaces the rest of the time. Commuter traffic jams during rush hours at both dawn and sunset see people coming from and escaping to the more humane confines of familiarity and pedestrian scale. However, the consequences of this daily ritual have placed enormous stresses on the small outlying towns and hamlets. The resulting problems include overcrowding and increased costs of development, snarled highways, skyrocketing land costs, increasing taxes, and steadily increasing costs for services and maintenance that are engulfing the familiarity and scale that were the reason for moving out in the first place.

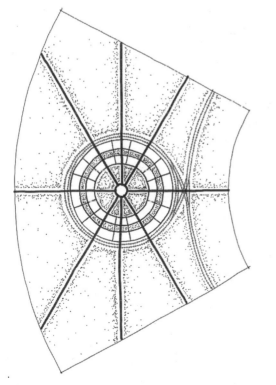
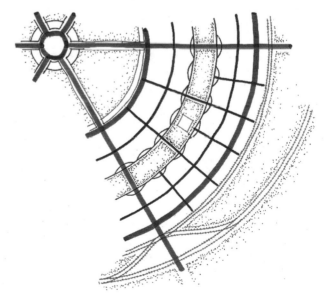

Sketch 1.3 Garden City Plan, 1898.

The wisdom of the ages that continues to make Charleston a thriving, walkable, downtown community somehow escaped the attention of the planners of Tyson's Corner and a myriad of other American cities and suburbs. The problem? We have too long mistaken aggregation for community and curb appeal for sense of place.

Community, in Terms We Can All Understand

Community has a variety of connotations, but first let's clear up a few misconceptions about it. Community is not a random accumulation of parts or sections loosely tied together by roads and waterways. Nor is it the homogenous glut of single-use interchangeable pods containing shopping centers, office buildings, housing, and open spaces that can be found without much effort in many American metropolitan areas. The result of this approach is that Orlando resembles Oshkosh, which resembles Oakland, which even resembles Ottawa—and the list goes on.

Community must also not be thought of as an alliance of special-interest groups all clamoring for attention and demanding their concerns be addressed. The divisiveness of this concept is the antithesis of community.

According to *Merriam-Webster's Collegiate Dictionary,* tenth edition, *community* is "an interacting population of various kinds of individuals (as species) in a common location" or "a group of people with a common characteristic or interest living together within a larger society."[4] Additionally, it can mean the area in which a population lives and may be identified with a way of life, such as a farming or fishing community, steel town, college or university town. A community may be known for some specific trait—innovation, ingenuity, determination, or traditional values and morality (as in the Amish communities of Pennsylvania). The term *community* also suggests a certain amount of interdependence, sometimes out of necessity, as during the colonial period when settlers in the New World banded together for mutual protection and social support.

In their book, *City Lights: An Introduction to Urban Studies,* E. Barbara Philips and Richard T. Legates argue that community has no agreed-upon meaning but that it usually refers to either (1) a group sharing a physical space, (2) a group sharing a common trait, or (3) a group bound together by shared iden-

Figures 1.4, 1.5 Which place says *neighborhood*?

tity and common culture and typified by a high degree of social cohesion.[5] If we are to use these definitions as a criteria for judging community, most of the post–World War II suburbs would probably not pass the test.

In all fairness, however, most of these areas to some degree do exhibit the more limited qualities of neighborhood. Again, for our purposes here, let's quote *Webster's*. It defines *neighborhood* as "a section lived in by neighbors and usually having distinguishable characteristics."[6] Well, in our market-oriented society the term *distinguishable characteristics* has been reduced to *product type,* and *neighbors* means *target market.* Much like a centrifuge, the frenzied growth since the 1940s has served to separate and distill the various segments of society into increasingly thinner bands or cross sections of socioeconomically similar peoples, placing them in residential areas of practically indistinguishable housing. The result of this lack of order, organization, and sense of place is that community as we have defined it has in a large part been lost.

Community as a concept can be interpreted as a sense of belonging, a way of life, and diversity with a common purpose. In modern times, technology has made the compact community unnecessary in the purely physical sense, and our resultant mobility has eroded our spiritual and emotional connection to our civic places. This emotional disassociation has allowed us to raze, in a wholesale manner, entire sections of our cities and communities in the name of redevelopment, leading to further psychic distress. All the while, we are creating acres and acres of new housing and shopping centers blithely named Rolling Meadows Estates or Foxhound Forest or Avalon Acres.

In the rush to accommodate demographic lurches, subdivision layout has been substituted for community design and shopping center trips for social interaction. In other words, community planners have been *reacting* to the frenzied pace of development, not managing or directing it. To a large extent, the talent of community planning has atrophied through disuse. We must begin again to think of our communities in terms of the human scale rather than the automobile scale. Attention to the time-distance relationship between our housing, employment, shopping, and recreation areas is critical if we are to achieve any realistic sense of community. Our cities and communities need to be of a finer texture, allowing more opportunity for interaction between our diverse peoples and thus enhancing our understanding of one another by identifying and focusing on the commonalities between us. Community, therefore, is belonging; community is a common purpose.

Community planners need to interpret their heritage and learn to apply it to the task of creating and re-creating the communities of today. George Tobey, in his book, *A History of Landscape Architecture: The Relationship of People to Environment,* says we need to establish goals that guide our planning efforts. He suggests that the values, habits, and objectives of the community's citizens must be addressed if community is to be achieved. From the physical standpoint, he suggests that good communities should adequately provide the means for moving goods, people, and information while allowing for the maximum freedom of choice in interaction between residents while providing for their health, safety, and comfort. He further states that good communities are adaptable to future modification because their image is maintained as a unified whole.[7] To these, other goals may be added that are tailored to a community's specific circumstances. The list is flexible and may change, but the end result should be the same: a methodology of workable parameters from which to approach the healthy growth of our communities.

What's the next step? Putting the goals into action in the design process. But to understand how this is accomplished we need to know what tools are used in community design. These tools are the building blocks that help us understand the subtle nuances of community form.

The Building Blocks of Community Design

For the esoteric nature of community to be realized, practical forms must be given to it. From a physical standpoint, the components apparent in successful communities can be inferred from Kevin Lynch's views in his book, *The Image of the City*. To Lynch, paths, edges, districts, nodes, and landmarks are the elements that give form to cities by evoking an image which is recognized, be it consciously or subconsciously.[8]

Paths, or corridors of movement, are the predominant form-giving element within a community and include walkways, streets, transit lines, canals, railroads, and interstate highways. They are the lifelines along which the majority of activity takes place and adjacent to which lie all the functions a community depends on: government, industry, commerce, and housing. In true communities there are networks of paths for automobiles, pedestrians, bicyclists, mass transit, and wildlife. Automobiles are not given priority over every other user. Street design anticipates a variety of users and attempts to create a balanced environment. Such terms as *boulevard, avenue, street, close, alley,* and *lane* connote a street design philosophy that when implemented, disperses traffic as evenly as possible, optimizing opportunities for citizens to choose the best mode and route of travel.

In the conventional suburban environment, paths are primarily designed for the automobile and seldom favor the

Metropolitan regions are finite with geographic boundaries derived from topography, watersheds, coastlines, farmlands, regional parks, and river basins. The metropolis is made of multiple centers that are cities, towns, and villages each with its own identifiable center and edges.

Charter of the Congress of New Urbanism

Figure 1.6 Path.

pedestrian. They are referred to by such terms as, *cul-de-sac, local street, collector,* and *arterial.* They are designed to accommodate faster and faster traffic at higher and higher volumes resulting in wider and wider streets. Traffic is concentrated on a few primary corridors, thus making gridlock inevitable. Where pedestrian paths are provided, they are primarily incidental. Sidewalks in subdivisions are viewed by developers as a burdensome extravagance. If walking paths are provided, they are usually limited to recreational areas.

Figure 1.7 Edge.

Edges are linear elements that are the boundaries between two kinds of districts. While not as dominant as paths, they are perceived as strong organizing elements. Edges are also transitions between two elements. They are lively, positive places or shared open spaces. They could be paths such as landscaped boulevards, or they could be creeks, farmland, or forest. In a regional application, a waterfront, a mountain range, and the boundaries between a floodplain and higher ground all constitute strong edges. They can be solid and impenetrable, resulting in abrupt differences from one side to the other, as an edge of a marsh, or they can be diffused and unfocused, as in the edge created by the limits of the urban services boundary of a municipality (sanitary sewer lines, water mains, etc.).

In the suburban environment there are few recognizable edges. This is one of the reasons suburbia is referred to as *sprawl.* Suburban edges are less perceptible. They tend to be characterized by a change in land use, sometimes signaled by berms, landscape buffers, privacy fences, and

Figure 1.8 District.

walls. If you're lucky, there may be a sign that tells you that you just crossed over a municipal boundary, but the letters may be too small to read at 45 mph.

Districts are areas that can be entered. You know when you get there. Buildings or structures within a district share certain recognizable commonalities and characteristics. Greenwich Village in New York City, the Mission District in San Francisco, and the French Quarter in New Orleans all exhibit separate and distinct scale, texture, and structural elements to the degree that they are easily perceived as a place. People use districts to help them mentally organize the layout of a city or town and to aid them in reducing a town or city of overwhelming scale to one that can be more easily managed. Districts exhibit a certain theme or visual clarity that evokes a distinct identity, such as a waterfront warehousing area, a downtown financial center, or a gentrified upscale neighborhood.

In suburbia, there are no districts in the traditional sense. There is zoning, but you can't really see that unless you look at a zoning map. Granted, you can tell when you enter into an office park or when you drive down a seemingly unending boulevard with used-car lot after strip commercial center after big-box retail. This lack of district identification probably contributes to the angst suburbanites express in letters to the editor and on radio call-in talk shows when yet another residential subdivision is proposed at its growth boundary.

Nodes are specific points in a community that have a name/place recognition value. They are points to and from which people travel, and very often they serve as the center or core of a district. Nodes are closely associated with paths and thus can also be found at the transition points between districts. Piccadilly Square, Times Square, and the Grand Mall in Washington, D.C., are all junctions of paths and exhibit the characteristics of nodes. Another important characteristic of nodes is that they are usually thematic in nature. Clusters of like uses tend to result in a discernable sense of association: again, Times Square and 42nd Street in New York for its theaters, the Grand Mall in Washington, D.C., for its government buildings and museums, and almost any seaside resort for its T-shirt shops.

In suburbia there are few if any nodes. Can you think of any? The intersection of two 8-lane divided boulevards with a traffic count in the hundreds per hour doesn't count. I suppose that shopping malls are nodes of a sort. They do concentrate numbers of retail outlets under one roof and offer junior high and high school kids a place to see and be seen on Friday night, but they suffer from a real sense of place and don't enrich the societal fabric of the community.

Landmarks are very similar to nodes, but are usually perceived as a single element, either structural or natural. They are the reference points used by all in navigating a path through the community, and they usually take the form of great public spaces, artwork, or a significant building. Landmarks usually contrast greatly with the background in which they are perceived, which enhances their visual importance in the landscape as beacons or reference points. They evoke a feeling of familiarity with a particular area and help to establish an identity for it. The Eiffel Tower, the Gateway Arch in St. Louis, and Telegraph Hill in San Francisco are all fine examples of landmarks.

In suburbia, landmarks are mundane visual reference points used to give directions to lost motorists: "Make a left at the second traffic signal, go 'til you see the elementary school, make a right, go past the fire station. . . . When you

Figure 1.9 Landmark.

see the water tower, take your next left and you're there."
Gives you goose bumps, doesn't it?

Even though Lynch spoke of these elements as the building blocks of cities, we feel that they are universal and relevant at the community scale as well. In other words, good communities, like good cities, will possess the same physical elements. In suburbia many of these elements are absent or are at least practically imperceptible.

In the past, these five basic elements were used through trial and error to create the memorable human places of habitation throughout the world. Change occurred slowly, almost imperceptibly during the life span of the average person. Good city and community design was rewarded with active use, embellishment, and longevity, whereas poor examples were reworked, eliminated, or abandoned. What has remained is a cumulative history of the best parts of city and community design.

The Tools of the Community Designer

Now that we have identified the elements of community, let's discuss how they are combined and organized in order to create better communities. First, we must recognize that they are the methods with which the viewer defines and orients him- or herself within a given space. Also, we must be cognizant that a well-designed space (or, for that matter, a community) must by definition exhibit the same principles of design that any true work of art exhibits: primarily harmony, gradation, contrast, and unity. While all successful works of fine art maintain these principles, they are created by artists who use the elements of line, direction, shape, size, texture, value, and color to organize the canvas into a perceptible image. In the same way, the community planner uses a distinct but uniquely dissimilar palette of spacial organizing elements, including axial design, hierarchy, transition elements, dominant features, and sense of enclosure to create a successful community.

What the Tools Do

Axial design is a strong visual and very powerful space articulator and usually tends to overpower the other organizing

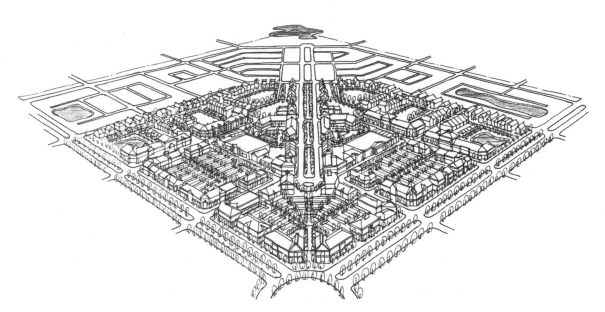

Sketch 1.4 Axial design.

elements. It is linear in nature, is used to establish order, and serves to connect two or more features or terminal points. While the concept of axial design is more closely associated with formality and rigidity, it can be used in more subtle ways to create curving vistas to direct one's view to a series of terminal points. One of the best examples of formal axial design is the town plan of Colonial Williamsburg. With the capitol building at one end and the College of William and Mary at the other end of Duke of Gloucester Street, shops, offices, and homes form the background of a very powerful relationship in spatial design. Whether it is used in a formal, symmetrical way or in an informal, asymmetrical one, axial design must successfully employ movement, function, and visual perception.

Hierarchy, or the gradation of design features, plays an important role in any spatial design. Utilizing a variety of sizes of spaces or outdoor rooms creates not only variety in the landscape, but helps the designer clearly delineate the more important rooms from the minor support areas. The effective use of gradation is one of the best methods one can employ in reducing a grandly scaled space to a more comfortable human scale and vice versa. Drama and excitement can be enhanced greatly with careful attention to hierarchical design.

Transitional elements join adjacent spaces. Exterior spaces can be seemingly endless and filled with a tremendous variety of objects, structures, and landscapes. However, they can be softened or blended by the use of transition elements. These elements are necessary if the space is to be considered complete or coherent. Because humans must be able to organize their environment so they can function in it effectively, the arrangement of the visual field is crucial to wayfinding and sense of place. Transitions are overlap areas that exhibit characteristics of both or all of the spaces that meet in a certain location. Repetition of a design element, similar sizing, coloring of architectural features, or landscape material—even the continuation of a paving pattern—are all examples of transitional elements.

Dominant features create contrast. Just as music crescendos to a climax and art needs a focus, outdoor spaces and communities are more effective and complete if a dominant element is discernable. This focal point gives a place a purpose; otherwise, the space is empty and unfulfilled. A focal point not only gives a space reason for existing, but in so doing creates unity within the space. The dominant feature of

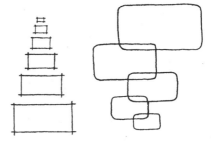

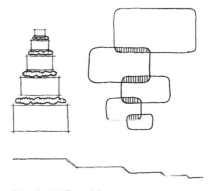

Sketch 1.5 Hierarchy.

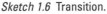

Sketch 1.6 Transition.

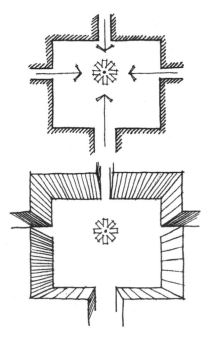

Sketch 1.7 Dominant element (top); enclosure (bottom).

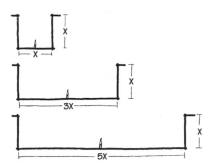

Sketch 1.8 Enclosure ratios.

a space or community completes the picture and creates a sense of the whole. However, too many dominant features within a given area create too many elements vying for attention, resulting in confusion. The single church spire of a medieval village, the way a baseball stadium is built around home plate, and the statue or fountain feature usually found in civic spaces create a center that all other elements of the space support.

Sense of enclosure is perhaps the single most important feature that results in the design of community spaces. Formed by the careful manipulation of the ground plane, the overhead plane, and the vertical or wall plane, enclosure can be created to fit the use or activity desired and thus establish the scale of the space. The activities or emotions that result from a walk down a friendly main street, a quiet conversation in an intimate townhouse garden, or a coin toss at the 50-yard line of a 60,000-seat stadium are all quite different, yet at home in their respective spaces.

In the same way, there is a direct relationship between the height of the vertical elements and the horizontal distance between them that must be respected in creating a functional yet comfortable space. When the height of the verticals is greater than the distance between them, one becomes more aware of the vertical elements themselves rather than the space they create. If the distance between the vertical elements exceeds four times their height, then a sense of enclosure is lost altogether. The most comfortable community spaces are those that fall between these two extremes at a ratio of two or three horizontal units to one vertical unit. With this ratio in mind, we can easily understand why shopping center parking lots and wide suburban parkways with extended building setback lines seem empty and undesirable, lacking richness of scale and texture.

The Spatial Components

The critical spatial components are circulation, open space, and structures. They are the primary aspects of spacial design that are manipulated by the designer to create ordered, contextual, and unique realms for human activity. No matter what the scale, the design process consists of the conscious arranging and rearranging of these three elements in the two-dimensional plane.

Circulation allows movement and mobility, enriching a static space, making it alive and fluid with ever changing experiences. However, overemphasis of this spatial use can eliminate the diversity on which good, functional spaces rely. The almost inevitable growth of the two-lane farm roads into six- and eight-lane commuter collector streets is an example of the overemphasis on function at the expense of perceived space and of how our suburban environments evolve into single-use sites or districts.

Open space, the seemingly void zone between vertical elements, can be perceived as positive, productive, planned, and functionally supportive or, conversely, as negative, wasted, unstructured, and deleterious. Too often in our suburban areas, open space is merely that area left over by mandated minimum setbacks and conveniently placed buffer areas between incompatible uses—a mere ploy to gain the approval of some regulatory authority.

In community design, open space must be thought of as the most ethereal of the fundamental building blocks in quality design. It should never be considered as an afterthought or as just the leftovers. If the viewer can perceive open space as a part of a larger composition, one that heightens the relationship of the other elements in that composition, then that space has been successfully designed.

Structures, the manufactured forms in which we live, work, shop, and play, are the destinations of our daily activities. They can be either harmonious and contextual or discordant and contrary. Open space, like water, is fluid and tends to escape unless held in place by strong elements and structures. Richly detailed architecture that strives to break down larger building walls into more human scaled projections and indentations creates texture and is therefore more successful at *holding* space than are monochromatic, slick, single-plane walls. Interest, in the form of shadows, reveal lines, and tactile surfaces, must be designed into walls if people are intended to comfortably use and relate to the spaces that surround them. As we have seen, the height of buildings with respect to the associated open space is pivotal in reinforcing a sense of enclosure. Likewise, the quality of an open space is further reinforced if the heights of the buildings enclosing it do not vary by more than 25 percent. However, unless the space is enclosed with a single building of uniform height, multiple buildings of exactly uniform height should be avoided in order to ensure variety and interest through shadows and

Sketch 1.9 Adjacent building heights should not vary by more than 25 percent of the smaller building.

Figures 1.10, 1.11 **Which space is integral and which space is merely leftovers?**

reveal lines. This type of building articulation also helps a person to reference his or her progress through a space. By merely projecting in the mind's eye the edges of buildings into the space, it is easy to approximate one's position and, in so doing, reduce its volume to human scale.

In Summary

Lynch's paths, edges, districts, nodes, and landmarks used in combination with the concepts of axial design, hierarchy, transition elements, dominant features, and enclosure are the building blocks and tools we need to create communities that are livable and dynamic. What we have described is classic urban design that should be applied to the community scale. A basic understanding of the ingredients necessary for successful community design must include forms and patterns that are flexible with regard to the common goals of the citizenry. Any prevalent theme or special characteristic that enhances the common heritage and familiarity promoted by the pedestrian scale will help to build an innovative network of environmental, cultural, and social systems that establishes context and rhythm while avoiding monotonous repetition.

Where Does Community Design Begin?

At a Glance

❖ Understanding the importance of context in community design

❖ Knowing what kind of information is available and where to find it

❖ Starting your education with a trip to city hall

❖ Understanding how your tax dollars have been hard at work

Community design begins with context. The context of a place is its history and, ideally, should be its future. And in order to understand the context you have to know where to look for it. Numerous types of information are readily available to anyone who wants to expend a little effort looking. Ideally, the information will identify what a community knows about itself and its environment and the constraints it has imposed on itself in order to protect both. As you analyze the many pertinent sources of information, you will understand the impact of proposed changes and evaluate the consequences of past decisions. Only when we thoroughly review all pertinent information are we ready to effect any changes to our communities.

Your Tax Dollars Hard at Work

Even if you are a tax hawk, you have to appreciate the amount of information that is available from the government. Federal, state, and local government agencies as well as local planning commission offices have a vast array of information available for your use . . . for a fee, of course! By highlighting the sources that follow, we do not mean to imply that they are the only ones you'll ever need, but they are a great place to start. Obviously, the issues of most importance in your community will vary depending on the part of the country in which you live. For instance, communities surrounding the Chesapeake Bay or located along its tributaries are affected by the regulations of the Chesapeake Bay Preservation Act. Municipalities in other environmentally sensitive areas may have more comprehensive growth management plans than those for whom uncontrolled growth is not yet an issue. The San Francisco Bay area and the City of Portland, Oregon, have established urban growth boundaries (UGBs) to arbitrarily set geographical limits on growth. States like New Jersey, Massachusetts, and Colorado have implemented smart growth initiatives that attempt to provide an overall vision statement for growth in these states.

The scale of a project will be the deciding factor regarding the kinds of information used. For example, it is unlikely that you would need regional economic indicators from a federal agency when the project is a 30,000-square-foot office building or a small commercial site. Nor would it be responsible to propose a mixed-use traditional neighborhood development without considering the availability of adequate sewer and water service. As we discuss the types of data and their sources, remember that their names may vary throughout the country, but the type of information is typical of what you will find with a little effort.

City and Town

City and town government is a primary source of pertinent community information. The types of data that can be obtained are comprehensive growth studies, zoning, and site plan and subdivision ordinances (including such addenda as landscape ordinances, zoning maps, tax and topographic maps, planimetrics, sewer and water service maps, master street and highway maps, and bikeway maps). Copies of these sources can be purchased or reviewed in the offices of planning or engineering services. They come in a variety of scales, from 1″ = 100′ to 1″ = 2000′. The maps are useful to the designer for creating accurate base sheets for design development and presentations to clients and public bodies. This also expedites the graphic representation of ideas that will ultimately be translated into detailed construction drawings.

Comprehensive Plans

Suburban sprawl or uncontrolled development is a heated political issue for many municipalities. Growth, when left to happen piecemeal, can consume valuable land resources and destroy irreplaceable natural treasures. Many states are requiring their municipalities to create and then regularly update their comprehensive plans to align with the state's growth vision statement. Many states have found it necessary to establish a formal statement of development and planning policy. Ideally, it should outline a comprehensive strategy for growth that preserves valuable land reserves while helping to foster optimum economic viability. It may address long- and short-term goals and explore future challenges while providing a platform for amendments to accommodate changes in technology and refinements in planning theory.

In order to simplify the task, the plan may break down the city or county into planning zones. Land-use acreage tabulations may be included for each zone with regard to single-family and multifamily units, commercial and industrial space, open space, and whether these are over or under target projections. The issues most commonly discussed include existing and proposed housing, transportation networks, environmental conservation areas, public facilities including existing and future schools, fire and police stations, libraries, parks and recreation facilities, sewer and water services, bikeways, overall drainage considerations, and economic development target areas and objectives.

Some of the more extensive comprehensive plans provide design guidelines for preferred ways of developing these ideas, with incentives such as cost sharing between the municipality and the developer for the extension of public utilities to a proposed development site. Others only state policies and objectives, stopping woefully short of creating a framework for action. Whichever type your municipality may have, the *Comprehensive Plan* is required reading for all who are contemplating land development or for those who just want to know what kind of vision your public servants have established for you.

Zoning Ordinances

Euclidean zoning was legitimized by the 1926 U.S. Supreme Court decision in the case of *Village of Euclid, Ohio v. Ambler Realty Company.* This case established a municipality's right to designate land-use zones and permitted uses within those zones. Today, modern *zoning* can be defined as the classification of land-use types that establishes a range of permissible development options for a piece of property. Simply stated, it establishes what can and cannot occur on a given property. These land uses are identified on a zoning map, and the permitted uses are defined in the zoning ordinance. The exact name of the use classifications may vary but generally include the following: office, commercial, agricultural, residential, industrial, conservation, recreational, resort, and historic preservation.

Zoning maps are usually drawn at a scale of 1″ = 200′ or 1″ = 400′ and are available at a municipality's planning department. During the initial stages of research, zoning maps are helpful in pinpointing appropriately sized parcels for an intended land use as well as determining which parcels could be considered for a change of zoning classification to allow a different and more intense use. Within each land-use category a range of factors with a graduated scale of use intensity is stipulated with regard to allowable conditions and specifications. For example, the uses outlined in the residential category range from high-density multifamily units to single-family detached dwellings on large lots. Each category includes a set of regulations defining minimum standards for layout, setback from the public right-of-way, allowable density in units per acre, parking space requirements, maximum building square footage, and so on. The compatibility of any proposed changes to the community must follow the guidelines of the zoning ordinance and meet all relevant criteria.

Standardized zoning codes have given us the suburban monoculture we enjoy today. The separation of uses originally intended to prevent slaughterhouses from sprouting up next to grandma's house has slowly become a behemoth that stifles innovation and sustainable growth. In fact, most of the traditional neighborhoods and memorable towns we love to visit (e.g., Charleston, South Carolina, and Savannah, Georgia) could not be built today under existing zoning regulations.

Subdivision Ordinances

The *Subdivision Ordinance* establishes regulations that govern how parcels of land are subdivided and developed. While it may include the procedure for the transfer of property titles, as a rule it will not deal with the actual placement of buildings on the lot. This is reserved for the site plan ordinance.

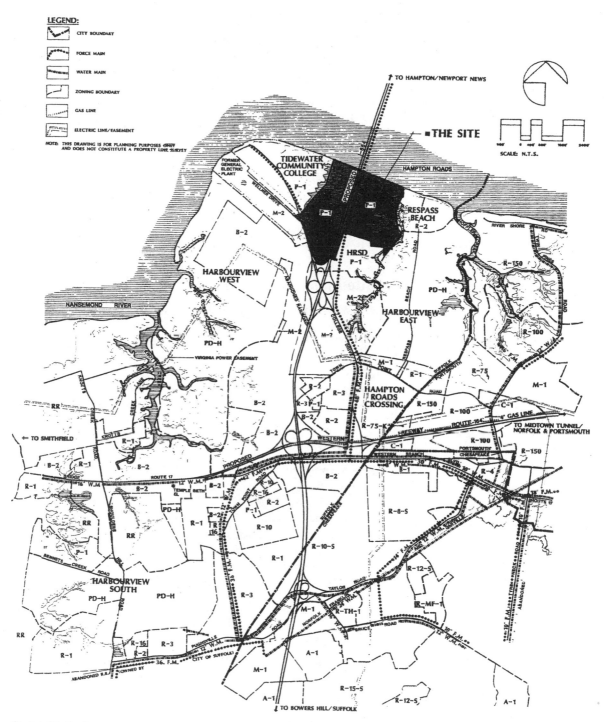

Sketch 2.1 Zoning map.

Adherence to the subdivision ordinance requires the development of preliminary and final subdivision plats, which are prepared to ensure all required improvements regarding street width and road location are carried out according to a municipality's *master street and highway plan*. Detailed specifications for streets and street signage, streetlights, traffic-control devices, sidewalks, alleys, driveway entrances, lot sizes, setbacks, easements, public sites, recreation areas, and so on are established to ensure that a uniform system is maintained. Also included are the rules for seeking a variance to any of the requirements in cases where meeting specific criteria may place undue hardship or burden on the property owner. More important, this procedure is an opportunity for imaginative designers to circumvent the standardized mandates in order to introduce the innovation of a better product.

Site Plan Ordinances

The *Site Plan Ordinance* is the set of guidelines that must be adhered to in order to obtain a building permit. It relates directly to the zoning ordinance in that it establishes the construction specifications (length, width, minimum and maximum square footage) for such things as parking spaces, lot coverage, stormwater management areas, drainage structure, street and curb details, and landscape requirements.

Maps, Maps . . .

Topographic maps at a scale of 1″ = 100′ can be found at the municipal surveyor's office. The contour interval may vary depending on the terrain, but will usually be between 1 and 5 feet and should identify all major high points and low points as spot elevations. Topo maps are useful because they provide a basis for preliminary engineering and feasibility analysis during the initial stages of planning. They provide an accurate source of topographic data without incurring the expense of a full-scale physical survey. They can be counted on for accuracy to within ±5 percent. However, this information should not be substituted for a complete site survey prior to the development of construction documents.

Planimetric maps (or just *planimetrics*) show the accurate placement of lot lines and such physical features as trees, buildings, roads, and ditch lines. They are usually at a scale of 1″ = 100′ and can be obtained in the survey and mapping department of a municipality or at the city or county engineer's office. While they do not necessarily show vertical topographic information, they are useful because they provide an accurate representation of the physical objects occurring in the landscape. Obviously, the more recent the map, the more current the information. However, older planimetrics are also helpful in gaining an insight into the past uses of a property and in determining the original lay of the land and its drainage patterns. Planimetrics can be used in conjunction with tax, zoning, and topographic maps to provide some initial impressions of a site.

Tax maps show the lot boundaries and their approximate area in acres, in fractions thereof, or in square feet. They also include the name of the owner and the estimated value of the property. Tax maps can be obtained from the city assessor's office and allow the community planner to identify current land uses and future trends for the area as well as whether a property is over- or undervalued. Tax maps also serve as a means to verify information gleaned from the planimetrics. In smaller municipalities, tax maps may be freehand-drawn, very obtuse, and not to be trusted as a reliable source for base sheet information. However, more and more municipalities are having them professionally produced to scale and are therefore as reliable as planimetrics. In any case, it is always a good idea to consult more than one source of information to ferret out any inconsistencies. Accuracy in base information is crucial to successful community design. However, surprises can and do occur, so it is wise to be as thorough as possible.

Sanitary sewer maps are a necessary source of information when contemplating infrastructure requirements for proposed growth. Their accuracy is limited, as they are only a diagrammatic representation of an overall layout. They can be obtained at the city engineer's office or public utilities department and show major trunk lines, gravity interceptors, and sanitary sewer force mains on maps at scales between $1'' = 1200'$ and $1'' = 1800'$. Individual sewer lines, manholes, and rim and invert elevations are shown on maps of $1'' = 200'$ to $1'' = 400'$. When used in conjunction with zoning and topographic maps, they provide a general understanding of the direction of flow, current capacity, and how far or whether a line can be extended. Service taps are made into a 4- or 8-inch pipe that allows the wastewater to flow by gravity into increasingly larger lines, collecting from a greater and greater area. Unless they flow directly into a treatment facility, they terminate at a pumping station, where the wastewater is gathered and pushed to a treatment facility. For those who can decipher them, calculations concerning existing pumping station capacities can be obtained from the municipal engineer's office. When the goal is to extend service into new areas, it is usually wise to have the sewer system designed by a qualified engineer who specializes in infrastructure. He or she can advise what, if any, modifications can be made to increase capacity. This information is useful when discussing the impact of growth as well as for long-range projections about future service needs.

Water maps are usually the same scale as sanitary sewer maps and generally can be obtained from the same sources. They show the location and size of all water lines, valves, and fire hydrants. Calculations of the amount of pressure available in each area can be obtained from the city engineer's office or the municipal water authority. Water maps are useful because they help to determine the availability of water and the cost of providing it to a site, and they offer crucial information with regard to project feasibility.

Many communities have established *master street and highway plans,* bikeway plans, and greenway plans. Streets and highways plans use codes and legends to categorize streets by the number of lanes, the presence of medians for divided and undivided boulevards, recognition of scenic easements, and so on. *Bikeway plans* show the network of paved surfaces designated as bikeways. This does not necessarily mean that the bikeway is a separate entity from a street or sidewalk, but only that it exists, on paper at least, as part of a community-wide system.

More and more municipalities are combining open-space preservation with the desire for *greenway corridors* in an effort to retain unique ecosystems while providing opportunities for recreation. Cities like Raleigh, North Carolina, have established extensive greenway systems that link several preservation areas to maximize their usefulness as productive ecosystems and recreational amenities. Guidelines established to respect the integrity of bikeways and greenways must be reviewed in order to maximize the opportunities they provide.

Overlay District Guidelines

Overlay district guidelines are usually established within the context of special circumstances. Many municipalities have developed regulations to maintain the integrity of historic districts, to protect environmentally sensitive areas, or to limit the impact of or prevent inevitable conflicts between certain

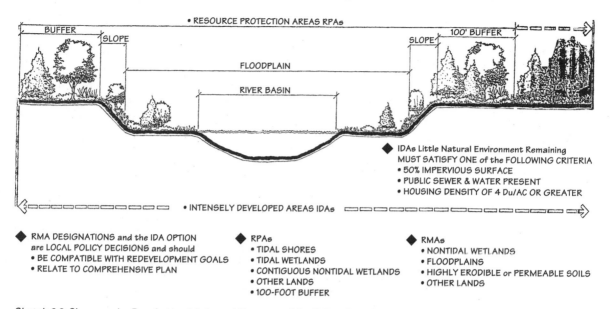

RESOURCE PROTECTION AREAS RPAs

BUFFER
SLOPE
FLOODPLAIN
RIVER BASIN

SLOPE
100' BUFFER

◆ IDAs Little Natural Environment Remaining
MUST SATISFY ONE of the FOLLOWING CRITERIA
• 50% IMPERVIOUS SURFACE
• PUBLIC SEWER & WATER PRESENT
• HOUSING DENSITY OF 4 Du/AC OR GREATER

INTENSELY DEVELOPED AREAS IDAs

◆ RMA DESIGNATIONS and the IDA OPTION
are LOCAL POLICY DECISIONS and should
• BE COMPATIBLE WITH REDEVELOPMENT GOALS
• RELATE TO COMPREHENSIVE PLAN

◆ RPAs
• TIDAL SHORES
• TIDAL WETLANDS
• CONTIGUOUS NONTIDAL WETLANDS
• OTHER LANDS
• 100-FOOT BUFFER

◆ RMAs
• NONTIDAL WETLANDS
• FLOODPLAINS
• HIGHLY ERODIBLE or PERMEABLE SOILS
• OTHER LANDS

Sketch 2.2 Chesapeake Bay Act restrictions. (*Courtesy of the Talbot Group*)

land uses. Cities such as Charleston, South Carolina, Savannah, Georgia, and Williamsburg, Virginia, have designated historic districts that are maintained by strict architectural guidelines. Design review committees must approve proposed changes or improvements prior to the issuance of building permits.

In other cases, municipalities are required to respect national guidelines in order to protect valuable resources that are shared by more than one state. As an example, the Chesapeake Bay Preservation Act affects communities in the Chesapeake Bay watershed by limiting encroachment on its tidal wetlands and tributaries as well as seeking to reduce and ultimately eliminate sources of pollution. Some states have their own preservation areas for which strict limitations on growth have been implemented (e.g., New Jersey's Pinelands Preservation Area).

Regional Planning Agencies

An excellent source of all things demographic, regional planning agencies have a wide variety of books, maps, and aerial photographs that can be purchased. Whether you are creating your own reference library or want information relevant to specific projects, this is one of your best sources. *Planning district commissions,* as they are sometimes called, provide a wealth of data on economic growth trends, as well as forecasts and inventories of human service resources. They also provide information about comprehensive management studies for physical and environmental planning as well as transportation. The information is not limited to regional specifics but is compared to national trends regarding economic growth and legislative initiatives. Studies are published on a variety of topics—elder housing, poverty, watershed analysis, water quality, solid waste disposal, energy resource management, hazardous wastes, scenic and open space opportunities, to name a few. They provide an invaluable service by gathering and analyzing the data that would be too time-consuming and tedious for community planners to do for themselves. You can find out if your area has a planning district commission by calling your municipal planning office.

The State

State highway standards apply to all roads owned by the state. Heretofore, they are improved and maintained by the state department of transportation, with the majority mileage of these roads being in rural areas. However, as towns and cities have expanded, these roads have remained subject to the standards established by that state's highway department. Design requirements for speed, width, allowable frequency of intersections, curvature and radii, maximum superelevation and vertical curve, design specifications for bridges, culverts, cul-de-sacs, pavement composition, and so on are provided in a publication that can be obtained from the state department of transportation.

The Federal Government

A myriad of information can be obtained from the various agencies and departments of the federal government. We won't list them here, but you can be sure that huge amounts of research and regulatory data are published each year. You will have to determine what sources of information are essential to your task. You can easily become overwhelmed by what is available, but with a little forethought you can determine exactly what you need. The sources that follow are a good beginning. If you find that you want or need more information, begin your search by telephoning or searching the websites of the agencies that have produced the information we list.

. . . And More Maps

The United States Geological Survey produces 7.5-minute quadrangle maps (USGS *topographic maps*) at a scale of 1″ = 2000′. Technically speaking, they are a polychonic projection subdivided at 10,000-foot grid ticks based on each state's coordinate system (longitude and latitude). They can be obtained from a U.S. Geological Survey office, online at the USGS website, or locally at technical supply stores that cater to engineering firms. In mountainous areas, USGS maps may be carried by merchants who sell hiking and canoeing supplies. The information is standardized to include generalized

Figure 2.1 USGS Topographic Map.

Figure 2.2 NWI map.

topography at 5- to 25-foot contour intervals, water bodies and their depth, streams and marsh areas, cleared and wooded areas, primary and secondary highways, light-duty and unimproved roads, and the general locations of buildings and cemeteries. USGS maps are useful as base sheets for large-scale conceptual planning. As a contextual source of information they provide a plethora of physical data to help the community planner maximize his or her research efforts.

The destruction of wetlands has been a source of much controversy. Regulatory legislation has attempted to classify wetlands according to productive water quality for wildlife habitat and groundwater recharge. The information provided by *National Wetland Inventory* (NWI) maps classifies wetland areas by ecological system, ecological subsystem, class, and subclass. Systems or types considered to be useful wetlands according to regulatory criteria is the source of continuing debate. NWI maps are produced by the U.S. Fish and Wildlife Service and can be obtained from that source or from technical supply stores that cater to the needs of engineering firms. They may also be available through your regional planning commission offices or the local office of the U.S. Army Corps of Engineers. These maps identify the general location and type of wetlands within the quadrangle window of the USGS maps at a scale of $1'' = 2000'$. This is a great advantage, as it allows the two to be overlaid, thus providing a source of base information for large-scale planning efforts. NWI maps are useful in that they provide a generalized inventory of possible wetland areas. However, detailed wetland analysis confirming the presence of wetlands must be done on a site-by-site basis by a qualified wetland scientist and verified by the U.S. Army Corps of Engineers.

Air Installation Compatible Use Zones, or *AICUZ maps,* diagram noise and accident potential (crash) zones in and around military airfields. They were developed by the Department of Defense in response to growing pressures for the development of land adjacent to military airfields. The zones coincide with the orbital airspace and that used for landing approach and takeoff. Each zone is categorized on the basis of noise intensity and crash potential. Compatible land uses are suggested to provide guidelines for surrounding development and to eliminate possible conflicts.

Civil airports have similar maps that identify high noise potential. You can obtain a copy of one from the airport manager's office or a local real estate association. (By the way, civil airport managers don't like to think of their maps as identifying crash potential. It makes them kind of nervous. So humor them and be sure not to mention the *C* word.)

Many cities are located along waterways and in coastal regions. Regulations for construction within the floodplain are necessary to protect the integrity of the floodplain itself and to prevent, as much as humanly possible, the likelihood of floods that result in collateral damage and loss of life. *Floodplain* is defined as any land area that adjoins a watercourse or body of water that is subject to inundation. These areas of inundation are delineated on *flood insurance maps* and flood boundary and floodway maps published by the U.S. Federal Emergency Management Agency as part of the National Flood Insurance Program. The U.S. Geological Survey also publishes flood-prone quadrangle maps, and the U.S. Army Corps of Engineers publishes floodplain information reports. The importance of these maps is obvious.

Aerial Photographs

Aerial photographs identify natural and human-made features for the interpretation, evaluation, and analysis of land resources. The level of accuracy required in the interpretation of existing conditions prior to land-use planning necessitates a vigorous inventory of site characteristics. While site visits are strongly recommended, aerial photographs allow the site to be seen in context with its surroundings. Also, site characteristics that may be inadvertently overlooked during a site survey will be faithfully recorded on film.

There are a variety of sources for aerial photographs. The federal clearinghouse for high-altitude and satellite photography is the Earth Resources Observation Systems (EROS) Data Center in Souix Falls, South Dakota, which is managed by the U.S. Geological Survey. The EROS center's holdings include some 8 million frames gathered from 1940 to the present and include photographs obtained from the National Aeronautics and Space Administration (NASA), the National High Altitude Photography Program (NHAP) from 1980 to 1987, and the National Aerial Photography Program (NAPP) from 1987 to 1991. Both NHAP and NAPP were supported by a number of federal and state agencies, including the Departments of Agriculture, Defense, and the Interior, which provided systematic coverage of the 48 conterminous United States. Strict flight parameters ensure minimum shadow and haze and no cloud cover.

The products available from the EROS center include black-and-white, natural color, and infrared photographs, film transparencies, 35mm slides, and some digital scanner data. The photographs are taken in stereo pairs—two overlapping high-resolution, stereoscopic photographs—which can be viewed three-dimensionally using a stereoscope.

The photographs are available in 9 × 9 inch contact prints as well as in (2X) 18 × 18, (3X) 27 × 27, (4X) 36 × 36 inch enlargements and 35mm slides. You can also order special print sizes. EROS provides a free comprehensive index on microfiche, which provides all the information you need to order. One helpful hint: Identify the map coordinates (longitude and latitude) of the area for which you want photographs on a USGS topographic map. This will be helpful when ordering.

The USGS has another product that combines computer-generated aerial photography with its quadrangle map resource. This product is referred to as a *Digital Orthophoto*

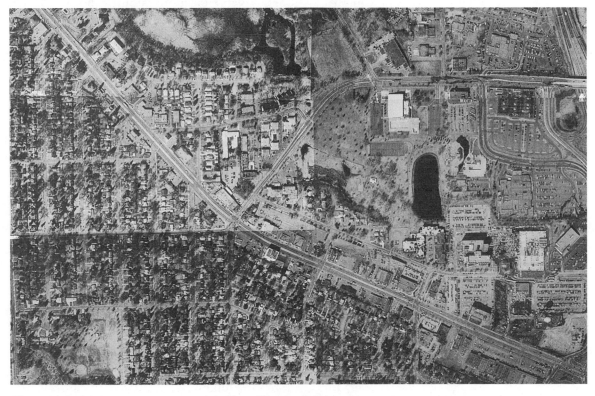

Figure 2.3 Aerial photograph courtesy of the Town Planning Collaborative.

Quadrangle (DOQ). It has been *orthorectified,* which means that it has been altered so that it has the geometric properties of a USGS topographic map. The images are at a scale of 1:12,000 and represent 3.75 minutes of latitude by 3.75 minutes of longitude (one-quarter of the 7.5-minute-quadrangle topographic maps). The standard DOQ is a black-and-white or color-infrared image. Four of them form a *mosaic* (overlapping images) and, when joined, cover the same area as one of the standard 1:24,000-scale topographic maps. You can obtain DOQs as digital files on CD and, in some cases, download them from USGS's website (for a fee, of course). Check out http://wmc.wr.usgs.gov/orthophoto_basic.html. For further information on aerial photos, contact the U.S. Geological Survey at the EROS Data Center in Sioux Falls, South Dakota, or visit www.terraserver.com.

Although the Terraserver website includes images from Russian satellites, you can access USGS images there, too. The site is set up so you can easily find most places in the United States and several locations around the world. You merely type in the name of a city or town and click on Go to get a list that shows the date the image was taken and the company that produced it. When choosing the image you want to see, double-click, and a message will prompt you to download the software to view the image. That done, a black-and-white satellite image loads onto your screen in stunning clarity. From this point you can choose to zoom in and see more or zoom out for broader context. The scale range is from 1 meter per pixel to 64 meters per pixel.

When you choose a USGS image, you have three options of what to view: (1) the photo created from the DOQ image, (2) the USGS topographic map of the area, or (3) a high-altitude, in-color, regional satellite image. Being able to switch back and forth between the topographic map and the aerial photo is very helpful if you are having trouble locating the area you want. Remember, even though the image looks big on your screen, it may be very small when you download it and print it out.

If you're short of time and just want to get an image to look at, you can download the USGS images directly onto your computer at no charge. You can convert them into a printable form, but you will probably need to download a series of images at 1 meter per pixel and piece them together. However, for accurate land planning, you need to purchase the digital file so you can use the higher-quality image. Remember that most of the images are not as current as you might like; they may be several years old. Some of the Terraserver images are more recent, but they are not as accurate in scale as the USGS DOQs.

If you want a more recent image or if you want to have a photo taken, there are companies that will accommodate you for a price. There are links from the USGS section at Terraserver.com offering numerous source names and website links to choose from; you can order online or by phone.

Other sources of aerial photography, however, may not offer the scale you want, the product you need (35mm slide, for instance), or be as current as the USGS products. In local offices of the U.S. Soil Conservation Service, black-and-white aerial photographs of the regions that they serve can be reviewed. You might also check the yellow pages of the telephone book. You may find aerial photography services that will take the pictures you need. It usually requires that you meet with the pilot/photographer to discuss the location and scale of the product you need, and don't forget to ask if a photograph of what you want already exists. There's no use paying for flight time if you can get a copy of an existing photograph.

Another source is the state highway department, which uses aerial photographs for transportation analysis and planning. Again, you are limited to the scale provided, but most often these photos are up-to-date and reliable.

Don't forget to ask your municipality if it has aerial photographs. Some do, but the information may be limited and not recent. Older photographs can be useful, though, when you are trying to analyze growth or verify land-use patterns within your community. Land that has been left in its natural state for a decade or longer may have some development constraints that have been overlooked. With these photos, you're probably going to be limited to viewing them on the premises. However, some cities have a complete set of aerials on mylar from which a blueprint can be made and purchased.

Soil Surveys

Soil surveys are published for each state by the U.S. Soil Conservation Service. They discuss soil description, physiography, relief, drainage, and issues relevant to the use and management of soils. They provide detailed guidelines as to how land can and should be used with regard to crops and pasture, beach and dune, marsh and woodland management, recreation, and wildlife habitat. Soil types and their properties are listed, including freeze dates, growing season, capability and projected yields of crops and pastureland, along with the possible commercial application of forest products. Within the pages of the soil survey are maps at a scale of 1 inch = ¼ mile. Soil information is superimposed on an aerial photograph and identified by an abbreviation of the soil name.

The soil survey is a useful tool because it provides a broad outline for land use by suggesting land-use possibilities taking into account soil type. The parameters for development recommended by the soil survey can influence recommendations by allowing the community planner to compare cost of development between alternative sites based on soil permeability, depth, salinity, and shrink-swell potential and with regard to the soil amendments necessary to accommodate nonrecommended land uses. For more conclusive results, soil borings will be necessary to confirm the exact conditions of each site.

Figure 2.4 Soil survey map.

The Corps

The mission of the U.S. Army Corps of Engineers ("the Corps") is to provide planning, design, and construction services for the military in both war and peace. However, as directed by Congress, the Corps also has a rather extensive civil works program. It provides comprehensive planning for river basin development, regional wastewater management planning, and regional water resource and floodplain management, including correction of drainage problems and flood control measures. It oversees beach erosion control and hurricane protection projects, performs damage control and rehabilitation assistance during natural disasters, and assists local governments in regulating floodplains. It administers federal laws regulating the use of the nation's navigable waters and grants permits for the discharge of dredged or fill materials into those waters as mandated by the U.S. Clean Water Act. It also is responsible for certifying wetland delineations and for providing local assistance to municipalities in complying with wetlands laws.[1]

In Summary

Thorough research is essential to effective community planning. Going the extra mile during the research phase and following up on that nagging question may make all the difference. The sources that you should consult will depend on the scale of the task as well as the goal you are trying to achieve. This chapter gives you some direction—a place to start. If you are new to the game, you will become more familiar with the kinds of questions to ask as you become more familiar with the process. Do not be afraid to do too much research at first. Better to do too much than not enough.

If you are a design professional, do not get too complacent. An old dog *can* learn new tricks. The old saying, "Pride goes . . . before a fall"[2] has been applied to many professionals who overlooked some essential element in their haste to get the job done. Because our communities are continually evolving, the romance with the past and the deficits ascribed to the present are but a snapshot in time. The communities of the future will combine the best of what we have learned only if we do not plan them in a vacuum. Understanding this, the importance of the research phase becomes self-evident. The sources we have briefly described as well as those you will find on your own provide not only context and continuity, but insight about the community as a whole and the growth patterns that we have established for it. Do your homework!

CHAPTER 3

What's the Process of Community Design?

At a Glance

❖ Understanding the importance of making community design a team sport

❖ Taking the raw information about the context of a site and creating analysis

drawings to make sense of what you have discovered

❖ Identifying the process of community design from concept to implementation

The process of community design requires cooperation between designers, financial, economic, and real estate professionals, municipal authorities, and the community at large. Growth is a politically charged issue for many burgeoning communities, and for any planning effort to succeed, a team approach is essential. The design team may vary, but it should include a landscape architect, a civil engineer, and an architect. Non–design team contributors may include an environmental scientist and land surveyor, an attorney, an economic analyst, a real estate broker, a banker, the land owner, and the developer. During the course of a project the team will expand to include the municipal planning director and his or her staff, members of the local planning commission, city council, the various review agencies of the municipal government, and interested community groups and individuals. For planning that involves federal or state regulations, someone from a federal or state agency may become involved in a plan review or inspection role. For example, wetland delineation must be confirmed by a representative of the Army Corps of Engineers.

For any community planning effort to be truly successful, it is essential that all those who influence the process be part of the team, especially the municipal authorities because of their crucial role as overseers of the community welfare. More and more, changes to our communities require some form of modification to existing zoning restrictions. Most often, these are granted as *conditional zoning,* whereby a city council will grant a variance to a particular zoning requirement in exchange for certain guarantees, or *proffers,* made by the land developer. For example, the developer may negotiate to pay the costs or a portion of the cost of extending public services (e.g., water, sewer) to the proposed development in exchange for the council's vote of approval.

The size of the team will depend on the scale of the project. Obviously, development of a neighborhood retail center on a small parcel would not require the same level of interaction as, say, a large master-planned community, but the planning procedure is generally the same.

The typical development procedure occurs when a land owner, be it an individual or a corporation, puts a parcel of land up for sale. Before an interested land developer buys the property he or she may contract the services of a firm that specializes in land planning to help define opportunities in accord with existing zoning restrictions and how the parcel fits into the overall plan of the community. Once the design professional identifies needed information, its usefulness depends on how it is analyzed.

The first step is a market assessment of the needs, demands, and trends of the community as a whole. An analysis done by a reputable firm that specializes in market trends is essential to determine the project's *absorption* and its fit with the community at large. The market analysis is also essential for obtaining financing for the project. For example, a market assessment to determine the need for additional single-family housing would evaluate such factors as land area required, zoning, number of houses already available in the area, the number sold in the past five years, and the price range. It will also include an analysis of economic factors, with special emphasis on the growth or decline of local and regional employment generators and the maximum number of persons presently employed versus the number of positions expected to be filled. From this, the economist will make certain assumptions by estimating the number of housing units needed community-wide and the market share that can reasonably be expected by the developer for the proposed project based on its location and the type of product it offers.

Subsequent to this or possibly at the same time, the land planner begins to gather site data. Detailed knowledge of the site and its surroundings is generated in graphic form. The overall assessments made at this stage will be a crucial element for the objective decisions made later. While there are no hard and fast rules on how this data should be recorded and presented, the following tools can be very useful.

Analysis Drawings

The *Surrounding Development Assessment* presents data gathered on existing and proposed developments as well as physical and market conditions. This information should be organized in a manner that can be quickly and easily understood, because it will serve as a critical tool in determining appropriate land uses and their locations. From it complementary, compatible, and perhaps expandable land uses can be identified.

An *Existing Conditions Map* identifies the physical constraints and attributes of the site. It is an inventory of all site features and regulatory constraints, such as topography, geology, soils, and climatic information; plant and animal life; and existing zoning both on- and off-site. It will have a description of the restrictive covenants and deed restrictions, if any, or other governing design criteria: local ordinances; state and federal criteria for environmental impact with regard to floodplain, air, and water quality; existing structures such as buildings, streets, and utilities; surface and subsurface drainage (hydrology); and unique features such as wetlands and archaeological or historic sites. This type of objective information is used as a beginning point for the next level of analysis.

A *site analysis* drawing combines the objective data of the existing-conditions map with realistic opportunities and somewhat subjective and intuitive design considerations. This is the stage where certain observations and judgments can be made about the site with regard to access, circulation, entry, views, visibility, orientation to surroundings, and existing and potential focal points.

A *character analysis* drawing assimilates all data gathered into a purely subjective document that subdivides the site into a variety of zones and identifies the inherent ambiance of each. This extremely valuable tool provides plausible justification for the location of specific uses in specific areas.

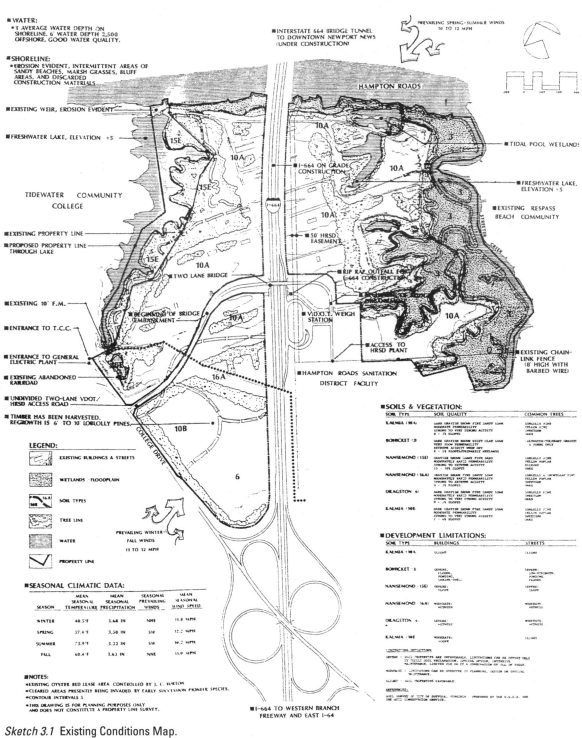

Sketch 3.1 Existing Conditions Map.

LEGEND:

- WOODLANDS
- OPEN FIELDS
- WETLANDS/MARSH
- SAND/BEACH
- WATER

■ EXISTING 100+ SLIP MARINA HAS LIMITED ACCESSIBILITY TO KEELED SAILBOATS DUE TO SHALLOW WATER DEPTH.

■ EXISTING OYSTER BEDS DISEASED BUT EXPECTED TO RETURN TO COMMERCIAL PRODUCTION.

■ EXISTING HOUSING ON WASHINGTON AVE. IN POOR CONDITION. TRANSITION/BUFFER AREA REQUIRED TO REDUCE VISUAL POLLUTION.

ENCLOSED VIEW

KINGS CREEK

PANORAMIC VIEW

SCALE: 1"=400'

CHESAPEAKE BAY

■ COAST GUARD HOUSING

■ DIVIDED AVENUE and IMPROVED BOARDWALK PROVIDE LINKAGE W/ DOWNTOWN.

TOWN OF CAPE CHARLES

HIGH SCHOOL ATHLETIC FIELD

HERITAGE ARMS APARTMENTS

■ EXISTING GOLF COURSE MINIMALLY DESIGNED & SPARSELY VEGETATED.

■ EXISTING CAPE CHARLES WELL SITE. EXPANSION POSSIBLE.

■ PROPERTY OFFERS OPPORTUNITIES TO CREATE THEME/IMAGE ON APPROACHING CAPE CHARLES.

■ PRIMARY VEHICULAR ACCESS RECENTLY WIDENED AND SURFACED. 8000' ± TO ROUTE 13

VA. ROUTE 184 (to U.S. Route 13)

■ WINTER WINDS (N.W. TO N.E.) N.E. WINDS MOST SEVERE DURING WINTER MONTHS 35 - 45 KNOTS POSSIBLE

■ POSSIBILITY FOR COMMUNITY FOCAL POINT/EXPANDED COMMERCIAL.

CAPE CHARLES HARBOR

■ BARGE DOCKS PROVIDE RAILROAD LINKAGE TO HAMPTON ROADS at LITTLE CREEK.

■ EXISTING OYSTER BEDS CONDEMNED DUE TO INDUSTRIAL POLLUTION.

EASTERN SHORE RAILROAD, INC.

■ U.S. COAST GUARD STATION

BAYSHORE CONCRETE PRODUCTS CORP.

BUFFER

■ HARBOR DREDGING SPOILS DISPOSAL AREA

■ NEW PUBLIC HOUSING MAY NEED SPECIAL SCREENING.

■ EXISTING CAPE CHARLES WATER TANK CREATE NEGATIVE VISUAL IMPACT FROM ROUTE 184 ACCESS.

VA. ROUTE 642 (to U.S. Route 13)

■ 6800' ± TO ROUTE 13 SECONDARY ACCESS LOCALIZED TRAFFIC.

■ EXISTING CAPE CHARLES SEWAGE TREATMENT PLANT W/EXPANSION POSSIBILITIES.

■ 150' DELMARVA LIGHT & POWER CO. EASEMENT

■ ACCESS BETWEEN NORTH & SOUTH PARCELS DIFFICULT- EN STREETS & BRIDGE HELD/SION MAY BE REQUIRED FOR IMPROVED ACCESS BETWEEN PARCELS.

■ EXISTING MANSION OFFERS GOOD OPPORTUNITY FOR GOLF COURSE FOCAL POINT.

■ DUNE AREA TO BE PRESERVED.

■ PRIMARY DUNE LINE

■ LITTORAL DRIFT OF BEACH SAND OCCURS IN A SOUTHERLY DIRECTION.

PANORAMIC VIEW

■ RAILROAD AND INDUSTRIAL AREAS CREATE VISUAL, NOISE AND AIR POLLUTION. STRONG BUFFER AND TRANSITION ZONE NEEDED.

■ MATURE MIXED HARDWOODS & PINES
- Red & White Oaks
- Tulip Poplar
- Ash
- Loblolly Pine
- American Holly
- Dogwood
- Shadblow

■ ENVIRONMENTALLY SENSITIVE EDGE CONDITION SHOULD BE PROTECTED & MAINTAINED.

■ DEFINED PUBLIC ACCESS TO BEACH DESIRABLE.

■ SOILS ON SITE ARE PREDOMINANTLY SANDS AND SILTS FROM THE PLEISTOCENE AGE COASTAL PLAIN STRATA AND IF PROPERLY DRAINED, THEY ARE GENERALLY CONSIDERED BUILDABLE.

■ 23 HISTORICAL SITES IDENTIFIED

■ EXISTING OYSTER BEDS.

■ EXTENSIVE SHORELINE EROSION- REPLENISHMENT MEASURES REQUIRED.

■ ENCLOSED POND SOON TO BE BREACHED BY BAY.

ENCLOSED VIEW

CHESAPEAKE BAY

ALLEGOOD POND

■ SUMMER WINDS (S. TO S.W.) COOLING BREEZES FROM S.W. NUMEROUS SEVERE THUNDERSTORMS AND OCCASIONAL HURRICANE DEVELOP

ANNUAL RAINFALL 40' - 50' INCHES

PANORAMIC VIEW

■ WETLANDS/MARSH/LAKE

■ OPEN FIELDS CURRENTLY UNDER CULTIVATION.

SOLAR ORIENTATION

MIDDAY
SUNSET SUMMER
SUNUP WINTER
FALL/SPRING
SUMMER

ENCLOSED VIEW

OLD PLANTATION CREEK

BROWN & ROOT, INC. (Owner)
THE BRITTON COMPANY (Development Consultant)
REES JONES, INC. (Golf Course Consultant)
GA/PARTNERS, INC. (Market & Financial Consultant)
ESPEY, HUSTON & ASSOCIATES, INC. (Environmental Consultant)

■ SILTING OF INLET LIMITS USE OF PLANTATION CREEK

Sketch 3.2 Site analysis.

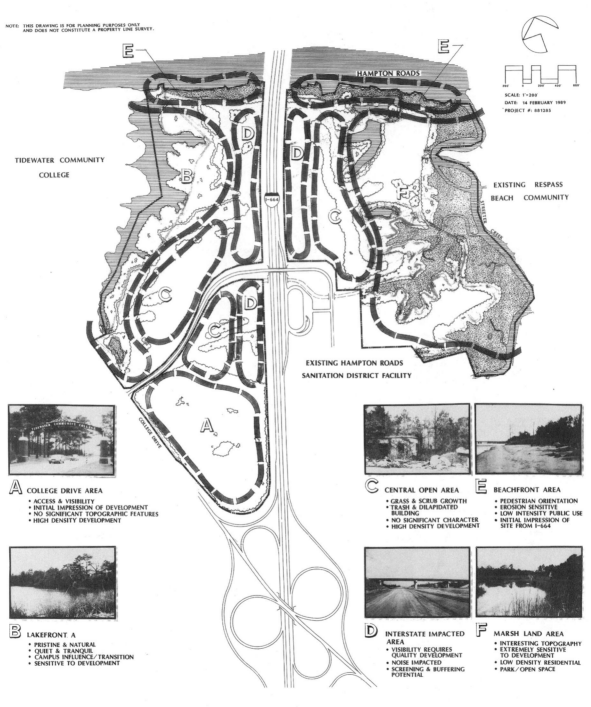

NOTE: THIS DRAWING IS FOR PLANNING PURPOSES ONLY AND DOES NOT CONSTITUTE A PROPERTY LINE SURVEY.

SCALE: 1"=200'
DATE: 14 FEBRUARY 1989
PROJECT #: 881285

HAMPTON ROADS

TIDEWATER COMMUNITY
COLLEGE

EXISTING RESPASS
BEACH COMMUNITY

I-664

EXISTING HAMPTON ROADS
SANITATION DISTRICT FACILITY

COLLEGE DRIVE

A COLLEGE DRIVE AREA
• ACCESS & VISIBILITY
• INITIAL IMPRESSION OF DEVELOPMENT
• NO SIGNIFICANT TOPOGRAPHIC FEATURES
• HIGH DENSITY DEVELOPMENT

B LAKEFRONT A
• PRISTINE & NATURAL
• QUIET & TRANQUIL
• CAMPUS INFLUENCE/TRANSITION
• SENSITIVE TO DEVELOPMENT

C CENTRAL OPEN AREA
• GRASS & SCRUB GROWTH
• TRASH & DILAPIDATED BUILDING
• NO SIGNIFICANT CHARACTER
• HIGH DENSITY DEVELOPMENT

E BEACHFRONT AREA
• PEDESTRIAN ORIENTATION
• EROSION SENSITIVE
• LOW INTENSITY PUBLIC USE
• INITIAL IMPRESSION OF SITE FROM I-664

D INTERSTATE IMPACTED AREA
• VISIBILITY REQUIRES QUALITY DEVELOPMENT
• NOISE IMPACTED
• SCREENING & BUFFERING POTENTIAL

F MARSH LAND AREA
• INTERESTING TOPOGRAPHY
• EXTREMELY SENSITIVE TO DEVELOPMENT
• LOW DENSITY RESIDENTIAL
• PARK/OPEN SPACE

Sketch 3.3 Character analysis.

Why We Need Them

The basic function of the analysis documents is to help the team understand the site's constraints and opportunities. They are also helpful exhibits at public meetings to provide community leaders with all relevant information as concisely as possible. Additionally, these documents help make the case for the viability of the proposed project to the financier who will provide the necessary funds; to the planning commission, board of supervisors, and city council to obtain approval and any zoning modifications; to the general public because, as we have discussed, growth issues can be so politically charged that early involvement of citizen groups helps to reduce future conflicts. The current controversy over suburban sprawl and the advent of alternative concepts to control, stem, or refocus the tide of growth in our metropolitan areas has created an atmosphere in which citizen involvement early in the life of a project is not only wise but essential. An informed public, therefore, helps to reduce the possibility of misinformation and hostility to change that is often vented in the editorial pages of the newspaper, on radio call-in talk shows, and at city council and planning commission meetings open for public comment. The intensity of emotion, often fueled by the media in order to sell a few more newspapers or boost ratings, places the burden of proof of need for any project on the community design team. The analysis documents provide verifiable evidence as a design tool, and they also establish criteria by which proposed development can be justified.

The final step in the research and analysis phase is the definition of a *program*. While clients may have a list of preconceived ideas they want to explore, it is the design team's task to clearly identify the goals and expectations for a project and blend them with the constraints and opportunities uncovered during the research and analysis phase. Ultimately, the program should relate the desired behavior or activities that are to occur within the subject site, place, or district with the needs of the community at large. But it is more than just so many tennis courts and parking spaces. It encompasses both technical and aesthetic criteria.

For example, a purely technical program definition may specify that certain activities are desired (e.g., the creation of a park that includes two tennis courts, four basketball courts, six soccer fields, picnicking for 50 persons, a tot lot, and parking for 75 cars). The aesthetic portion of this same program may outline the desired emotions that visitors to this park should experience (e.g., the park should provide a beautiful, relaxed atmosphere for family fun). While each portion clearly defines the park's goal, blending them together communicates a true vision of the requirements of the park.

Therefore, before beginning any design an adequate program is mandatory. In fact, you might say that if you have a good program you have already begun the design phase. However, because the program forces one to focus on the project's intended goals, it should not be detail-driven or inflexible. The program should be fluid and subject to change as new information is discovered and as new opportunities present themselves.

The Design Phase

The design phase is the creative and problem-solving phase of community planning. It is the next logical step in the process, whereby the information from the market assessment and the analysis documents is put to the test. *Concept ideation* is the attempt to relate the goals of the program to the needs of the market and the constraints of the site. Simply put, it is the vision: the mechanism for creating order out of chaos.

During the design phase, innovative concepts are investigated by developing and refining alternative approaches or solutions that address the specific issues. At this point it is good to remember that there is never one perfect plan. The optimum solution will probably be the one that is the best marriage of the market-driven goals of the program and the desires of the community—not necessarily the one that makes the prettiest picture. Also, factors such as environmental regulations, architectural style, technological standards, socioeconomic diversity of the population, and the needs of the market are constantly fluctuating. Solutions that worked two years ago (and in some cases a few months ago) may not adequately address the concerns of today's communities.

Alternative solutions can take the form of freehand graphic sketch plans, and land-use types are often shown as bubble diagrams. The positioning of these land uses will ultimately serve to enhance and facilitate a scenario of best-possible compatibility with adjacent properties. The effects of each alternative should be identified and the concepts analyzed with regard to direct, indirect, and cumulative impacts on internal, adjacent, surrounding, and nearby neighborhoods.

The number of solutions will vary, but during the initial exploration it is not uncommon for there to be as many as 10 possible solutions, many of which will eventually end up in a crumpled heap on the floor.

For example, one option may address the goals of the program but fail to meet the needs identified in the market assessment. A subsequent solution may meet these requirements but fail to meet some technical aspect of the site plan ordinance with regard to transportation (e.g., distance between traffic lights and the maximum allowable lot coverage as stipulated in the subdivision ordinance).

The Design Charette

A *charette* is a brief, intense design workshop in which the design team works together with municipal staff, city coun-

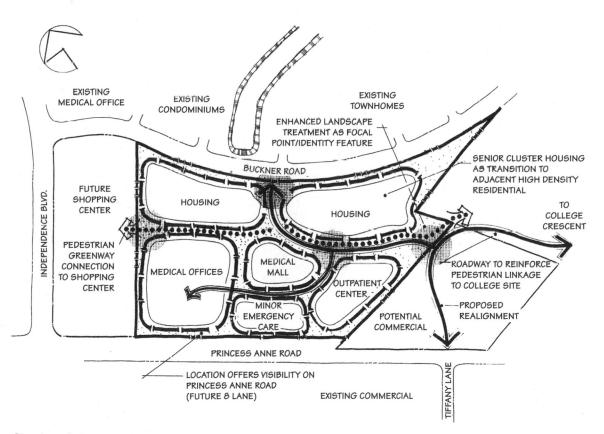

Sketch 3.4 Bubble diagram.

Project Profile: Midtown Center, Madison, Wisconsin

Location: Madison, Wisconsin
Client: City of Madison, Wisconsin
Planning firm: Town Planning Collaborative
Project size: 79 acres

Key Features:

- The initial phases will include mixed-use, apartment, and townhouse building types to form the geographic and market center of the new neighborhood.

- Later phases will include single-family homes that will compete with the influx of more conventional house types.

- A regulating plan to graphically depict private land and the public realm.

- Thoroughfare standards providing graphic descriptions of public rights-of-way, articulating typical layout of travel lanes, parking, sidewalks, and public spaces for a uniform urban fabric for the community.

- Architectural standards that illustrate building massing and plan layout for the variety of building types addressing the plan's ability to accommodate a broad diversity of housing, retail, and office use.

- Standards for platting by accretion that allows incremental development over time.

Project Approach:

The goal of the project was to develop a town center on a greenfield site outside existing city boundaries. The town center needed to be compact with a variety of activities and places to live for people of all ages. The plan needed to result in a place that has a decreased dependence on the automobile, provides a greater proportion of open space to development space, and has a greater level of convenience and amenity for residents. The design team used a week-long charette process to set the framework for the City's High Point/Raymond Neighborhood Development Plan. This process was a requirement for annexation of the property and coordinated effort between public officials, the public, nonprofit organizations, and multiple land owners. The project has spurred additional new traditional development prospects in the Madison metro area. While the project is more oriented to conventional builder methodologies than to high design, it does guide building types to be consistent with the urban form and allows construction without stringent design review processes.

cil members, the land owner, the developer, and all interested citizens in order to produce a plan that addresses the needs of the community. The charette may last a few days or as long as a week. The charette process typically begins with a public meeting where a formal presentation of the project is made in order to provide all the *stakeholders* with the issues that must be addressed. Afterward, the design team may hold individual meetings with key community members to ask specific questions that have not been answered during the research and analysis phase. The design team typically establishes a working studio near the site where the pen-to-paper work will be done. This studio is open to the public and often has a display area in which current scenarios can be viewed and commented on. Public meetings are often conducted by the design team corresponding to various stages of the conceptual design process. These feedback meetings are essential because they let the stakeholders know that their issues are being listened to and seriously considered even if they do not always end up on the final plan. The level of citizen involvement may vary for each project, but planning professionals would be remiss to ignore what people want and need their communities to be. Interested community groups and individuals who have participated in the planning process tend not to be hostile to projects they have had a hand in creating. If people feel as though they have had a voice in the process and perceive that their concerns have been addressed, they will be more supportive and accepting of change and growth. The goal of the charette should be to balance the public's need for involvement while using every opportunity to increase their understanding of good design so they can better participate in the process. However, unless an experienced facilitator conducts the charette, it may become confusing and result in a total lack of direction.

The final plan is the result of the creative exercise: merging the research data, program, goals, site factors, and stakeholder input. Ideas are refined into as many viable solutions as are needed, remembering that there is no such thing as a perfect plan—only a better one. After all the client and community reviews are complete, the final concept plan is created for presentation for the various stages of public approval. Once municipal approval of the concept has been gained, the next step of the design phase is plan refinement, or the *preliminary subdivision plan.*

The Preliminary Subdivision Plan

Using the broad-brushed recommendations proposed in the concept plan as a guide, the preliminary subdivision plan applies the specific criteria for development found in the site plan, subdivision, and zoning ordinances to create a more detailed representation of the project. While it can still be freehand in nature, it should be done to scale and with specific attention paid to the design criteria governing streets (curve radii, parallels, tangents, etc.).

For example, elements of the preliminary subdivision plan would include numbers of required parking spaces, any landscape buffer requirements, maximum allowable lot coverage, stormwater retention or distribution facilities, and location of ingress/egress points. This stage tests the quality of the concept. A good one will require very little modification. However, mistakes in drawing scale at this stage may necessitate time-consuming and expensive changes later on. Once complete, the preliminary plan is submitted to the municipal planning agency for review.

At this point, the plan is examined by municipal planners with specific regard to how it addresses and complies with established regulations in the various municipal ordinances or any overlay district codes that have been newly created for the project or that may already be in force. If the designer has done his or her homework, very few changes should have to be made.

After the preliminary plan is approved, the *hardsheet* is produced. The hardsheet mathematically establishes the elements of the concept, creating a true vision of the built environment. On it, all lines and curves are computed using known reference points such as established property lines or survey benchmarks. *Benchmarks* are monument points field-located by the survey crew to establish the horizontal and vertical elevation of a known point (e.g., a large tree or manhole cover).

When creating a hardsheet for a parcel of land, the preliminary plan is used as a guide. By first calculating the centerline of the streets, the draftser will follow municipal regulations (minimum distances between reverse curves, minimum radii of street returns, cul-de-sac bulb sizes, minimum lot sizes, setbacks, etc.) to create an actual plan that will accurately represent the built product. It includes the *metes and bounds* of existing property lines as well as the topo-

Figure 3.1 Public meeting. *(Photo courtesy of Town Planning Collaborative)*

graphic contours, public right-of-ways, streets, utility structures, and utility easements.

This then, is a second test of the concept's quality. However, even with the best concepts, it is common while creating the hardsheet to find subtle errors that were made during the conceptual phase. For example, in the process of finalizing a conceptual plan for a golf course community done by another firm, the authors found that the course had 19 holes. A closer examination of the drawing revealed two #9 holes in addition to a number of substandard-sized housing lots unacceptable to the provisions established in the local subdivision ordinance. This type of mistake, although innocent, resulted in additional design costs to the client in order to adapt a supposedly finished design before the final subdivision plan could be done.

The original plan was graphically superb, but it lacked design substance. Remember that a pretty picture doesn't always represent reality. But the opposite is also true; the quality of the graphic presentation can make or break a design concept. A timely and needed design solution may be rejected because it is presented with inadequate or poor graphic techniques. Nondesigners have enough trouble visualizing the final result from a two-dimensional drawing. Their task shouldn't be compounded by having to look at a poor graphic presentation. It is therefore paramount that review boards such as planning commissions and city councils be given the best possible product from which to base their decisions. Good graphics are very important, but they should not be used to camouflage poor design. With the approval of the preliminary subdivision plan, the design phase ends.

The Implementation Phase

With the design phase ended, the implementation phase begins. The hardsheet is used to create the *final subdivision plan,* the *subdivision plats* of each individual lot within the parcel and as a reference source in the field for the survey crews during construction stakeout.

The *final subdivision plan* is an accurate scale representation of a proposed land use. It is used in formal presentations to public bodies and reviewing boards to gain final approval. A *subdivision plat* is the recording document that establishes property ownership, utility easements, and public rights-of-way. It is used to delineate individual parcels of property and is required by municipalities for the recording of land ownership, its transfer, and as the document of final design approval that goes into the public record. It is used as the basis for the field stakeout of the physical survey and to establish what is referred to as a *takedown,* a portion of a subdivided parcel of land that is bought at a given time. For instance, a client's attorney will discuss a loan with a banker for a certain portion of land recorded in a subdivision plat. The takedown for this loan may be only 22.8 acres of a 100-acre site. The attorney can request a loan for only the amount needed to make improvements to that portion of the project. This method is particularly helpful to control the costs of phased development while maintaining legal land boundaries. With the approval of the final subdivision plan, the design phase ends. At this point, the hardsheet is used to create the construction documents. It would be appropriate at this point to distinguish the difference between the terms *plan, plat,* and *plot.* A *plan* is a method of action, a way of doing things, to achieve a goal. A *plat* is a recordable document that gives form and detail substance to a plan. A *plot* can refer to a two-dimensional graphic either hand-drawn or produced on a computer, and it can also be used to mean a piece of land.

Construction documents provide detailed information about the specifics of the implementation of the project for the various contractors who may be involved, and they must be placed on record and approved by municipal engineering review personnel to verify compliance with city regulations. Section views, or *profiles,* are used to locate and establish the parameters of in-ground elements such as sanitary sewer lines, stormwater management facilities, water lines, and streets.

Site-specific construction plans represent a building or a configuration of attached buildings on a single site. They will show building attachments, topographic information for site grading, sanitary sewer and water hookups, street ties, landscaping and signage, and so on. Subdivision construction plans are two-dimensional, representing the plan (horizontal) and profile (vertical) alignment and elevation changes of site features such as streets and sidewalks, sanitary sewer and water lines, and stormwater management elements (manholes, catch basins, etc.). These documents graphically represent to the municipal review engineer that the proposed solutions for the site are not only efficient but have been designed to safeguard the public health, safety, and welfare.

The approved construction plans are then used in the bidding and negotiation phase in order to find a suitable contractor to build the project. After awarding a contract, the construction phase begins. A survey team is called in initially to *stake out,* or establish, the elevation of the land form, then the location of sanitary and storm sewers, water lines, streets and sidewalks, and ultimately the footprints of the buildings. As each stage is staked out, implementation can occur. The timetable for completion depends on the size and complexity of the project and a number of other variables (product availability, weather, scheduling of subcontractors, etc.).

In Summary

The process of community design can take many months or even years. The politics of these deals are such that many projects never even make it off the drawing boards. But for those that do, many steps must occur before the idea results in a completed project. Making community design a tcam sport is essential for the process to go forward with vision and deliberate action. No one group should dominate the process, nor should any one group's voice be excluded if the project is to be truly successful. Each member of the design team must come to the table ready to work without professional rivalry raising its ugly head. Elected officials must learn to look beyond the mandated minimums of current regulations in order to serve the best interests of the community—not the best interest of their reelection campaigns. Citizens and neighbors must be ready to express their opinions but also to listen to what others have to say. Land owners, developers, and financiers must recognize that following the path of least resistance over the last half century has created places with a short shelf life. It can be done. It is being done successfully in many places, but not enough. The process has procedures and nomenclature; it requires analysis and consideration. It takes meetings; plans need to be drawn and redrawn. It takes professional creativity and bureaucratic oversight to get it done. The result is up to you and me. Are you ready to get started?

CHAPTER 4

What Is the Language of Design?

At a Glance

❖ Learning to speak the language of community design

❖ Understanding where to look for inspiration and how to distinguish good ideas from bad ones

❖ Creating and understanding a set of consistent graphic symbols to convey the ideas of design

❖ Recognizing how the design process works and some tips for making it work for you

Until now, we have discussed the basics of community design and what generally happens during the process. But knowing the mechanics doesn't necessarily tell us much about the creative nature of design. What goes on in the designer's brain? What does the designer bring to the task? What is creativity, anyway?

Creativity, as it relates to community design, is not so much a talent as it is the learned ability to solve a problem. It is asking the right questions that enable one to see the big picture and identify a theme. Creativity is the spark that gives life to the raw elements. It is that point at which the dead elements of the research and inventory phase begin to come together and reveal design patterns. For the community designer, the act of being creative is a process of blending the *program,* that wish list of ideals, with the constraints of existing conditions.

Creative thinking can be a struggle. The key to it, however, is just to begin. Whether pruning a tree, climbing a mountain, or creating a community, the first step is to take the first step. One must find the diseased branch or the one that is most out of balance with the tree and cut it off. One must choose the easiest access to the mountain and go there. One must identify the givens of a project and use a theme as an underlying structure in the planning process. In each example, the first step is taken, then that step is assessed before proceeding. We might call this approach to creativity the STARR method: *STudy* the problem. *Act* on the finding. *Reassess* the situation. *React* accordingly.

This act of being *creative* can thus be interpreted as *design.* For our purpose, the two words are interchangeable. Creative planning is design, and one who designs is a designer.

The act of designing is very inertial. The phrase "The tendency of a body at rest tending to stay at rest and of a body in motion to stay in motion" can be applied with ease to design. It is an active process. Inspiration may be difficult at times, which is why adherence to the program is so important. It can be the mechanism that helps the designer jumpstart a cold brain. And, as any good designer can tell you, once the process of design begins, it is like a freight train running downhill. Its fast and furious. That's a simple enough definition, right? But it doesn't tell us what design is.

The concept of design scares a lot of people by inferring some sort of mysterious art practiced only by the most gifted minds. Simply put, design is the conscious and subconscious mind wrestling with a puzzle and trying to resolve it. This process can be all-consuming at times. In fact, you can get so absorbed in a particularly troubling scenario that you dream about it when you are asleep. Just because you leave the office at five does not mean you leave the puzzle at the office. In fact, the subconscious ponders it for so long that a flash of insight may occur at some of the most unlikely times, and wham, you better have a pencil and paper handy. Every good designer should keep a pencil and paper handy at all times, especially on the nightstand! That space of time between turning off the light and dropping off to sleep is prime brain time. Maybe as we are trying to put everything aside for the night, the usually mute voice of the subconscious can be heard. Or maybe we are just freeing brain space to work at a higher capacity without so many interruptions.

Design is not a mystery at all. It is the graphic exploration of issues, a process of discovery that leads to *eureka*—that coalescing of ideas that sets humankind apart from the beasts . . . *reasoning.*

Let us not confuse the term *graphic* with *art,* either. While some designers are artists, not every designer is an artist, and an artist is not necessarily a designer. Designers draw to see the possibilities, to make the connections. The brain-hand-eye coordination allows designers to see what they are thinking. The result should be a plethora of both good and bad solutions; design can be a messy business. Every good designer should have a pile of wadded up paper on the floor.

The goal of this chapter is to encourage you to be a problem solver by showing you tools that will help you define the issues and lead you down the path to discovery. We will also pass along some tricks of the trade that we have found to be the most helpful and that you will see utilized in the chapters that follow.

If you are an old hand at this process, maybe we can remind you of some of the basics. If you have been crunching numbers too long, maybe we can help you unlock some of your more intuitive skills that have been boxed up and stored in the attic of your brain. If you are new to the game, we can equip you with the tools that will help bring your best instincts to bear on the task. Finally, if you are not a designer but want to understand it so you can be a better participant in the process, we want to let you know what you will see and how to understand it. Remember that no one has the corner on intuition. Although it may come easier for some, the rest of us have to work pretty hard at it. In the end, you will find that with experience you can cultivate a talent for it. Find what works for you and stay with it. To that end, the best way for us to help would be to show you what designers do and why. Hopefully, if we do our job right, you will be able to glean the best of what we have to offer and add it to your own bag of tricks.

Program, Get Your Program Here

The program is the culmination of what the client hopes to accomplish with the site as well as the opportunities that are evident from the research and analysis phase. However, in many cases it is the designer's responsibility to ask the client more questions and then to temper the initial vision with input from the ultimate users, if possible, as well as to meet the demand as identified by the market research. Moreover, needs must be separated from desires: needs are *threshold conditions* whereas desires are *electives*. The program should be organized to segregate the technical requirements from the aesthetic desires. But it does not stop here. As the creative juices get flowing, the process of discovery may reveal new possibilities. That's why it is so important for the program to be flexible enough to incorporate new opportunities as they present themselves. As the designer focuses on the task, the program guides the action. As the designer focuses on the task of creativity, the program guides the action; it gives direction to that creativity, literally making something out of nothing. The design program works similarly to a program one receives at a Broadway play or some other special event— it clues in the audience to the sequence of events they will witness and, in some cases, the goal that the performers hope to achieve.

As in our example, the program must be formally written down so that it can be referred to often. In fact it should be posted in a prominent place so that it can serve as a kind of checklist to keep the designer from forgetting anything.

At this point, the designer should not be overly concerned about the details. Although it is important that concepts be as realistic as possible to coincide with cost constraints, design should not be detail-driven. Early concepts should deal only in broad generalities. The details tend to work themselves out as the concept is further refined.

How does design begin? The program has been established. The research data has been analyzed to identify the opportunities. What now? How do we jump-start creativity?

The Inspiration of Design

Design, much like writing, making music, and creating art, is very kinetic; however, it sometimes needs to be helped along. Inspiration is the grease that can get the freight train of design moving, but it is not always easy to come by. It's true that if you have a good program, the battle is half won, but calling up your inspiration is equally important.

There are three sources of inspiration: the natural world, the manufactured world, and abstract thought. As we consider these, don't expect us to create a new science. The goal is to get you to think in unaccustomed ways, to open your eyes to the obvious and not so obvious. Every design attempted should build on what we know already. This is not only smart, it is the way our communities have evolved and adapted over the years.

The Natural World

The beauty of the natural world is unmatched for inspiring creativity in all but the most closed mind. Whether it is the perfect geometry of a shell we find at the seashore, the playful sound of the meandering brook in the forest, the rich color of the desert landscape at sunset, or the intricacy of the veins in a leaf from your own backyard, inspiration abounds if we only look for it.

In the natural world we find not only beauty, but economy of energy—doing the most with the least with little or no waste. For example, it is no accident that a tubular column is the strongest structural element. The next time you are out-

side look at a reed or a tree trunk. In both cases, maximum weight is supported by the least amount of mass. The cactus is another example. Its trunk and leaf are merged, thus reducing the surface area subject to moisture loss and enabling it to survive in the most hostile environments.

Figure 4.1 Inspiration from the sea.

The bubble is perfect in form and design. It maintains a perfectly round shape with an almost magical consistency. Each individual, whether large or small, is exact in symmetry and proportion. Spherical as a single element, it takes on a crystalline, almost angular structure in mass. If you look close enough, say at the froth of the ocean or the dishwater in your own sink, bubbles take on an almost honeycomb appearance. This six-sided configuration, composed of six triangles (the basic building block), is the element that makes possible the geodesic dome of the Epcot Center at Florida's Disney World.

Nature abounds with energy and simplicity, providing multiple solutions to common problems. The wings of a bumblebee and an eagle differ dramatically in size, structure, and composi-

Figure 4.2 Inspiration from the land.

Figure 4.3 The wings of the bumblebee perform flawlessly.

tion, yet each performs its intended function flawlessly. Nature repeats successful solutions. It's no accident that there are no three- or five-legged animals—but there are numerous no-legged creatures and multi-legged ones.

Nature loves balance and symmetry. In every living thing, nature attempts to create the perfect solution (body size and shape) to satisfy a particular problem (program). All trees of a species attempt to branch in a certain pattern (the perfect solution in a perfect world), but no two are exactly the same. The forces of wind, disease, and foraging animals all modify and customize in their own slight way each individual tree.

In the mineral world it can be said that beauty is a product of both strength and weakness. Erosion caused by wind and water exploits weak seams in rock, whereas hardened forms resist the inexorable, relentless efforts of these forces. The result: glorious valleys and sleepy, serene deltas.

With nature as a guide, don't be afraid to think in ways that are new and unique. If a meandering stream helps you to see a better hierarchy of circulation, go for it. If the cell pattern of a leaf leads you to construct a better town plan, hurrah! We need the innovation.

The Built Environment

It seems to be politically correct to find fault with the built environment. Nevertheless, there is much to celebrate and imitate. As we look for inspiration in the manufactured world, we need to incorporate the best of human endeavor into the continuum of design. The successful communities of the past and present reflect not only the essence of our relationships with one another, but the organizing elements we use to create form and function.

We have already mentioned Charleston and Savannah, which have capitalized on their historical significance, as well as resort towns like Seaside—towns that have been given a lot of attention in the recent past in regard to what communities of the future should emulate. More recently, the town of Celebration, Florida, has captured national attention because it reminds us of the way towns used to be built and can be again if we have the will to do it. Thousands of tourists visit these places every year just to experience them—to walk down their streets, to shop, eat, and to dream about what it would be like to live in such a place.

The point of this exercise is to analyze places like these and explore why they are preferred to more conventionally designed places (no one wants to vacation in suburbia!). We need to ask ourselves the following questions: Why are some of the more traditional towns from the past still functional and desirable today? Why have the ceremonial boulevard and the customary location of the marketplaces at key intersections of travel stood the test of time? Why do the resorts, the theme parks, the historic areas attract droves of us to their

Figure 4.4 Seaside, Florida.

Figure 4.5 Places like this have economy of scale and give attention to detail.

quaint and crowded streets? Is it not the economy of scale, the attention to detail and spatial definition, that creates a feeling of community? Do they not make us feel at home in comfortable relationship with one another and with ourselves?

In our travels as well as in our daily lives we should constantly be aware of our surroundings, taking note of our reactions to the spaces through which we move. We can learn from the built environment by asking ourselves what works and what doesn't. What could have been done to make it better? It is not enough to simply identify a problem; that's easy. As rational, thinking human beings we should always attempt to imagine a solution to the problems presented. Only through this active involvement with our manufactured world can we possibly begin the process of eliminating features that don't work. If we can't eliminate them, then at least we can ensure that we do not employ them again.

As we do this, we learn from the successes of the past, but also from the *blunders,* which are the true teachers because their unabashed consequences speak so loudly. One need not look much further than the nearest hamburger alley to be faced with how not to do it. The philosopher spoke well who said, "Those who cannot remember the past are condemned to repeat it." I don't suppose Santayana was thinking of community planners when he uttered those words.

Figure 4.6 Hamburger alley in suburbia.

Abstract Thought: The Emotional Connection

Inspiration is not always limited to what we can see and touch but can often be inferred from emotions and feelings, which are abstract concepts. The psychology of how users perceive a space or the community in which they live can have obvious ramifications. Research suggests that the quality of spatial definition affects perception and use. If joy and excitement are the emotions desired, the elements of color, texture, pattern, and surprise should be utilized. If introspection and reverence are wanted, then smooth, curving lines and rolling topography should be used. The use of water, shade, and the color green are calming, soothing, and reassuring. Sharp angles, hard surfaces, and hot colors can stimulate feelings of excitement and anticipation. Concepts like perfection can be represented by certain basic shapes (e.g., circle, equilateral triangle). The grand buildings and public spaces remaining from antiquity that incorporate these ele-

Figure 4.7 Rolling topography inspires reverence and introspection.

ments inspire us with their intricacies and simplicity. Yet the key to their success and livability is their inherent ability to adapt to change. As each new generation embraces them, they continue to serve as testimonials to the emotions they inspire.

Drawing What We Think

In order to think conceptually and understand graphic communication techniques, one needs to know the graphic language of community design. This language represents the various elements of design and visually describes the functional relationships of a place.

Nondesigners have difficulty interpreting two-dimensional plans. The plan (i.e., the view from above) can be quite confusing to the casual observer accustomed to experiencing only the pedestrian scale. Therefore, a good plan must be descriptive and informative simultaneously. Every line should mean something and correspond to an item in the program. The language of design, therefore, consists of the graphic symbols that represent the building blocks of community. All the disparate elements of the built environment must be represented using some discernable and distinct symbol. Each designer may have his or her own style, but the key is to maintain a consistent repertoire.

In order to use Lynch's paths, edges, districts, nodes, and landmarks as the building blocks of community design and axial design, hierarchy, transitional elements, dominant features, sense of enclosure and the spatial components of circulation, open space, and structures as the tools of design, we must associate them with a graphic designation. During the conceptual phase of the design process, each symbol should reflect its inherent activity and be bold, simply conceived, and convey the essence of the element in a very generalized manner. The graphics must distill

Figure 4.8 Versailles, France. Photo taken by Robert McDuffie.

complicated patterns, land uses, and activities into very simple images that are easily drawn and readily understood.

Hand-drawn, manual design is preferred to computer-aided design for conceptual plans so that the designer can be in touch with the scale and shape of the site. It is very difficult to obtain the tactile interaction needed for the creative process while working with a mouse and a display screen because there is no spontaneity. The designer is removed from the design surface, and that can hinder the effort. Every designer should have plenty of pencils, markers, and paper.

Symbolism for Substance

Paths are linear elements and represent both vehicular and pedestrian movement. They are free-form, either continuous, dashed, or dotted, with arrows to denote direction. Whether major arterial or neighborhood street, urban thoroughfare or meandering woodland trail, each should denote a degree of usage that is unique and clearly communicates proportion and hierarchy.

Edges, like paths, are linear. Because they represent boundaries that are either soft or hard, real or perceived, they are important organizing elements. They can be represented in a variety of ways, including with dashes, dots, hatches, or stipples.

Districts encompass areas of commonality. Although less defined, they should be continuous, fluid, and graphically serve as a background for more focused, active elements. A pastel color wash works nicely for this because it provides translucent substance.

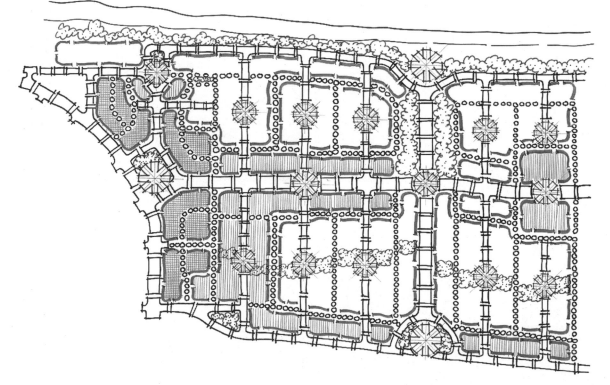

Sketch 4.1 Concept plan.

Nodes are specific points of recognition. They are destinations and very often represent the core or center of a district as well as a transition between two districts. Because they are closely associated with paths, they can be represented by dashed circles or bulbs within a path.

Landmarks are important reference points. By nature they are attention-getters and should reflect this special status graphically. Asterisks, stars, or other symbols that scream "Look at me!" are appropriate.

Axial design is represented by a strong linear connection. It creates a clearly recognizable order connecting two or more features or terminal points.

Hierarchy is a gradation between outdoor spaces. It is depicted by a series of shapes ranging in size from small to large and can connote the difference in scale between similar uses (e.g., transportation corridors).

Transitional elements are the overlap areas that exhibit the characteristics of two distinct spaces. They blend or blur the edges and help us make sense of what we see when we pass

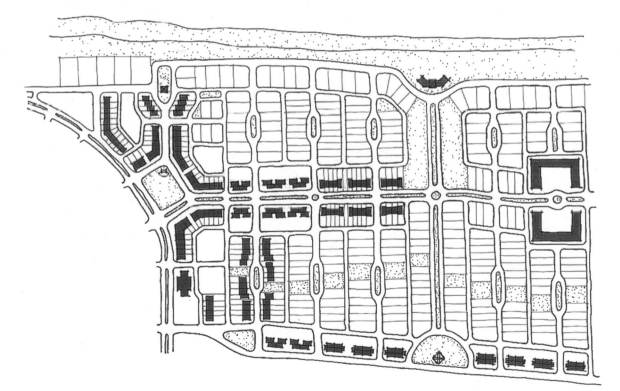

Sketch 4.2 Preliminary plan.

from one space to another. Transition can be represented by the repetition of a building form, a landscape element, or even a paving material.

Dominant features are focal points. They create hierarchy and contrast. They command attention and may become landmarks. They give space a reason for existing. Dominant features are represented similar to landmarks and can be either at the terminal points of an axis or at the center of an open space.

Sense of enclosure is the single most important spatial characteristic. It is interpreted as the relationship between the horizontal and the vertical. It has the ability to emote

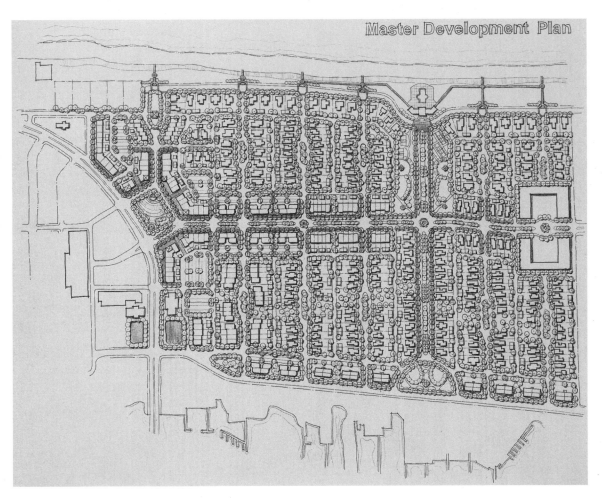

Sketch 4.3 Illustrative master plan.

comfort at the proper scale and stress when the space is out of proportion with its intended use. Sense of enclosure is not as readily shown in the plan view, but it can be interpreted when building massing or landscape elements are used to define an outdoor space.

Circulation and *paths* are essentially the same. They represent different means of movement, whether vehicular or pedestrian. A hierarchy of circulation systems is essential for good design and is the basic method for giving order to a community. Circulation can be represented by either lines, dashes, or dots depending on the volume and type of traffic.

Open space can be a void, leftover space where the lot was too small, was a funny shape, or where environmental constraints prohibit building. Then again, open space can be a series of well-placed, appropriately sized commons that provide residents a variety of choices for relaxation, play, and interaction.

Structures are buildings and can be represented by any number of geometric shapes. They can be long or short. They should be sized appropriately to represent the scale of the proposed use and to create human-scaled spaces. Other useful symbols include the following:

- Trees or natural buffers can be represented by circles, fluid curves, or random continuous lines.

- Screens, whether natural or constructed can be represented as a jagged or picket fence–type line.

- Water, whether streams or the edges of lakes, is usually represented by the universally recognized standard for watercourses—a long dash and three dots.

- Topography will be drawn in two ways: existing and proposed. Existing topography is represented by short dashed lines with every fifth contour shown slightly longer and heavier. Proposed topography is represented as a continuous line linking existing contours of the same elevation. Contours do not cross as a rule, except when an outcrop is being illustrated.

- Property should be represented as series of long lines with two dashes interrupting it at regular intervals.

- Utilities can be drawn as a continuous line interrupted by the first letter of the utility being shown (*S* for sewer, *T* for telephone, etc.).

- Views, whether positive or negative, can be represented by two lines emanating from a point with an arrow at the end. An arc can be drawn between the lines.

Design: How Does It Work?

How does design work? As research data is gathered and analyzed, it is being loaded into the conscious and subconscious mind. There it begins to coalesce with our preconceived notions, our experiences, and our emotions. We mull it over. We wrestle with various outcomes. It can be a very strenuous and energy-consuming process. Sadly, there are no magic words that will make it easier; it requires intense concentration to channel all of one's energy into solving a problem. But several things will help you get through it and make it work for you.

- Get the pencil moving! You won't get anything done until you do. Right, wrong, or indifferent, nothing happens until this occurs. There is such a thing as studying something to death. Sometimes you just have to start slugging away at it.

- Starting slowly is best. There is no reason why one should not warm up to the effort. Just as a sprinter loosens up before a race, so you should spend a few minutes thinking about your plan of attack.

- Start with the elements of the site that are more readily and easily solved. In other words, work from the given to the unknown, from the general to the specific.

- Let your hand and eye react together so that you are almost an observer of what is going on. Once you get going, you can ask yourself if it feels good. If it does, ride the wave until it breaks.

- Look at the site in terms of circulation, open space, and structures—but independently of one another. Optimize each system irrespective of the others. Then begin the process of overlaying each to identify opportunities and conflicts, ultimately blending them to an optimum solution.

- Make connections. Learning to see the connections between seemingly unrelated elements is a skill.

- Constantly questioning the status quo is the critical path to creativity. Always test yourself and your emerging solution. Ask questions: "Have I missed an opportunity? What if I were to do this? Can I get another 10 percent here or there? What happens when I add, subtract, increase, reduce, intensify?" Get the picture?

- Do not get too attached to any one solution, either. No plan is perfect. With each succeeding pass over the concept, a new piece of the puzzle fits into place. In fact, sometimes you find solutions to as-yet-unrecognized problems. You recognize you have done it only when you are evaluating your solutions with a critical eye. Serendipity is so sweet.

- Don't be afraid to leave a particularly challenging scenario when you are just not getting anywhere with it. It is better to take a break and come back fresh than to keep hammering at it and get frustrated. Take a break. Have an adult beverage. Relax. A lot of tough problems have been solved on the back of a cocktail napkin.

- If you are pressed for time and you can't afford to take a break, try walking around to the other side of the table. Rethink your approach. Readjust. Recalibrate your thinking.

- Think on your feet. Design should be done standing up. The phrase "thinking on your feet" is aptly spoken in the realm of design. Refining the details can be explored while sitting down, but the initial thrust to come up with viable concepts and the key to good design is *activity,* which is best accomplished standing up.

- In learning to distill our creative energy within the movement of eye, hand, and arm we are similar to an athlete whose concentration is brought to crescendo in competition. A good designer should break into a good sweat while designing. The exhaustion is invigorating.

- Ultimately, we should ask ourselves how what we are proposing will fit into the community. What problems are we solving or creating? Is there a better way? Is the community supported, served, benefited, or enhanced? We have to consider the bigger picture, the larger issues. If it is good for the community, it is good for the individual, and the designer has done the job right.

In Summary

In this chapter we have learned that community design is problem solving. Often, there are so many barriers to producing good design solutions that the path of least resistance has led us to vinyl villages of franchised architecture surrounded by seas of asphalt. The endless pursuit of mediocrity has an alternative. We must study ways of doing better, act on our findings, reassess the situation, and react accordingly. In order to do this effectively we need to recognize that most of us need inspiration from outside of ourselves. The world around us is replete with examples of both good and bad solutions. Inspiration is ours if we know where to look.

The natural world has many beautiful and functional organisms. The manufactured world has much we don't want to repeat, but there is a lot of good, too. Our minds need to be fully operational and our emotions are key to how we feel. Both working together help us to comprehend how abstract concepts can move us toward good design.

Learning the graphic language of design is essential if we are going to put all of it together and communicate our ideas effectively. Creating our own or interpreting the drawings of others requires a thorough understanding of how the building blocks of community are represented on paper. The more we exercise these skills, the more insight we gain. We must train our minds as we train our bodies if we want them to master a task.

CHAPTER 5

What Is the Framework of Community?

At a Glance

❖ Understanding that community design must accommodate both pedestrians and automobiles

❖ Establishing a framework for circulation that provides options for movement

❖ Learning how to put the automobile in its place

❖ Creating places where people want to walk

❖ Understanding the infrastructure needs of community

Community, like any structure, must have a framework that supports it and gives it physical form. Circulation systems, both vehicular and pedestrian, are not only the essential paths that allow movement, they are the bones, if you will, around which the organism of community grows. More than an exercise in engineering technique, roads and pathways can serve as necessary evils or as conduits for the lifeblood of the community, providing access, service, and security for residents. Superior circulation design creates the mental pattern or image of a community. It is the one element that truly creates individuality and establishes character.

Not that the other issues we have discussed are less important, but we have to admit that community planning continues to be predominantly influenced by the automobile. In too many places, traffic engineers have become the de facto community planners. You don't have to be a genius to look at our communities and figure out that traffic engineering has, more than any other factor, subdivided our communities into commuter hell. One need only try to get from point A to point B in any town for this to become crystal clear.

The physical organization of the region should be supported by a framework of transportation alternatives. Transit, pedestrian, and bicycle systems should maximize access and mobility throughout the region while reducing dependence upon the automobile.

Charter of the Congress of New Urbanism

In larger metropolitan areas, one can trace the sequence of development back to a central-core grid system. After World War II, a modified or flexible grid came into fashion due in part to its successful use at a planned unit development (PUD) in New York called Levittown. This in itself was a radical break with the tradition of the times. In the 1960s and 1970s PUDs came to be more accepted, with far-reaching changes for society. Curvilinear roads, looping collector streets, short, curving cul-de-sacs, and a reliance on the hierarchical system became commonplace. This approach worked well until the PUDs in any given area began to build out and the inevitable traffic congestion resulted.

In the 1980s, the exclusive community came into vogue. Every development had to be a *private* this or a *lifestyle* that, complete with gatehouses both real and ceremonial. These usually relied on a single entry point, which led to a large-loop collector road with smaller imitations of the larger con-

Figure 5.1 Suburbia is dominated by the automobile.

cept serving as the pattern for the individual neighborhoods. At the beginning of a new century, we are looking back to a simpler time and place. The neotraditional town exhibits the traditional values of neighbors, friends, and family, with a de-emphasis on the automobile by attempting to enhance the pedestrian environment and promote mass transit.

Vehicular circulation consumes an estimated 30 percent of our developed areas. It is the most expensive feature of community development and creates vast expanses of pavement—literally a no-man's-land for the pedestrian. But lest you confuse us with the frenzied wackos who believe that the automobile is inherently evil and is destroying the planet, let's approach it from a rational standpoint. Down deep we all know the real problem lies not with our cars but with the way our towns and cities are structured.

Because the automobile is such a strong influence and promises to be so for a long time to come, roads and parking

Figure 5.2 Residential streets should foster interaction between neighbors.

must be approached calmly and logically. This is one of those situations when a little dreaming can be helpful. We've seen what traffic engineering has given us: the Los Angeles Freeway, the Atlanta Loop, I-95 through New York City, and the Washington Beltway. Good circulation responds to topography, water bodies, wetlands, and public utilities to enhance movement within the community. Properly utilized, it can create harmonious unity to reinforce variety and wayfinding. But if used incorrectly, circulation does a very good job of creating discord and confusion. The problem is that too often it is patterned after highway standards, resulting in very costly, inflexible design. In addition, the local circulation tends to follow or respect zoning lines just as much as it does parcel lines, and this reinforces the separation of uses and community divisiveness. A better approach would be to balance street design requirements for safe and efficient movement with the scale of the application. For example, residential

Figure 5.3 In suburbia, residential streets are often microfreeways.

Sketches 5.1, 5.2 **Which plan reflects a unified community design?**

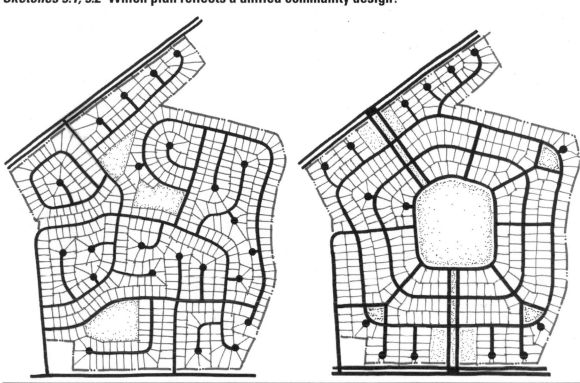

streets should be intimate, should foster interaction between neighbors, and should be designed or customized for community conditions. They should not resemble microfreeways.

Basic Patterns

On a neighborhood scale, circulation patterns in our developed areas generally take on one of four basic forms: grid, radial, hierarchical, or looping. More typically, each neighborhood will be designed by using a combination of two or more of these basic types.

The Grid System

The *grid system* is designed to disperse traffic as uniformly as possible by providing multiple options for both pedestrians and vehicles. It has been much maligned due to its seeming rigidity, monotony, and indifference to topography. It can, in fact, be relatively easy to adapt it to topography. With its beginnings in the militia towns of the Greeks and Romans, it was easy and quick to construct, its primary aim being to allow rapid movement from one side of town to the other for defensive purposes. How ironic that, given its beginnings, the grid system is now thought of in terms of congestion and inaccessibility—gridlock, as it were. It was also used with frequency in the American Midwest with its abundance of level land. An extreme version of this street pattern is found in San Francisco, with streets seeming to defy gravity in their head-on orientation—literally straight up and down the hills.

The success of the grid lies in its predictability of intersections, which gives the traveler clues and reference points in wayfinding. With the north-south streets as named boulevards and the east-west ones as numbered connectors, it becomes almost impossible to lose one's way. All one needs to be able to do is count. Moreover, in a grid system, because of the even distribution of traffic, practically every foot of frontage on the street is usable and functional in that all the streets are directly accessible from the immediately adjacent privately owned land—something not necessarily true in suburbia. A pleasant by-product of this even distribution of traffic is less reliance on specifically designed collector streets—they are simply not needed as much.

Exciting spaces can result when two grid systems converge. Again using San Francisco as an example, a walk up and down Market Street reveals interesting triangular intersections and green spaces. Overwhelming vertical spaces are created by the adjoining skyscrapers. New Orleans, with its grid system bending in response to the shape of the Mississippi River, creates a physical and psychological link to that great waterway to which the city owes its existence.

The grid is usually very walkable for the pedestrian for reasons cited previously and the fact that it creates a variety of ways to go from one destination

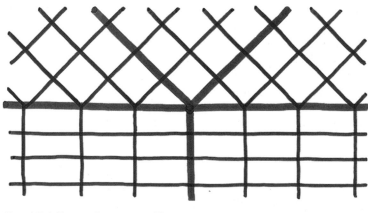

Sketch 5.3 Converging street grid systems.

to another. However, repeating the block pattern too often can be very expensive and land-consuming. For example, when New York City is mentioned, one thinks immediately of the world's largest collection of giant skyscrapers. But an equally astounding fact is that the island of Manhattan is perhaps 45 to 50 percent covered by asphalt pavement. All this, and yet there is still never a parking space to be had!

Radial Systems

The *radial system* is a series of streets emanating from or focusing on a central point or zone. From a functional standpoint, this system can usually be found to originate from old farm-to-market roads where produce and livestock were transported to a central area for sale or shipment. This system works well to create a community heart or focus, thus functionally and figuratively unifying an area. It works best in combination with a set of circumferential roads that create concentric circles about the center. This is, in fact, nothing more than a modified grid system resembling a polar projection map of longitude and latitude lines. Radial streets allow the most direct route to and through a central point. In large areas, these radial farm-to-market streets have evolved into the major collector streets that carry the bulk of the traffic for the area leading to peak periods of congestion at the central point.

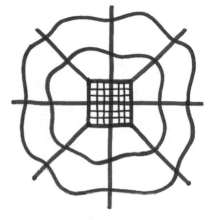

Sketch 5.4 Roads creating concentric circles about a center.

While most cities have some form of radial system emanating from the older city core, this system has not been applied to the outlying areas and probably should have been used much more as a design approach. This could have helped create *focused* suburban areas rather than the sprawling format that has occurred. In some cases, this system has been superimposed over a grid to create some very dynamic urban spaces. Washington, D.C., Paris, and the original Daniel Burnham plan of 1909 for Chicago incorporated this concept as well as most of the more organic, less-planned core areas of cities such as Boston and London.

Hierarchical Systems

The *hierarchical systems,* also known as the *branching system,* is a pattern of circulation structured much like a tree in that smaller roads or branches lead to increasingly larger collector roads. This concentration of traffic on fewer and fewer roads

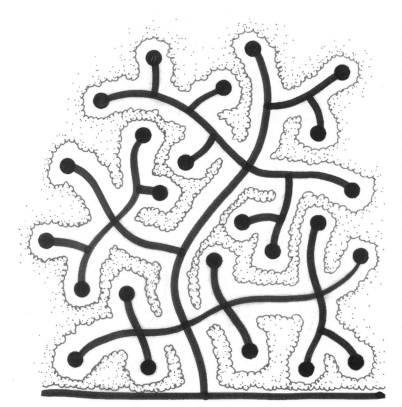

Sketch 5.5 Hierarchical street system.

ensures an eventual overload of the system because it creates few, if any, alternative routes of access to a particular place. Instead, choke points are created, as there is essentially only one way in and one way out of an area. Because traffic is being directed to one or only a few points of circumferential movement, navigating around the choke points is very difficult. This also tends to isolate certain areas from the community at large, reducing their psychological link with or incorporation into the fabric of the community. Hierarchical circulation systems came into design prominence with the advent of the large planned unit developments in the 1960s, which persist in massive numbers today.

Hierarchical systems rely heavily on cul-de-sac streets, which can be used quite effectively when you want to pull some amenity, open space, or wooded area into a residential area. Neighborhoods that can boast of such amenities are usually those with higher-priced homes, as cul-de-sac lots tend to be more expensive. When used in large-scale residential neighborhoods, wayfinding for visitors and residents alike can be exasperating, as all areas tend to look the same. This problem can be somewhat overcome if an identifiable spine road or collector loop is employed to create a discernable structure that literally holds the system together.

Hierarchical systems function best within small-scale residential environments consisting of a limited number of housing types and dwelling units. They also work well for areas adjacent to tidal waters, on lakes, or in areas of substantial topography. All of these areas are typified by an undulating edge beyond which no development is possible; therefore, using cul-de-sacs or closes that branch off a neighborhood street is a typical solution. By keeping through traffic to a minimum, they help reduce noise and conflicts between pedestrians and automobiles at the extreme end of the system. They are also very economical, as they allow the maximum amount of development area per minimum length of street.

Looping Systems

Like the hierarchical system, *looping systems* can be more readily utilized for individual neighborhoods than for community-wide applications. When used in combination with the hierarchical system, a strong sense of place can be achieved for the neighborhood—but, again, not necessarily for the overall community. Neighborhoods built using this format usually are typified by a primary entrance road that leads to a central organizing roadway from which the residential streets stem. Looping systems have been widely used in planned unit developments because they provide a strong organizing framework, but they can also be very effective when utilized within communities limited by standard euclidean zoning. Despite the single-entry feature, this layout distributes local traffic somewhat better than the branching system, especially the farther away from the entry one travels. For this reason, roadway widths can be somewhat smaller than those found in the hierarchical systems. However, as in the hierarchical system, all traffic is forced to a single point, with the end result being the same: traffic congestion.

To a limited extent, this system can be applied in a linear fashion, especially in areas where large through streets or highways bisect an area, with access to adjacent areas limited by topography, wetlands, or water. In these instances, the primary role of such a system is to provide additional right-of-way frontage for development and to provide for a parallel

Transit corridors, when properly planned and coordinated, can help organize metropolitan structure and revitalize urban centers. In contrast, highway corridors should not displace investment from existing centers.

Charter of the Congress of New Urbanism

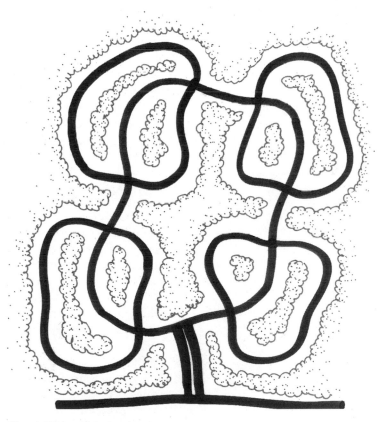

Sketch 5.6 Looping street system.

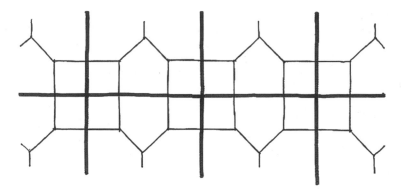

Sketch 5.7 "Minibeltway" around intersection separates through traffic from local traffic.

access system to the main road. This form has been widely adapted to successfully create linear office parks along major thoroughfares. They are successful for this reason: exposure to and visibility from the main road are possible, while access to the office sites is channeled and controlled at fewer points. This allows the larger traffic volumes on the primary roadway to be separated from the traffic around the office sites. However, the gains from such flexible access are lost by the inability to identify a center or focus of the development itself.

As previously stated, our existing neighborhoods and communities have been structured using one or more of the four basic circulation patterns. Whether this has been in response to such things as topographic anomalies, wetlands, or the location of existing utilities, we need to evaluate the strengths and weaknesses of these patterns to determine how they can help create the type of community framework we want. All can and should be utilized.

Classifying Streets

The function of a street dictates its classification; this in turn dictates its design volume and construction requirements. Streets can be either private or public; however, larger streets are more likely to be publicly owned and maintained. Residential street design standards may vary slightly among older municipalities, but in communities developed since the 1950s, wider street sections are the norm. This change occurred as a result of the implementation of federal highway standards based on civil defense guidelines. During the 1950s, transportation planners studied the impact of aerial bombing on European cities during World War II. Tight street grids made them ideal targets because they provided concentrated areas for destruction. These lessons were then applied to planning for nuclear conflict. Wider streets were deemed necessary for potential mass evacuation prior to, and cleanup following, a nuclear strike.[1] The casualties of this thinking have been the communities who have lost their uniqueness, their sense of individuality, and their sense of place. Streets have become solely the domain of the automobile. The grid pattern has faded from use and the alley has become all but extinct in the suburban realm. Alleys can, however, be found in fashionable redevelopment or gentrified areas, serving as private rear-access drives for upscale homes.

CSD Pattern

In conventional suburban developments (CSDs), street classification has evolved and has come to be defined in hierarchical terms, each type representing a higher volume of vehicular traffic. This has produced three primary types of streets: minor streets, collector streets, and arterial streets.

Minor streets are courts, cul-de-sacs, or short loop roads that directly serve residential homesites. These typically have a 40- to 50-foot right-of-way width and contain two travel lanes, with an additional pavement section wide enough to allow on-street parking.

Collector streets have a 60- to 100-foot right-of-way and are three- to four-lane roads that connect residential areas to arterial streets. At the lesser right-of-way width, dwellings have been oriented toward the right-of-way, but at greater widths they are oriented toward side streets or sited with their backs to the collector. Commercial uses usually occur at the intersection of arterials and collectors.

Arterial streets have right-of-way widths of 100 feet or greater. They are designed for the movement of high volumes of traffic between nodes with commercial or industrial functions. They usually always consist of a divided roadway of four or more lanes with a defined median in the center. Cross-access is limited to median breaks located at intersections and are 500 or more feet apart. Generally, no dwellings front directly onto arterial streets. Dwellings that do face arterials are usually preexisting conditions; otherwise, they are most often accessed by a frontage road. This practice is fading from use because of the expense of maintaining separate, parallel roadways. Most of these frontage roads are absorbed as arterials are widened to make way for more traffic moving at higher speeds.

TND Pattern

In traditional neighborhood developments (TNDs), the nomenclature of street classification has more variety. This is not to suggest that streets do not function in a similar fashion or that the streets capable of higher traffic volumes so prevalent in standardized suburbia have been replaced, but TND streets are intended for smaller volumes. This is due to the fact that a network disperses traffic on more streets rather than concentrating it on fewer streets. To understand TND street classification, one must realize that streets are considered to be the domain of both the motorist and the nonmotorist alike. Streets are intended to help define the neighborhood, creating a sense of place. They are interconnected, reducing through traffic on any one street and providing more than one way to get to a destination.

TND streets tend to have a narrower pavement width, but they provide both travel lanes and on-street parallel parking. This technic helps to slow traffic and thus improve safety for pedestrians. Sidewalks are provided on both sides of the street and separated from the street by a planting verge. Shade trees are regularly spaced in the verge to help define the street edge and moderate summer temperatures.

TND street types are defined by their use and location, as is true for conventional suburban development, but TNDs use the following terms: *neighborhood streets, alleys, drives, roads, avenues,* and *boulevards.*

Neighborhood streets provide two-way vehicular movement. On either side of the street is a planting verge for street trees and a sidewalk. There is no median separating travel lanes. Parallel parking is provided on one or both sides of the street. Rights-of-way along neighborhood streets may vary between 30 and 60 feet (*right-of-way* being measured as the distance between the back sides of both sidewalks).

Alleys, or lanes, are narrow, one- or two-way service corridors providing access to the rear of residential lots. In TNDs, the alley is used to store and pick up garbage cans, run utilities (usually underground), and park vehicles (either in garages or in small parking areas at the rear of the house). Alley right-of-way widths vary, but may be as much as 30 feet. There are no sidewalks along alleys.

Drives are roads that separate a developed area from a nondeveloped area. Along the developed edge, a drive may have curbs and gutters; the other side of the road may be more rural in character, perhaps having a wide shoulder or a drainage swale. The right-of-way width will depend on the number of travel lanes used.

Roads serve as access to a residential neighborhood. The character of a road may be rural, with shoulders and swales on either side, or it may have curbs and gutters, planting verges, and sidewalks on one or both sides.

Avenues are the equivalent of CSD collector streets. They may have more than one travel lane in each direction and have a tree-planted median separating opposing traffic. Avenues usually have a terminating vista at the center of a neighborhood where a public building or monument is located. Avenues may have on-street parallel parking on both sides. They most definitely will have sidewalks separated from the travel lanes by a tree-planted verge.

Boulevards are the equivalent of CSD arterial streets. They are large, multiple-lane roadways often having a wide, planted median in the center separating opposing travel lanes. Boulevards will not have on-street parallel parking, but they will probably have sidewalks separated from the roadway by a planting verge irregular in width that allows the sidewalk to meander rather than being rigidly parallel to the pavement edge.

Design Considerations

Street and roadway layouts have an impact on the community far beyond their costs of construction; they create the mental image one is left with after visiting a place. This being the case, they should be designed with special attention to their appropriateness, orientation, and amenity potential. A number of design principles must be followed to ensure that this occurs and that successful, functional, yet aesthetic circulation is realized. However, assuming that the primary network of roads already exists in the majority of our communities, wholesale redesign is neither feasible nor practical. But new road projects and the development of raw land are continual, resulting in an ever increasing suburban sprawl. Therefore, let us discuss some of the finer aspects of road design. These points are not hard-and-fast rules that are required from a technical standpoint; they are desirable design approaches that can lead to a better community.

Project Profile: Hillsborough Township, New Jersey

Location: Hillsborough Township, New Jersey
Client: Hillsborough Township
Architect: Looney Ricks Kiss Architects
Project size: 33.5 acres
Project type: Main Street master plan

Key Features:

- A new traffic rotary at the southern end of the town center and a new gateway building at the northern end.

- The main street is divided into several traditional downtown blocks through the introduction of new streets, a plaza, and a town green.

- Existing vegetation, new buildings, and other streetscape and landscape elements are used to reinforce the scaling down of the existing automobile-scale highway corridor into the proposed pedestrian-scale downtown blocks.

- The town green, plaza, and rotary will feel like a series of outdoor rooms by pulling new buildings up to the sidewalks and placing parking to the side and rear of buildings.

- Benches, sidewalk cafés, tightly spaced rows of shade trees, and decorative street lights and signage will reinforce the pedestrian-centered character.

- Apartments over Main Street shops will generate day and evening activity.

Project Approach:

The goal of the master plan was to transform a one-quarter-mile length of Route 206, a suburban highway corridor, into a more livable Main Street and traditional town center. In order to accomplish this, the team produced an economically and socially realistic vision that would be both pedestrian-friendly and have a strong community character and identity. This included input from citizens via the creation of an electronic town hall. Using this medium, a community vision survey was conducted enabling citi-

zens to compare and select preferred designs for streetscapes, public spaces, buildings, signage, parking lot uses, and activities. After the survey data was analyzed, stakeholder meetings were conducted to show and explain the results of the survey and obtain feedback. The mas-

ter plan was created based on citizen recommendations to establish a township focal point for employment, recreation, entertainment, commerce, and government activities, with options for walking, bicycling, and mass transit as alternatives to automobiles.

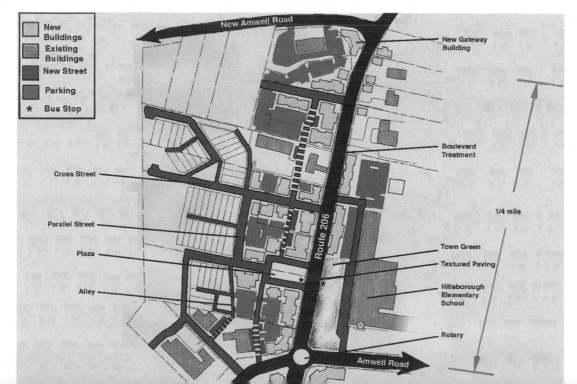

Legend:
- New Buildings
- Existing Buildings
- New Street
- Parking
- ★ Bus Stop

New Amwell Road

New Gateway Building

Boulevard Treatment

Cross Street

Parallel Street

Plaza

Alley

Route 206

1/4 mile

Town Green

Textured Paving

Hillsborough Elementary School

Rotary

Amwell Road

Figures 5.4, 5.5 **Which neighborhood leaves a better lasting image?**

- Identify areas where roads cannot be placed (marshes, steep slopes, historic/cultural places of significance, etc.).

- Identify those areas most suited to uses such as housing, commercial centers, and offices, and attempt to link them in as many ways as possible.

- Identify the most convenient access points and determine the desired lines of travel. That is, determine desired points of destination from the site and lay out internal circulation accordingly.

- Promote access and land-use integration within the community. In recent years, road systems have been designed to identify individual developments from the outside and to discourage casual access from the local collector street. This might still be important, but we may need to reconsider or reduce this emphasis to promote a stronger connection to the community at large and to instill a greater sense of unity among various developments.

- Reemphasize boulevards. These wide, landscaped roadways create a feeling of grandeur and can easily be combined with an alley system. This dual system works well in high-density areas that allow public parking along the street, and the alley provides access and services to the housing, commercial, or office uses that front the boulevard. If land area and/or costs are critical, the alley can be one-way to reduce its size. When used in tandem with the alley, the boulevard width can be reduced because the alley decreases the level of use along it.

- Streets should be designed to keep the driver's attention focused on the road and to make movement easy and enjoyable. The necessity for access between points A and B is no reason that the trip can't be pleasant and aesthetically appealing. Significant buildings, open space, entryways, and so on should all be considered as focal points.

- Through traffic should be separated from local/residential traffic but should remain part of the community. Otherwise, dissociation from each occurs. A system that separates these two forms of traffic can actually reduce traffic for both.

- *Superblocks,* larger areas surrounded by streets but allowing no through traffic, were once hailed as the road system of the future. Originally designed to separate vehicular and pedestrian traffic almost totally, super-

Figure 5.6 The texture of the surroundings should complement the design speed of a roadway.

blocks are now thought to be neither necessary nor advisable. They have been shown to be dangerous spaces for pedestrians and to increase traffic congestion in areas that surround them.

- The concept of friction should be understood and applied with care. *Friction* is anything that restricts the flow of traffic by requiring vehicles to stop and start. Using the design of streets to slow or calm traffic increases pedestrians' sense of safety and reduces the likelihood of traffic accidents. Traffic-calming devices used to create friction are numerous. These may be things as simple as adding street trees, changing the pavement at pedestrian crosswalks, or providing a narrower street. Or they may be more-complex changes that actually alter the geometry of the street to deflect a vehicle's path. Examples of this type include offset midblock yield points, bulbing at midblocks and intersections, traffic circles, roundabouts, and parallel parking on one or both sides of the street. Boulevards, avenues, and other collector streets require somewhat less traffic calming. Through streets and other residential streets require more.

- Good circulation requires giving thoughtful consideration to such things as sight lines, transition, wayfinding, visual clues, and reference points. Circulation design should work to create an interesting and informative system that utilizes subtle elements as well as technical ones.

- The *visual grain,* or texture of the surroundings, should complement the design speed of the roadway. The lower the speed, the more texture can be discerned from the vehicle. At higher speeds, texture is more likely to be missed or unappreciated, meaning that larger elements and spaces will be better perceived and appreciated at higher speeds. This should be carefully planned and not allowed to happen at random. It is for this reason that

Figure 5.7 The terrain should guide roadway design. National Park Service photo.

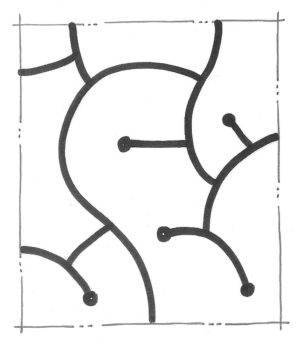

Sketch 5.8 A branching pattern lacks a sense of order.

Sketch 5.9 An identifiable spine or loop road creates a discernable structure.

the slick office tower adjacent to an expressway can be visually striking, whereas at the pedestrian scale it seems strangely out of place.

- In neighborhoods, a delicate balance exists between the optimum amount of street and the lot size. The larger the lot, the less total amount of street is necessary; the smaller the lot, the more street is required. However, on a per-lot basis, just the reverse is true: larger lots require more street and smaller lots require less.

- Street design should not create double- and triple-fronting lots. *Double-fronting lots* are those that front on a local neighborhood street but have as their rear lot line the right-of-way of a major collector street. *Triple-fronting lots* have the same characteristics as the double-fronting ones plus additional frontage on an entrance road into the neighborhood.

- It is generally less costly as well as less destructive to the land to lay out roads parallel to topographic contours or at right angles to them. Otherwise, the *diagonal layouts* created are more difficult to implement and result in awkward building sites. Although in many cases their use cannot be eliminated, in all cases they should be minimized.

- In rolling terrain, the terrain itself should guide the design to create interest and excitement. By simply following the lay of the land, a much more dramatic landscape can be achieved. On level land, the designer must, through the manipulation of the road layout and structure location, instill a sense of drama or experience that comes naturally in areas with rolling terrain.

- Short cul-de-sacs should be of smaller right-of-way width, reducing construction costs and impervious surfaces. However, overuse of cul-de-sacs at the expense of other minor streets should be avoided. This practice can exacerbate traffic problems by requiring wider collector roads and thus eliminating any cost savings.

- Because circulation is the prime method of wayfinding, there should be an underlying order or logic to its design. Otherwise, chaos results. Too often, confusion is purposefully created to inhibit cross-access and to force traffic to specific collector streets. Historically, emphasis has been placed on patterns designed to reinforce the separation of uses; however, this leads to further traffic concentrations that rely on only a few through streets.

- Conscious effort needs to be made to reinforce, not sever, the ties between residential areas and their supporting commercial and office areas.

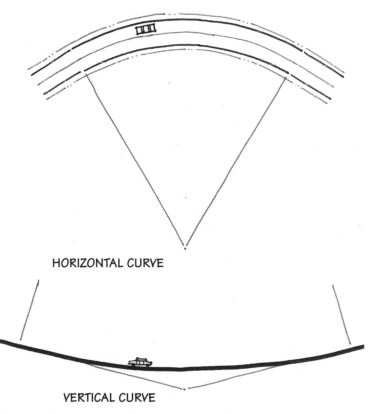

HORIZONTAL CURVE

VERTICAL CURVE

Sketch 5.10

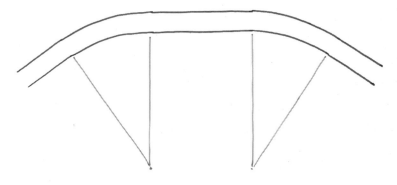

BROKEN-BACK CURVE

Sketch 5.11

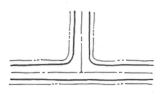

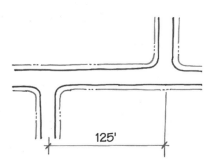

125'

Sketch 5.12 Intersections.

Technical Considerations

To this point in this chapter we have addressed only the grander design issues relating to the total community. However, a number of technical parameters are either commonly accepted as standards or dictated as mandates by the municipality. We attempt here to be as generic as possible while emphasizing that every municipality adheres to slightly different standards that must be verified prior to any design.

- Streets are usually crowned in the center for positive drainage and may utilize a curb and gutter system or roadside swale to channel surface runoff to an outfall and to act as a visual and physical barrier between vehicular and pedestrian spaces.

- Curbing is usually 6 inches high, although a 4-inch rolled curb is sometimes used. Grassed swales and shoulders can be found in areas with low-density development.

- Pavement width varies; however, 24 to 30 feet from curb to curb is common for a 50-foot right-of-way. A right-of-way of this width usually allows parking on one side of the street, and a 60-foot right-of-way allows parking on both sides of the street.

- Streets are laid out using a system of horizontal and vertical curves. Depending on the right-of-way width and design speed of the road, the minimum centerline radius of a horizontal curve can vary from 75 feet for a 50-foot right-of-way to 250 feet for some state-maintained highways. Vertical curves provide positive drainage and enable the designer to adapt a road to topographic conditions.

- Broken-back curves and reverse curves are usually designed with at least a 100-foot tangent or straightaway between them to allow recovery time for the motorist and additional braking space.

- Intersections should intersect at right angles, but many cannot. It is considered unsafe, however, to design an intersection with less than 30 degrees of deflection. Also, intersections should be either directly opposite one another or at least 125 feet apart from centerline to centerline.

- The curved section connecting two streets or street returns at intersections should not be greater than 10 to 15 feet for most residential streets as measured on the right-of-way. A 10-foot radius equals a 20-foot curb radius. Why? This ensures that motorists are forced to stop when required and makes the crossing distance for pedestrians as direct and short as possible.

- In CSDs, cul-de-sac lengths vary, but generally should not exceed 1000 feet in length. The right-of-way dedication of cul-de-sac bulbs or turnarounds is usually required to be 100 feet in diameter with an 80-foot curb diameter. These are usually required for school buses, fire trucks, and garbage trucks, but should actually be considered on a case-by-case basis to allow flexibility and interest in the land plan. For example, on short cul-de-sacs, the school bus rarely accesses the street, remaining instead on the community collector street. Therefore, it does not require a turnaround sized to accommodate it. Likewise, fire trucks stop at the nearest fire hydrant. Thus, on a short street they are more likely to stop at a hydrant location along the collector street. In other words, the standard solutions mandated by traffic engineers are not necessarily the best solutions for a given situation.

- In TNDs, cul-de-sacs are rarely used because they prevent connectivity. If cul-de-sacs must be used, pedestrian and bicycle access should be provided through the dead end of the street to allow connections to the neighborhood street beyond.

- Other types of cul-de-sacs are *hammerhead, shunt,* or a modification of both that allows smaller vehicles to make a continuous circle but requires larger vehicles to back up. A center island with landscaping can dramatically improve the appearance of cul-de-sacs if the larger diameter is required. These, however, are usually frowned upon by municipalities because it is sometimes unclear whose responsibility it is to maintain them (the city or the neighborhood). This should not necessarily prevent them from being used, but be aware that there may be some negotiation with city officials to determine whose responsibility it is to maintain them. In TNDs, a *close* is the preferred solution. A close is similar to a cul-de-sac but has a wide, planted median in the center that accommodates the vehicle-turning radius required by most municipalities.

- The amount of traffic must be considered when designing a road network in the community. Most intersections of minor residential streets don't require turn lanes, but larger intersections serving employment or retail centers do, especially those accessed by divided roadways. A good rule of thumb for minimum requirements for these turning lanes is 150-foot vehicle stacking with 150 feet of transition space. This may require additional right-of-way dedication along a property frontage.

- *Trumpet intersections* are an at-grade solution, allowing some traffic to continue to move even when through traffic is stopped by traffic signals. They can also aid in creating a sense of place by providing space for entrance icons, landscaping, and water features.

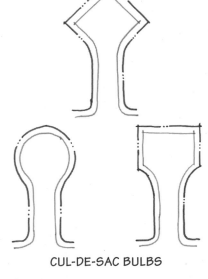

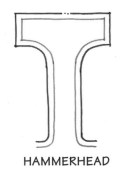

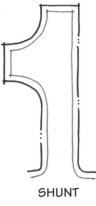

CUL-DE-SAC BULBS   HAMMERHEAD   SHUNT

Sketch 5.13

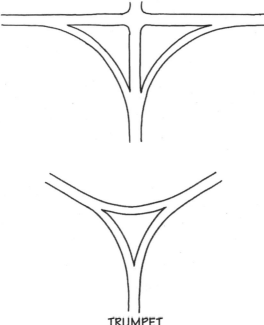

TRUMPET

Sketch 5.14 Trumpet intersections.　　　　　　　　*Sketch 5.15* Rotary intersection.

- *Rotaries,* like trumpets, are good placemakers. Indeed, some of the more memorable examples of urban design contain at their heart a rotary intersection. Largely ignored and denigrated by traffic engineers, they allow single-way movement around a center island (a focal point) and do not require signalization at lower traffic counts. Rotaries are especially useful for intersections of 500 to 1000 trips per hour and work well in residential areas, especially if the center area becomes a landscaped park.

- Intersections should not be placed on a high point such as a hilltop, and the gradient within 100 feet of intersections should not exceed 10 percent for residential streets or 2 percent on larger streets. However, if there is a choice between having an intersection at the hilltop or slightly below it, the hilltop is the better of the two because it has better visibility. For similar safety reasons, intersections on tight curves should also be avoided. These are just some of the detailed design criteria in effect in most municipalities, and the solutions offered here should not be construed as the final word on

Figures 5.8, 5.9 **Where would you rather take a stroll after supper?**

detailed design. For that information, consult your local engineering standards.

Pedestrian Circulation

Getting people out of their cars and onto their feet is an issue that has been discussed at length in just about all of the planning journals and has been the topic of a few books. Walking is not only the best form of exercise, but it's the best way to meet our neighbors. Meeting our neighbors makes for better community. It's more than providing a sidewalk along every street. It's more than establishing biking, fitness, and walking trails in abandoned railbeds, greenways, and parks. Most of what we call *pedestrian ways* are sterile and inhospitable environments, especially those located along busy thoroughfares. Extremes of heat and cold, sun and shade, wind or the lack of it, and glare can adversely affect use. Because of this, you don't see many people using sidewalks in suburbia anymore. There's just something unnerving about walking along a four-lane collector street subject to wide swings of microclimate with automobiles speeding by only a few feet away. It leaves one feeling exposed.

One contributing factor is that building facades are too far away from the street. The suburban building setback requirements rob us of the enclosure and scale that make us feel comfortable. And to compound matters, there is nothing separating us from the automobiles except 2 or 3 feet of grass. The typical suburban street design sequence goes something like this: four-lane divided arterial, sidewalk, 10 feet (if you're lucky), landscape strip, parking lot, building. The kind of design sequence that most pedestrians prefer goes like this: street, on-street parking, tree-planting verge, sidewalk, building, parking lot. The difference that is understood, albeit subconsciously, by the pedestrian is scale.

Another problem is the absence of a reason to use sidewalks in suburbia. They don't really go anywhere people want to go. Even if they did, getting there wouldn't be a pleasant experience because of all the aforementioned reasons.

Bikeways and fitness and walking trails, on the other hand, have their own unique problems. While they are usually located away from automobiles and parking lots, their relative seclusion and lack of a destination contribute to a perceived lack of security, thus discouraging use. As William H. Whyte observed in his study of small urban places, people want to go where other people are.[2] They are drawn to popular shopping, recreation, and entertainment centers to interact with and observe others. One need look no farther than the local shopping mall to see this in action. Jane Jacobs offered some insight into this phenomenon in her book, *The Life and Death of Great American Cities*. She suggested that there is a correlation between the amount and variety of activity associated with a sidewalk and whether people use it.[3] She introduced the concept of *networking of activities,* which is the integration of both the amount of diversity included along the walk and the variety of interest it offers to potential users. An *intricate mutual support* or *functional mixture* must develop before there is an incentive for pedestrians to use it. And, she stressed, the more diverse the activity and opportunity, the more pedestrians are likely to use it.

How do we put it all together to come up with a specific strategy for creating pedestrian ways that will be used? Here are a few guidelines:

- Remember the preferred sequence: street, on-street parking, tree-planting verge, sidewalk, building, parking lot. Obviously, this isn't possible in every situation, but remember that pedestrians like spaces with an intimate scale.

Figure 5.10 In suburbia, valuable land is wasted as underused parking lots.

- The ultimate goal is to meet the user's need for enclosure while providing a safe, comfortable, and interesting place to interact with others.

- Pedestrian ways should be integral circulation routes to specific destinations in the community. They must go where people need and want to go.

- Plan for novelty. Create alternate routes to the same destination. Allow for individual variation. People get bored if there is only one way to go.

- The concept of networking can be used to create a cohesive balance of function and amenity along the way. A hierarchy of social gathering spaces adjacent to or bisecting the pedestrian artery will enhance its usefulness to the user.

- A choice of activities, both active and passive, provides something for everyone.

- Every location is unique. Avail yourself of every opportunity to enhance the walking experience. If we want people to get out of their cars, it has to be convenient, worthwhile, and perceived as a gain rather than a sacrifice.

Parking

Parking lots are perhaps the major contributor to the visual chaos that afflicts most of our urban and suburban areas. Accommodating the car has become the prime directive for most of our traffic engineers, municipal planners, and site-plan review personnel. Parking layout should be designed with purpose and logic that can be instantly understood by the motorist. Layout should be clear and somewhat predictable, with the focus being limited to finding a parking space, not interpreting the ramifications of the layout.

However, too much of a good thing can have deleterious effects. To ensure an ample supply of parking, municipalities require an excessive amount of spaces, especially for commercial uses and usually for peak use of only one week of the year: December 18 to 24. This mentality actually encourages more vehicles, more trips, and more pavement. Rather than solving the parking/traffic problem, this approach creates it.

For efficiency's sake, a parking lot is consolidated in as small an area as feasible, grouping as many spaces together as possible. In our commercial areas this has led to larger and larger parking lots, further distancing the shopping center from its servicing collector street. What has resulted are great expanses of asphalt or concrete, usually filled to only one-quarter or one-third capacity 98 percent of the time. This fiscally irresponsible act causes much valuable land to be literally wasted and unproductive. In addition, from the environmental standpoint, larger areas of impervious surfaces cause more stormwater runoff, which leads to either more pollution of local streams or at the very least the consumption of precious land dedicated to stormwater retention or groundwater recharge devices.

The alternative is to build only those spaces truly needed to support commercial space or to build more retail in the

In the contemporary metropolis, development must adequately accommodate automobiles. It should do so in ways that respect the pedestrian and the form of public space.

Charter of the Congress of New Urbanism

space formerly dedicated to parking. This would not only return more tax dollars to the municipal treasury, but the commercial areas would benefit by enhanced visibility due to a location closer to the local collector street. Less land would be consumed for commercial uses, which would free up land for some other use, thereby increasing land use efficiency.

The negative impact of parking lots can be reduced more effectively through dispersion rather than through the landscaping Band-Aids employed by most municipalities. Although somewhat more expensive to construct, more parking areas with fewer spaces in each are aesthetically more pleasing. As a general rule, most people will not walk more than 300 feet to a destination. If applied, this knowledge would not only improve parking lot layout, thus creating more efficient parking lots, but it would also enhance the visual environment by eliminating the sea of parking we all loathe.

In commercial and office areas alike, parking bays should be oriented *toward* the building; that is, the travel lanes should be perpendicular to the facade of the building. This enables people to access the building entrance without crossing multiple travel lanes and parking bays. Psychologically, this ability to *see* the front door makes the distance traveled on foot seem shorter. The converse of this not only makes the trip seem longer, it requires people to walk between parked cars, which creates a sense of apprehension and insecurity.

When multiple bays are employed or required, it is wise to include a landscaped island every three or four whole bays if possible to discourage any diagonal movements across the parking lot by motorists. Such movements create safety concerns for motorists and pedestrians alike, as cars approaching in such a manner are not expected and can lead to an overreaction on everyone's part. Such an island should extend the entire length of the parking bay and be wide enough to support large shade trees. This technique not only provides much-needed green space in a typically inhospitable environment, but it also helps pedestrians orient themselves by breaking up the sea of asphalt into smaller "ponds."

One-way systems should be avoided to maximize space utilization and to reduce the confusion factor that normally accompanies such arrangements. Angular, one-way systems invariably lead to inefficient layouts and result in awkward triangular areas that are used for landscaping. Not that landscaping is bad, but this layout results in areas that are usable only for landscaping and nothing else. From a design standpoint, in these cases the designer is a servant to the plan, not master of

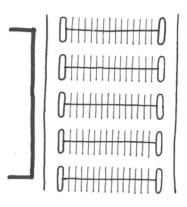

Sketch 5.16 Parking should be oriented toward the buildings.

it. Besides, no matter how well planned the parking lot, invariably a conflict will occur when a wrong turn is made.

Parking areas should be a flow-through design where possible, enabling the motorist to exit from a confined area without requiring a reversal of direction. Continual forward motion through a parking area is far preferable to a dead-end type in which, if all spaces are occupied, backing up is required. When long dead-end parking areas cannot be avoided, some form of turnaround should be provided. A small hammerhead arrangement can provide a convenient method of escape from a full parking lot while at the same time solving the problem of where to put Dumpsters. In this way, the Dumpster doesn't become the focal point of the parking lot. This solution works well for apartment sites. The true advantage of the arrangement, though, is that a turnaround can be provided with no loss of parking spaces.

If parking lot visibility is considered a negative, and if viewing the building it serves is deemed more aesthetic, then it would stand to reason that replacing one with the other would improve the visual quality of our commercial corridors. By simply requiring that parking occur at or behind the *building setback line,* with no parking permissible between the building and the street, a grand improvement to the visual qual-

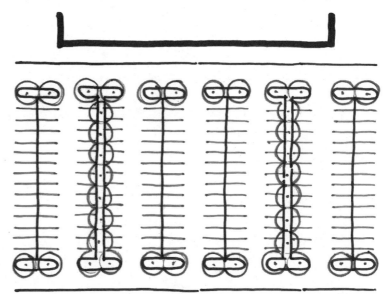

Sketch 5.17 Landscape islands discourage diagonal movements across parking lots by motorists.

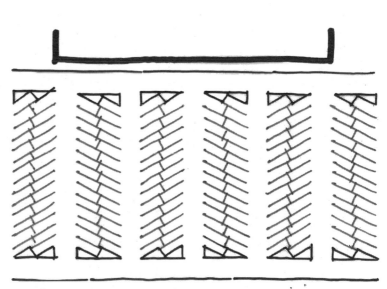

Sketch 5.18 Angular parking systems are inefficient.

Project Profile: The Belle Hall Study, South Carolina

Location: Mount Pleasant, South Carolina

Clients/Sponsors: Charleston Harbor Project; NOAA; South Carolina Coastal Conservation League; South Carolina Department of Health and Environmental Control; Town of Mount Pleasant

Planning firm: Dover Kohl and Partners

Testing center: The Johns Ecological Research Center

Project size: 600 acres

Project type: Sprawl versus traditional town: environmental implications

Key Features:

- Stormwater runoff variables were tested using a computer model that would compare rates of stormwater runoff for each type of development pattern.

- The analysis attempted to predict the volume of water leaving the site during a storm, the amount of sediment in the runoff, the levels of phosphorus and nitrogen in the runoff, and the chemical oxygen demand, which can place stress on surface water by limiting the oxygen supply in a water body.

- The TND scenario performed better than the CSD scenario. The volume of runoff in the CSD was 43 percent higher than that in the TND.

- Sediment loads were three times higher in the CSD scenario, and the nitrogen and phosphorus loadings and the chemical oxygen demand were all higher.

- The vegetated areas at the periphery of the TND scenario were found to absorb the pollutants before they reached the nearby creek.

Project Approach:

The environmental impact of conventional suburban development (CSD) and traditional neighborhood development (TND) were compared for a hypothetical project in Mount Pleasant, South Carolina. The sprawl scenario, while complying with best management practices for stormwater, was characterized by single-use pods containing one kind of lot and building use each, with no distinct edge disturbing all but token amounts of land. The large, irregularly shaped blocks used cul-de-sacs and depended on one way in and out of each pod. Big-box retail shopping strips with large parking lots and numerous out-parcels characterized the retail areas. Open space consisted of the leftover space between the pods and around regulated wetlands; much of the natural habitat was lost. The traditional neighborhood development was characterized by a compact form with a distinct edge. An interconnected framework of streets and alleys created walkable neighborhoods proportioned to allow a 5-minute walk to the town center. Parks, squares, and public spaces were faced by fronts of buildings and perimeter open spaces, and wildlife habitat was preserved.

BELLE HALL
SPRAWL SCENARIO

BELLE HALL
TOWN SCENARIO

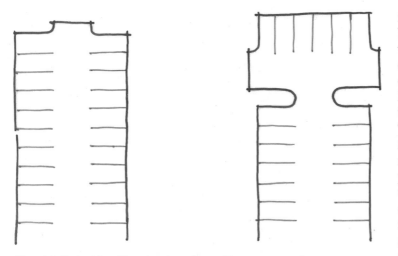

Sketch 5.19 Avoid parking that doesn't provide a turnaround.

ity of our developing areas can be achieved. This concept would also be useful for our existing corridors that front an overabundance of parking and lack the sense of scale and place that is so prevalent in suburbia. This is a good point to keep in mind when, in 20 years or so, many of those old strip shopping centers have outlived their usefulness and are destined for demolition. What a great opportunity to reverse the relationship and construct buildings that can provide greater visibility while improving the streetscape!

Public Utilities

In the real world, whether something can be built or not depends on how we address such concerns as the availability of public utilities (water, sanitary sewer service, etc.), the intricacy of stormwater management, the concern for environmental impact, and the adequacy of the current circulation system. The requirements for these services vary across the country because each region has a unique set of problems and opportunities. The extent of their availability is dependent on community needs and the density of development.

Residents of larger, more densely populated communities expect a high degree of convenience. Water and sewer service are expected and are provided for a price. The lack of adequate supplies of potable water can be a serious limitation to responsible community growth. So much so that many communities have had to place strict limitations on the use of water. The desert Southwest, for example, is no stranger to serious debate over water rights and its acceptable uses. Arguments over rights to the water of the Colorado River break out anew each time there is a drought in the states that depend on it for their water supply.

Sanitary sewer service can be a very costly part of growth, depending on the type of system required. Access to an existing system, its capacity, and whether or not it can accommodate an increase in flow are serious considerations. Topography must also be considered. For instance, in hilly areas gravity helps to move things along, but in the flatlands pumping stations are required to keep things flowing.

Smaller, more rural communities tend to be more self-sufficient. Well water and septic fields are the norm rather than the exception, and stormwater management consists of roadside ditches, farm ponds, and local creeks and lakes. But with this seeming simplicity come inevitable state and local regulations for lower density to allow for adequate septic fields and water quality requirements for freshwater wells.

Stormwater Management

All living creatures need water to survive. Humans, however, seem to place an extremely high value on its aesthetic quality. We pay large sums of money for houses on the beach, lake, or river. If we can't afford to own one ourselves we rent one of these jewels during the summer so we can enjoy the restful, almost hypnotic effects of being near the water. There is no shame in it; it's historical. From the Moorish water gardens at Grenada to Lawrence Halprin's Ira's Fountain in Portland, from the fountains of Versailles and Vaux-le-Vicomte to the tumbling, bubbling, gurgling forest stream, we are entranced by water. But when it comes to stormwater management we tend to approach it with an out-of-sight, out-of-mind mentality. We get too bogged down calculating the size of a pond required for a 100-year storm, forgetting it's water that we would gladly pay an arm and a leg to appreciate somewhere else. Until recently, the only concern about stormwater was how fast large quantities of it could be removed from streets and parking lots to prevent flooding. Now the quality of that water must be regulated.

When it rains, pollutants such as lawn and garden fertilizers, petroleum products, litter from roads and parking lots, soil, debris, trash, pesticides, and a variety of other waste and chemicals are washed into the storm drains of our communities. These pollutants end up in the streams, lakes, rivers, aquifers, bays, and oceans, where they affect water quality and marine life. The issue of what to do with stormwater became more complicated with the enactment of the National Pollutant Discharge Elimination System (NPDES) in November 1990. This new federal regulation requires local governments to reduce the amount of pollutants in their stormwater runoff.

Figure 5.11 Ira's Fountain in Portland, Oregon. *(Photo by Mendy Lowe, courtesy Lawrence Halprin)*

It isn't our intention here to discuss the technical aspects of this procedure; there are others more qualified than we to provide those lessons. Our focus is to highlight ways to make stormwater management facilities an asset, not just a necessity. There are two kinds of management facilities: dry ponds and wet ponds. A *dry pond* captures a large quantity of stormwater and slowly releases it until it is completely dissipated. A *wet pond,* as the name implies, holds water at consistent volume, allowing only the excess to escape through an overflow pipe or a spillway. Between storms, dry ponds can be rather unsightly, as they collect debris and litter. Wet ponds, costing a little more to construct, have more potential as an amenity and as a wildlife habitat.

Too often, though, these *engineered* stormwater management areas have more function than form. Drainage ponds and channelized canals can become community eyesores that need to be fenced and screened to keep them out of sight. But this is a terrific waste of a good resource. Retention and detention

Figure 5.12 A tumbling, bubbling, gurgling mountain stream.

ponds can be effectively used as amenities and, when designed with a little imagination, can help to create healthy, functional wetlands with both vegetative and animal diversity for all to enjoy. In fact, regulatory and permitting agencies look with much favor on projects that address both regional stormwater management and wetlands replacement and mitigation.

As a sales tool, strategically located lakes and ponds are superior assets in the fierce competition among single and multifamily housing developments. Aesthetically appealing as focal points, streams and lakes can help establish community character and enhance the perception of the built environment.

In Summary

Establishing a framework upon which communities can grow must accommodate both pedestrians and their automobiles. Successful examples of this can be found in many pre–World

Figures 5.13, 5.14 **Which stormwater device is a visual asset to its community?**

War II neighborhoods that used design techniques to create well-defined streets and public places. Because the automobile was less predominant, the focus was on the pedestrian. But today, we all love our cars and the ease of movement they offer, and we have let them literally drive the design of our communities. We have created seas of asphalt parking lots to service big-box shopping centers—parking lots that are never filled to capacity but are nonetheless required by our zoning codes and ordinances. This heavy-handed approach is not limited to commercial areas, however. It is applied with equal vigor to residential areas as well. Today's suburban neighborhoods boast excessive pavement widths, ostensibly for better access for emergency vehicles; the result is higher speeds that endanger neighbors and their children.

The alternative to this is to return to methods that create neighborhoods with a sense of place. Street design must provide interconnected circulation that creates focal points for reference and community identity. Building setbacks and planting shade trees will reinforce pedestrian scale along the street. Parking lots must be scaled to humans and located so that buildings take more prominent positions along the roadway. Stormwater management must reflect attention to more than technical criteria. Water resources can be artful and efficient if given enough thought.

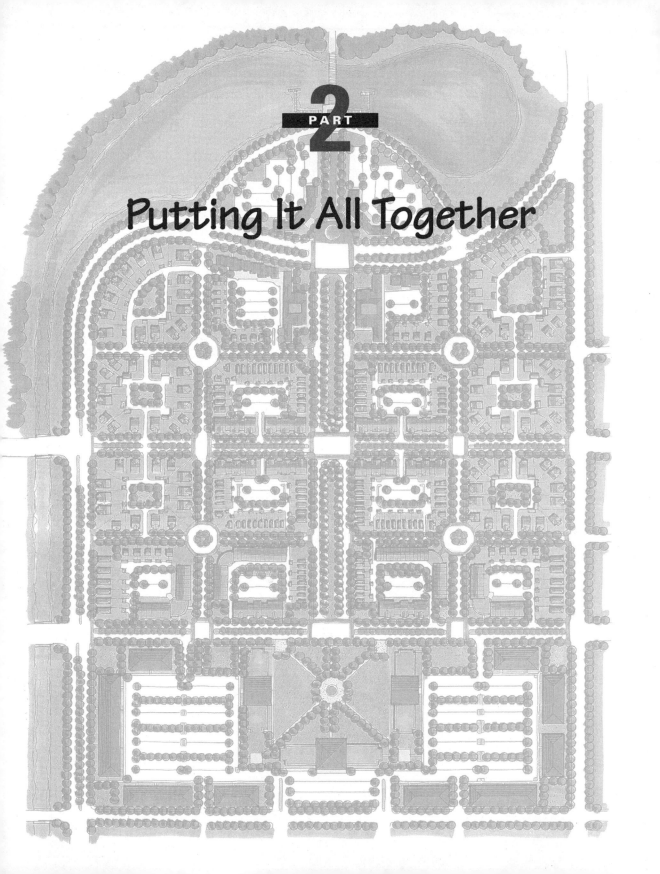

PART 2

Putting It All Together

Where Would You Rather Live?

At a Glance

❖ Understanding neighborhood as the fundamental building block of community

❖ Identifying the various forms of housing that make up our neighborhoods

❖ Exploring the differences between conventional suburban development and traditional neighborhood development

❖ Using recommended design parameters to create livable neighborhoods or to re-create existing ones

Where would you rather live? I'm not talking about a particular city or even a particular region of the country. I don't want an answer like "the beach" or "the mountains." No, I'm talking about a place much closer to home: I'm talking about *neighborhood*. Neighborhood is the fundamental building block of community. It is where we experience our family and friends. We shop, go to the movies, and stroll in the park there. We send our kids to school there. It's where we meet for PTA, soccer, little league, and church. It's where life happens. It's interaction. It's the place where we tell people we live. We don't say, "I live on Elm Street." We say, "I live in Shady Lawn" or "Dolphin Quay" or wherever we may call home; we save the street name for addressing letters or for the little map we draw when we send out invitations to our kid's birthday party.

In Chapter 1, we offered *Webster's* definition of neighborhood as a place of distinguishing characteristics where neighbors live. Well, we know that neighbors live there, but what about those distinguishing characteristics? What are the kinds of things that, when taken together, form a neighborhood? The Charter of the Congress of New Urbanism gives us insight into what a neighborhood should be. It states that neighborhoods should be compact and pedestrian-friendly. They should contain a mixture of uses so that many of the daily activities of living can occur within walking distance of one's home. The streets of neighborhoods should be interconnected networks designed to encourage walking. They should have a broad range of housing types and price levels so that a true mix of society is possible, which provides opportunities for strengthening personal and civic bonds essential to authentic communities. Public gathering spaces in neighborhoods should be distinctive and centrally located to reinforce community identity. Neighborhoods should contain different types of open space, ranging in size from small parks to village greens, tot lots to ballfields, conservation areas and open lands to community gardens. Workplaces and places to shop, schools, the library, post office, and other civic buildings should be within walking or bicycling distance so that residents and their children have a range of options for getting where they want to go rather than having to depend solely on their automobiles.[1]

As we move through the next few chapters, we will begin to understand how the principles that apply to making good neighborhoods are the starting point for building true communities. We're going to see how the basic building blocks of paths, edges, districts, nodes, and landmarks can be seen in the built environment. We're going to start seeing that when we use axial design, hierarchy, transitional space elements, dominating features, and enclosure, we build human-scaled places. We are going to see how the spacial components of circulation, open space, and structures can be used to create better places to live.

Where We Live

Housing is the most prevalent form of structure in the community. After all, it's where we live. And since the mid-nineteenth century the suburb has provided consumers the opportunity to express their individuality and freedom of choice by offering a variety of housing types and styles. The diversity possible in suburbia is an extreme example of market forces dictating architectural styles and the amenities that accompany them. Although many variations exist, there are four primary types of housing: *single-family detached* (still the most desired form of family living), *single-family semide-tached* (duplexes, triplexes, zero-lot-line units, cluster homes, etc.), *townhouses* (the suburban rendition of the urban row house, usually 4 to 10 units attached), and *apartments* (low-rise, midrise, or high-rise).

The concept of condominium ownership has tended to blend the various types of housing, blurring the distinction between them. It is not uncommon to see developments of single-family detached condominiums or even single-family detached fee-simple units served by private streets.

This will be the sequence of our discussion: First we will talk about single-family detached and semidetached houses. We will compare them in light of conventional suburban development (CSD) versus traditional neighborhood develop-ment (TND) patterns. We will provide a series of observations found in CSDs and then offer TND alternatives. We will do

Within neighborhoods, a broad range of housing types and price levels can bring people of diverse ages, races, and incomes into daily interactions, strengthening the personal and civic bonds essential to an authentic community.

Charter of the Congress of New Urbanism

Figure 6.1 Conventional suburban development. *(Photo taken by Wesley Page.)*

the same for single-family attached (townhouses) and then complete the chapter with principles for multifamily/apartment uses.

Single-Family Detached

Single-family detached dwellings are perceived by many as the ideal housing type in the modern industrial world. These consist of freestanding structures with yard space on all four sides. However, this form of development is the most expensive and

Figure 6.2 Traditional neighborhood development, Harbor Town, Memphis, Tennessee. *(Photo courtesy of Looney Ricks Kiss Architects.)*

land-consuming form of housing, requiring large amounts of road construction, utilities construction, and land clearing. In addition, the increased amount of runoff from the excessive road construction increases the likelihood of surface-water pollution.

Suburban neighborhoods are usually developed as a separate parcel following existing property lines, with only one or two points of access, and situated on the site in a random fashion. Since suburbia generally grows from areas of higher concentration toward areas of lower concentration, the density generally *increases* as development reaches farther out. Zoning requirements generally regulate a range of housing sizes and types. The market provides a variety of housing styles and price ranges, thus enabling the maximum number of people to be able to afford a detached unit.

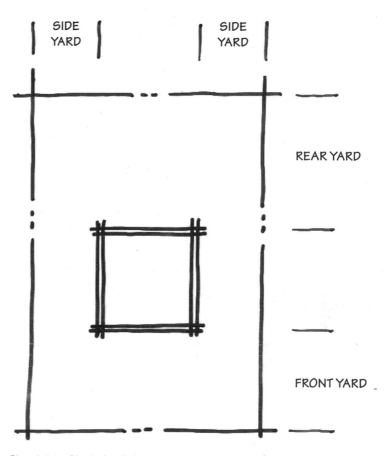

Sketch 6.1a Single-family house and lot.

Design Parameters

- Single-family lots usually range in size from 3500 square feet (SF) up to estates measured in tens of acres. Typical lot size thresholds are 4500 SF, 6000 to 6500 SF, 7500 to 10,000 SF, 12,000 to 15,000 SF, 20,000 SF, 30,000 SF, and 40,000 SF.

- A front yard setback of between 10 and 50 feet is usually required.

- A side yard setback is usually at least 5 feet or more.

- A rear yard setback generally requires 10 or more feet.

Project Profile: The Peninsula, Iowa City, Iowa

Location: Iowa City, Iowa

Client: City of Iowa City

Planning firm: Dover Kohl and Partners

Project size: 70 acres plus surrounding open space

Project type: Traditional neighborhood

Key Features:

- A compact form and a distinct edge yielding to large, continuous preserved areas.
- An interconnected network of tree-lined streets.
- Alleys allowing automobiles to be stored in garages at the rear of homes.
- Homesites with a clear front and rear.
- Small, walkable neighborhood blocks.
- Public parks and squares within easy walking distance of homes.
- Preservation of open space, views to the river, and wildlife habitat.
- A neighborhood center for small retail buildings and a town center open space.
- A set of graphic design guides to convey key design conventions for building scale and proportion, facades and key details, civic structures, public greens, and streetscapes.

Project Approach:

The goal of the project was to create a neighborhood that would respect and preserve the nature of the land where it was to grow and reflect the traditional Midwestern building type so prevalent in the older neighborhoods of the area. The site is formed by an oxbow in the Iowa River and boasts scenic views in all directions from the hilltop. The site is characterized by gently rolling topography and is edged by green spaces that include ravines with mature stands of trees and a golf course abutting the north and east sides of the site. The city purchased the land and established the open space park and commissioned the plan. The design team conducted a seven-day charette with elected officials and community residents.

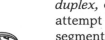

Single-Family Semidetached

Known by such names as *cluster homes, zero-lot-line (z-lot),*
duplex, or *triplex,* the semidetached single-family home is an
attempt to provide affordable single-family housing to a large
segment of the population. This is accomplished by eliminating one of the side yards and building the house on the property line itself. In recent years many new and innovative forms
have been developed in California, Florida, Texas, and in a
number of exclusive resort areas. Great effort has been expended to create living environments that are both spacious
and functional, exciting yet practical. The goal of this type of
housing is to incorporate as many features of single-family
detached as possible, but at densities that approach those of
townhouses.

Design Parameters

- The lots for these units are typically 35 to 50 feet wide.
- They maintain both a front and rear yard, although at
  least one side yard is eliminated.
- These are typically built and sold *speculatively,* meaning
  that the buyer has a limited number of options or up-
  grades that can be added to the basic structure.

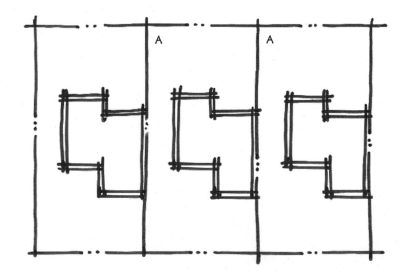

Sketch 6.1b Zero-lot-line houses. The elimination of side yard **(A)** reduces
lot size and cost to develop, with little or no reduction in house size.

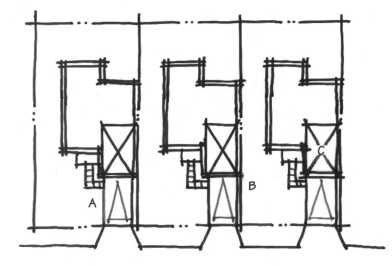

Sketch 6.2a **(A)** Minimum front-yard setback requires front-yard parking. **(B)** Typical architectural solution thrusts the garage door forward of building entrance, thus dominating the facade. **(C)** The garage door can consume 30 to 75 percent of the building facade.

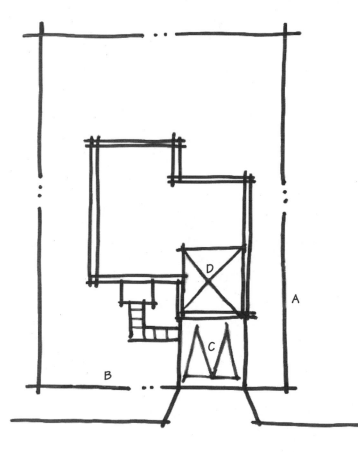

Sketch 6.2b **(A)** Zero-lot-line side yard usually contains no windows or doors to ensure privacy to adjacent unit. **(B)** Minimum front-yard setback literally requires front-yard parking. **(C)** Single-car driveway encumbers 20 to 35 percent of lot width. **(D)** Double-car garage encumbers 35 to 60 percent of lot width.

The primary task of all urban architecture and landscape design is the physical definition of streets and public spaces as places of shared use. Individual architectural projects should be seamlessly linked to their surroundings. This issue transcends style.

Charter of the Congress of New Urbanism

- With densities approaching 8 units per acre (U/A), the land plan must be well designed to minimize the impact of a potentially crowded site.
- Site amenities are mandatory if these units are to be marketed effectively.

Development Patterns

The conventional suburban development patterns used for creating many neighborhoods in the last 50 years abandoned the traditional neighborhood development patterns that evolved over several centuries. In the last decade of the twentieth century, a resurgence of interest in the traditional methodology led to the creation of neighborhoods that create not only a sense of belonging for their residents, but an improved quality of life. We are going to explore how these patterns apply to where we live. We are going to compare the CSD to the TND pattern to discover specific design guidelines, the goal being to explain how the conventional pattern creates a hindrance to true neighborhood design and then to offer a traditional alternative that is a better solution.

CSD PATTERN

Setback requirements and the need to accommodate automobiles have affected the architecture of single-family housing by thrusting the garage forward of the house proper and thus presenting the car accommodations in stronger light than the front door itself. Forced minimum setbacks require front yard parking. Requiring a home to be set back more than 20 feet from a street almost ensures that all off-street parking will be situated in front of the house. In larger lots, this may not be a problem because the distance between the house and the driveway reduces the impact of the parked cars. However, in the case of smaller single-family lots, the streetscape becomes consumed by driveways and parked cars.

Two-car garages can consume from 30 to 75 percent of the building facade, seriously degrading the image of the neighborhood, especially in higher-density single-family developments. This results in an overemphasis on the garage doors.

TND ALTERNATIVE

When mandatory setback requirements are relaxed, it allows the house to be located closer to the street than is normally

Figure 6.3 Suburban streets are dominated by garage doors and parked cars. *(Photo taken by Wesley Page)*

deemed acceptable. This not only provides for a larger rear yard, but encourages a garage door placement at or behind the facade of the house, thus emphasizing the front door, not the garage door. Ideally, placement of the garage door at 16 feet or more behind the facade of the house would result in the cars being parked *between* the houses rather than in front of them.

De-emphasizing the garage door by encouraging side-loading garages in both larger lots and higher-density situations greatly reduces this visually negative situation. This is encouraged only when it is not possible to locate the garages behind the front of the building. Direct vehicular access to the rear yard is an added benefit of this arrangement.

CSD PATTERN

Smaller lot scenarios result in unneeded tree removal to accommodate positive drainage requirements as mandated by many municipal engineers. In many communities, surface drainage

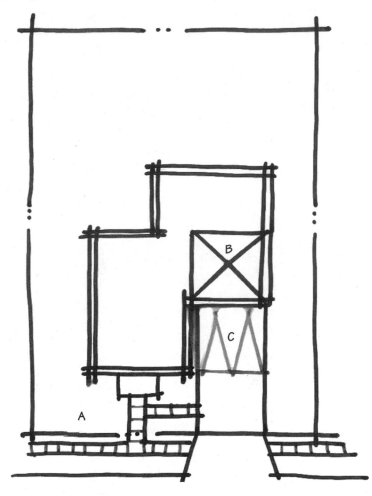

Sketch 6.3a **(A)** Reduced setback puts visual emphasis on building and not the garage door. **(B)** Recessed garage de-emphasizes door and creates a parking niche, reducing emphasis on parked cars. **(C)** If garage is recessed enough, the automobiles can be parked behind the building line.

must move forward from the rear of the lot to the front and occur within the boundaries of the site. The method most often employed to accomplish this is to require drainage swales around the house, typically following the side lot lines and requiring the removal of any object in the path of the swale, trees included. For adjacent lots, this results in twice as much land being disturbed to accommodate surface drainage along side-lot lines. Some filling of the rear portion of the lot to ensure the movement of this surface water is also normally required.

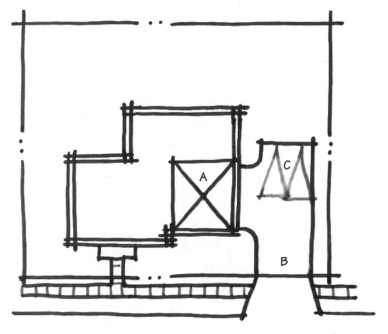

Sketch 6.3b **(A)** Side-load garage further reduces view of garage door. **(B)** Parking apron doubles as front-door courtyard. **(C)** Side-load garage allows forward entry into the street rather than having to back into the street, thus making the movement safer.

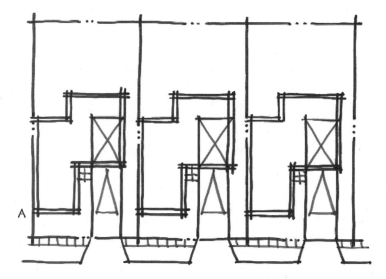

Sketch 6.4a **(A)** Recessed parking reduces view of cars from the street. **(B)** Forwardly oriented front door increases street surveillance, enhancing safety. **(C)** Larger rear yard results from forward house shift.

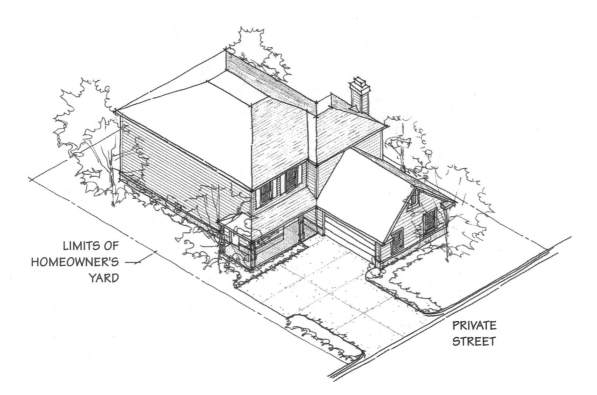

LIMITS OF
HOMEOWNER'S
YARD

PRIVATE
STREET

Sketch 6.4b One option that de-emphasizes the garage door.

TND ALTERNATIVE

Encouraging combined or shared driveways for adjacent homesites and using side-load garages reduces the amount of pavement required for each house and provides a larger infiltration area for surface drainage. This also orients the garage doors away from the street, de-emphasizing automobile storage.

CSD PATTERN

Residential subdivisions are often constructed adjacent to major collector streets and boulevards, which results in the homesites on the perimeter having double fronts: backyard adjacent to the collector street, front yard on a residential street. These double-frontage lots usually require the installation of expensive landscaping and/or fencing just to make the homesites marketable. Even then they are most likely the last to be sold and built upon. And, when finally developed, what

Figure 6.4 Cars are parked in carports on this Harbor Town street. *(Photo courtesy of Looney Ricks Kiss Architects)*

is the presentation to the street? What is the legacy of the developer to the neighborhood? Usually a 6- to 8-foot-high solid-wood fence built on the right-of-way line perhaps a mere 10 feet from the nearest travel lane of the collector street. This typical site design solution has done much to dissociate neighborhood from neighborhood and reinforce suburbia's sprawl image.

TND ALTERNATIVE

Orient the sides of lots to the collector street and serve them either with a common shared-access drive or a short cul-de-sac. This not only presents a better face to the collector street, it also reduces the number of lower-value lots that are impacted by the collector street. *Flag lots* are another method of accomplishing this within the bounds of most ordinances.

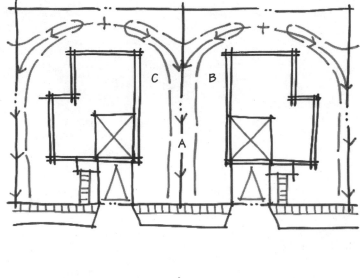

Sketch 6.5a **(A)** Combined drainage swales centered on the common property greatly increase the amount of undisturbed area around the houses. **(B)** More trees can be saved as a result of less land disturbance. **(C)** Amount of disturbed land between houses can be reduced by one-half.

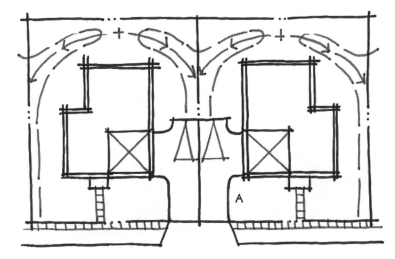

Sketch 6.5b **(A)** When used in conjunction with side-load garages with shared driveway, there is a greater potential to save more trees in front of the houses.

Figure 6.5 Deep front yard setbacks help to make the garage door more prominent than the front door.

Figure 6.6 Reducing front yard setbacks leave room for alleyways and rear yard garages.

Figure 6.7 Fort Suburbia? The backsides of two suburban neighborhoods are separated by a collector street.

NEIGHBORHOOD STREET

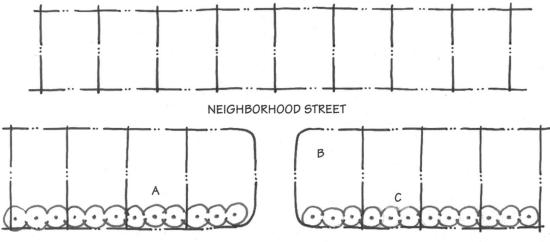

COLLECTOR STREET

Sketch 6.6 **(A)** Rear of units overlook major roadway. **(B)** Double- and triple-frontage lots usually must have increased setbacks to distance houses from major roadway.

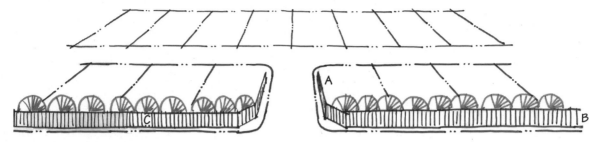

Sketch 6.7 **(A)** Privacy fences 6 to 8 feet high present a negative image to the community. **(B)** Continuous fencing disassociates residential area from major roadway and makes the street a more dangerous environment. **(C)** More often than not, fences are not maintained equally, giving a deteriorating look to the neighborhood.

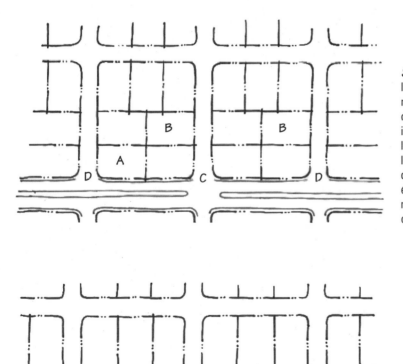

Sketch 6.8 **(A)** Side orientation to collector street creates a better street and neighborhood image. **(B)** With a side orientation, fewer homesites are impacted by their proximity to the collector street, making fewer discounted lots necessary. **(C)** Median break defines primary neighborhood entrance. **(D)** Multiple access points to neighborhood diffuse traffic and reduce choke points on the collector street.

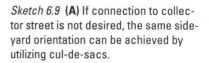

Sketch 6.9 **(A)** If connection to collector street is not desired, the same side-yard orientation can be achieved by utilizing cul-de-sacs.

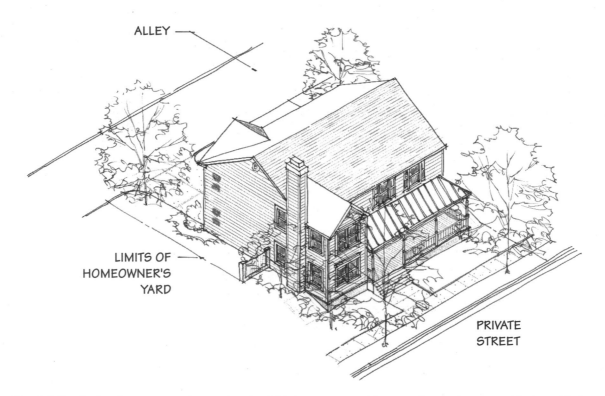

ALLEY

LIMITS OF
HOMEOWNER'S
YARD

PRIVATE
STREET

Sketch 6.10a Placing the garage on the rear facade of this home accessed from an alleyway lets the residents, not their cars, own the front yard.

In the case of smaller single-family lots, the streetscape can be greatly enhanced by using alleys to serve rear-oriented garages. Coupled with a reduced front yard setback and a reduced street width to allow on-street parking for visitors, a radical change in the image of our neighborhoods can be achieved. This is especially suitable for urban areas or areas that desire to become more urban.

Townhouses

Townhouses evolved as high-density housing in cities, originally serving as a transitional element between the commercial/industrial districts and single-family areas. With the advent of suburbia, the design style has been copied and applied in great numbers to outlying areas, where townhouses are clustered into separate and individual pods. Today, their main advantage is that they function primarily as a means of enhancing density while providing more-affordable housing.

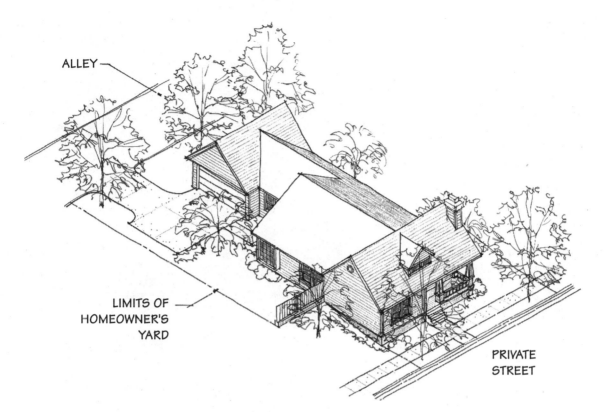

ALLEY

LIMITS OF
HOMEOWNER'S
YARD

PRIVATE
STREET

Sketch 6.10b This side-loading rear garage creates enclosure for the backyard.

Whether sold in fee simple or as condominiums on a private street, this form of housing eliminates all side yards except for the end units. In most situations, the townhouse is a two-story unit with a paved parking area in the front and a small fenced yard containing a storage building in the rear. However, in resort, areas where views are desirable, 2½- to 3-story units are commonplace, with attached single-car garages. In urban areas they are used to recoup high land costs.

Design Parameters

- In years past it was common to build 10 to 12 units in a single block, but in recent years a maximum of 6 to 8 units has become the norm.

- The unit typically maintains a 20-foot front yard setback from the right-of-way, principally to provide parking space for one or two automobiles.

Figure 6.8 Cars are stored in the rear of these town homes in a more urban community, creating an elegant streetscape.

- An equally sized rear setback is also provided so that the owner may have a small personal space.
- Common sizes range from 14 to 16 feet minimum to 24 to 30 feet maximum width.

Development Patterns

CSD PATTERN

Typically 20 to 28 feet in width, these units practically ensure that the entire front will be consumed by the parking pad and cars. In this case, green spaces and front yards are relegated to a 4- to 8-foot strip between the parking pad and the front of the building or a minor strip of yard extending to the street between end units. Automobile parking is always at a premium in townhouse developments because there are no guest-parking spaces; essentially, every space is designated for a unit. Continuous off-street parking leaves no on-street visitor parking.

When more than six units in a row are used, the street image becomes one of continuous buildings separated only by an expansive parking lot. Pavement from the front of one building to the front of another and very little or no green space create the feeling of living in a parking lot. In many cases, there may be a 90-foot-wide paved area between units facing each other across a street. This number increases to 100 feet when a 60-foot right-of-way is required, as it is in many municipalities. A severe

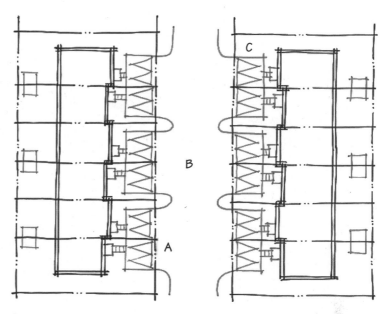

Sketch 6.11 **(A)** Continuous off-street parking creates a veritable parking lot with few, if any, guest parking spaces. **(B)** The space between the building fronts is filled with 90 to 100 feet of continuous pavement. **(C)** Typical layout results in minimal front yard landscaping space.

Figure 6.9 The front yard of suburban town house neighborhoods is often a sea of concrete.

Figure 6.10 Alleys in the rear . . .

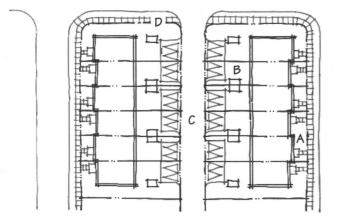

Sketch 6.12 **(A)** Elimination of front yard parking opens view of the building facades and increases landscaping space. **(B)** A reduced front yard gives a larger, more usable rear yard. **(C)** A sense of private access is enhanced when a rear alley is utilized. **(D)** A reduction of paved area between the buildings can be achieved even while providing on-street guest parking.

streetscape is made even more so by regulations that require a minimum of two parking spaces per unit.

TND ALTERNATIVE

The introduction of alleys for unit parking and service and freeing the street for visitor parking can greatly improve the visual image of the townhouse street. Coupled with a reduced front setback and a corresponding reduction of street width, the paved area between units can be narrowed from the typi-

Figure 6.11 . . . can allow a reduced front yard setback.

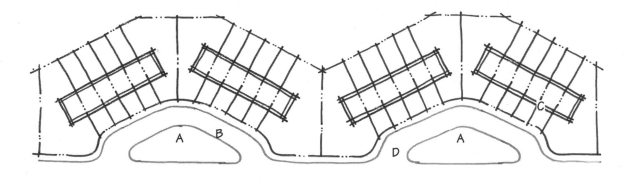

Sketch 6.13 **(A)** A mounded and landscaped island screens parking areas and garages from the primary circulation. **(B)** Ample guest parking is available at the back of the landscaped area. **(C)** A varying building placement creates a visually more interesting and appealing streetscape. **(D)** A sense of belonging and shared interest is fostered by the common-access drive.

cal 100 feet to 30 feet, and the front yard green space can be increased from 4 to 12 feet.

When density is not the prime motivator of the development, variety in site layout can be achieved by incorporating an eyebrow form of parking and circulation. This method separates unit parking and access from the primary circulation of the development. It also creates excellent landscape areas that can effectively screen the parking area from the internal circulation while providing ample on-street visitor parking.

CSD PATTERN

Mandatory front yard parking forces placing a building farther back on the lot, creating an awkward back-wall-to-back-wall situation in which the rear walls of the two units may be only 20 feet apart, with the second-story windows overlooking the yard space of the opposite unit. This ensures that access to the rear yards for service persons like meter readers and repair people will be difficult, often requiring them to walk down narrow passageways flanked by privacy fences or else requesting to pass through the unit. This can present a problem for the homeowner for such simple tasks as taking out the trash or cutting the grass.

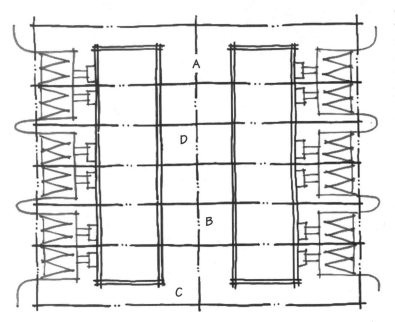

Sketch 6.14 **(A)** To accommodate the front yard parking, rear yard privacy is sacrificed. **(B)** Back-to-back arrangement allows second-story windows to overlook the corresponding rear yard. **(C)** Access to rear yards for interior units is possible only through the unit or across the rear yards of the adjoining units; a problematic endeavor when fences are involved. **(D)** When a 5-foot-access easement is employed, the result is usually an unmaintained, overgrown, and unprotected no-man's-land.

TND ALTERNATIVE

When side orientation to a public street is utilized with private rear access to serve rear-loading garages, the front can be either a public street or a green space. Coupled with a reduced-width public street, this provides a better street presence for the units, and visitor parking can be easily accommodated on the street. While it appears that much additional pavement would occur in this situation, remember that private streets can be constructed less expensively than public streets. This also solves

Figure 6.12 With the parking in the front, the rear of suburban town homes is often a maze of privacy fences.

the rear yard access problem, which now can be accomplished with no loss in density as measured in typical development scenario terms.

If, in addition to the more normal-width residential streets, the community collector street is not too large (60 to 80 feet versus 90 feet plus), townhouses can be oriented directly to it, especially if on-street parallel parking is allowed. The units themselves can be served from the rear by either a private street or a reduced-width public street. The private street or alley, when utilized in conjunction with garages, can create a usable rear yard space that is architecturally screened from the unit to the immediate rear. While this is not a new concept, its application in modern suburban America has been limited.

CSD PATTERN

Townhouse developments are normally designed as separate entities, freestanding and segregated from their surroundings,

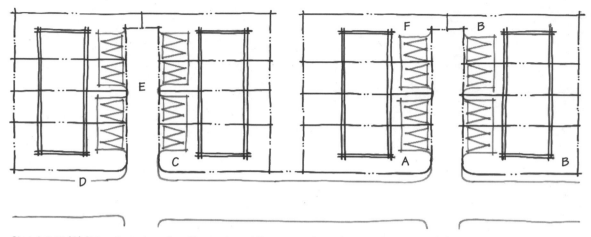

Sketch 6.15 **(A)** Side orientation of parking to the public street reduces its negative impact. **(B)** Units can be designed with the front orienting to either the green space or the parking court. **(C)** The primary view from the public street is of the buildings themselves, low side-yard fencing, and green space. **(D)** Ample on-street parking is available to visitors. **(E)** Private street or public alley provides resident parking. **(F)** Garage parking is possible with a relaxed setback requirement.

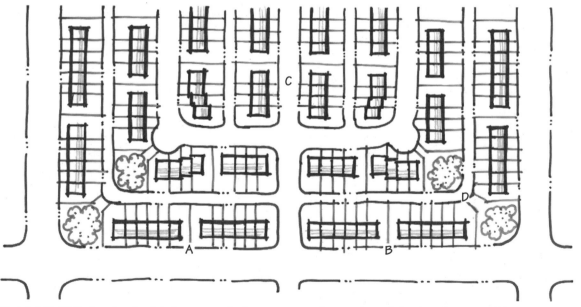

Sketch 6.16 **(A)** Reduced setback helps to contain the street space by creating a defined vertical edge. **(B)** View from the collector street is of the building facade rather than the parking areas. **(C)** Alley provides resident and services access to units. **(D)** Corner spaces can be utilized as very accessible and highly visible neighborhood parks while improving the image of the intersection.

with little or no access between them and either higher- or lower-density residential housing. When ill sited and with little attention given to where they are located with respect to schools, commercial sites, or employment areas, they can seem extremely forced and totally out of place. In other words, their purpose as a transitional land-use element has been forgotten or abandoned.

TND ALTERNATIVE

Townhouses should be transition neighborhoods with a required number of street ties to adjacent neighborhoods to better connect all housing areas. This establishes and reinforces a sense of community between various housing types rather than separating neighborhoods into individual enclaves. It is not necessary to extend every street from one neighborhood into another, but you should connect enough to encourage a certain amount of interaction between neighborhoods. After all, prudent planning should require some manner of access between neighborhoods in the interest of fire protection and safety.

CSD PATTERN

In too many instances, blocks of townhouse facades are continuous and lacking in architectural variation. The windows and doors are all the same; the roofs are all either gables or hips; the dormers, if any, are in the exact same place as on every other home. Using variations of these elements is one of the principles of urban design that is very often eliminated by developers because they perceive them as driving up costs. What remains, then, are rows and rows of identical facades, making each group of homes indistinguishable from the ones across the street.

TND ALTERNATIVE

Slight variations in building setback and height, coupled with architectural variety and diversity in landscaping, can provide distinction for each unit group. Rooflines can be mixed: one group can have hip roofs; one can have gables; both can have dormers or not. End units can be one-story instead of two, allowing the them to be handicapped-accessible. Placing groups with a one-story unit on the end is a good way to step down the architecture of the buildings to the corner of a street. Window types that have a residential character should be used, mixing in some bay windows as a premium. Providing a mix of

Project Profile: I'On, South Carolina

Location: Mount Pleasant, South Carolina

Developers/clients: Vince and Tom Graham

Planning firms: Dover, Kohl and Partners; Duany and Plater-Zyberk and Company

Project size: 250 acres

Key Features:

- The new neighborhood is situated between quarried lakes and freshwater sloughs that lead to the saltwater marshes of the Hocaw Creek and Charleston Harbor.

- A continuous public waterfront and marsh front.

- A wide range of dwelling sizes and types, including live/work units.

- Mixed-use buildings located on a public green.

- A graphic-design town code that sets key design conventions for building scale and proportion, facades and key details, civic structures, public greens, and streetscapes.

Project Approach:

The goal of the project was to create a traditional neighborhood development that reflected the area's historic context and respected its proximity to the city of Charleston. The design team began the project by visiting several historic towns, including Savannah, Georgia, and Charleston, South Carolina, to analyze building types and neighborhood framework. They then conducted a seven-day-long charette in Charleston, with the developers meeting with elected officials, municipal staff, and residents of the neighborhoods adjacent to the site. The team developed the master plan and a graphic design code to guide development into traditional low-country building types.

front-porch sizes and variety in the style of the columns sets off unit entryways. Moreover, even though codes often limit the number of connected townhouses to six, not all groups have to contain six. Any number of units can be used in a group.

Apartments

With the exception of the core areas of the inner city, where multistory apartment buildings are commonplace, most new apartments are two- to three-story walk-up structures. The garden-style apartments found in suburbia are designed to serve the needs of singles, young couples, and transients by providing starter living quarters at an affordable price.

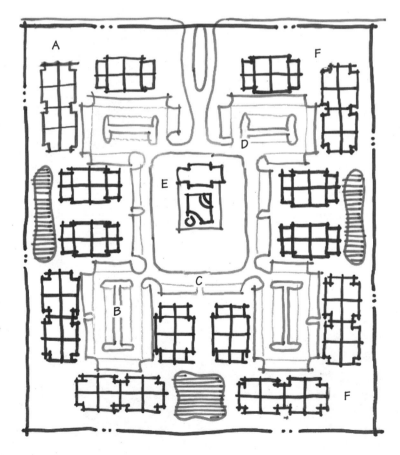

Sketch 6.17a Internalized parking. **(A)** Strong street exposure allows for highly visible landscaping and architectural design. **(B)** Parking areas are screened from exterior views. **(C)** Lower infrastructure cost with internalized services. **(D)** More direct access to entrance/exit possible with internalized parking. **(E)** Centralized recreation area is more accessible to all units. **(F)** Exterior orientation of structures maximizes off-site views.

Design Parameters

Historically, access to the individual units was from a central corridor or breezeway. In recent years the trend has been toward separate direct access for each unit or shared access with another unit to enhance privacy and create a sense of individuality. Structure height is generally related to concerns for fire safety and the height that can be easily accessed by fire-fighting equipment.

Two basic principles apply to the site layout of apartment complexes: internalized parking or externalized parking—*ins* versus *outs,* if you will. In other words, the buildings can ring the outside of the site with the parking areas internalized or they can be clustered to the center around an amenity with the parking oriented to the exterior. It is rare for one style to be used exclusively over the other. Most sites exhibit elements of both.

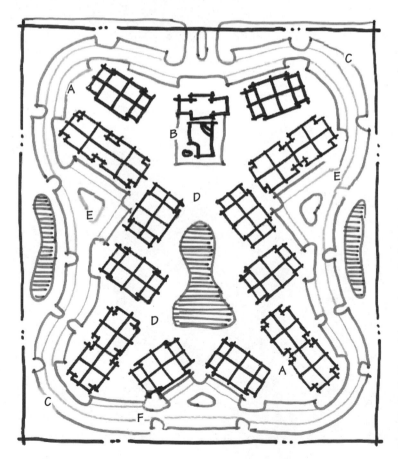

Sketch 6.17b Externalized parking. **(A)** External parking requires increased setbacks for the buildings, which reduces the impact on adjacent properties and allows three-story construction. **(B)** All buildings maintain direct access to community building and recreation area without crossing any parking areas. **(C)** For residents, views of the parking areas are minimized, while for neighbors or passersby, the parking is fully exposed. **(D)** More flexible building arrangements are possible with external parking. **(E)** Higher infrastructure costs are probable with external parking. **(F)** For rear structures, access to the site entrance/exit is long and convoluted.

Figure 6.13 Suburban apartment buildings are often grouped around a common green space . . .

Figure 6.14 . . . with the parking lot surrounding the perimeter of the site.

INTERNAL PARKING SCENARIO

This method is used more often when proximity of parking spaces to the front door is an important feature; no one wants to carry their groceries too far in the rain. Because fewer parking spaces result when parking is oriented to the center of the site, this method is usually employed for two-story buildings with densities of 12 to 16 units per acre. Internalized parking is also employed when direct access to an off-site amenity (e.g., a beach or ski slope) is desired.

EXTERNAL PARKING SCENARIO

More parking is provided by orienting the parking to the exterior of the site, thus making this method ideal for higher-density (16 to 36 units per acre) three-story apartments. These apartment complexes tend to be on-site amenity-driven, with pool, community building, and tennis courts in proximity to the building cluster. Longer walks from the parking space to the front door usually result from this layout.

Development Patterns

CSD PATTERN

The overwhelming negative impact of parked automobiles is the primary aesthetic failure in most apartment complexes. By focusing on automobile accommodation, an exciting, stimulating human environment is usually sacrificed. Immediately upon entering most apartment sites, one typically finds oneself driving in a parking lot no wider than 62 feet from curb to curb and driving in lanes 11 to 12 feet in width. If one lives at the rear of the site, and some of the sites can be very large, just getting out in the morning can be an arduous task.

TND ALTERNATIVE

To reduce the impact of parked cars, it is necessary to rethink conventional layout. This is most critical at the front of the site, through which the vast majority of the vehicles must pass. Separation of the through traffic from that of the immediate units in order to reduce this conflict is the most effective method to accomplish this—via stub parking, eyebrow parking, and sequestered parking.

Stub parking utilizes limited parking areas situated between individual buildings and accessed by an internal street or private road. This personalizes the parking for individual buildings, creating a stronger sense of ownership and responsibility

Figure 6.15 An apartment building in Harbor Town, near Memphis, Tennessee. The building relates to the street, not to the parking lot. *(Photo courtesy Looney Ricks Kiss Architects)*

on the part of the residents while discouraging unauthorized use by nonresidents.

Eyebrow parking, as with the townhouse example, performs in much the same manner as stub parking except that these parking areas retain two access points to a collector street and provide an opportunity for a significant green space between the parking and the street. The resulting configuration literally forms an eyebrow shape that not only separates the traffic, but also creates a more dynamic visual orientation of the buildings, in that few if any buildings front directly on the collector street. Instead, they are arranged in an accordion-like fashion to form large outdoor rooms that foster a sense of ownership by residents. The angular orientation of the unit to the roadway also makes this layout flexible and adaptable to irregularly shaped sites.

As the name implies, *sequestered parking* establishes different systems for both the immediate resident parking and the through traffic. Near the entrance of the site, the two systems diverge, allowing through traffic unimpeded access to the rear

Sketch 6.18 **(A)** Individual parking areas are designated for specific structures. **(B)** Individualized parking areas discourages use by nonresidents. **(C)** Internal community collector road provides direct access to entire site while enabling on-street parking for nonresidents. **(D)** Views along the collector road are of green space and building, not parking lots.

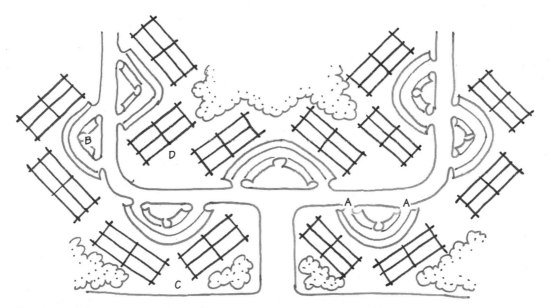

Sketch 6.19 **(A)** Each parking area has two points of access to the collector road, facilitating traffic flow. **(B)** "Eyebrow" parking provides designated parking for specific buildings. **(C)** Landscaped island helps buffer parking areas from collector road, improving views. **(D)** Angled orientation of buildings at internal collector road creates more dynamic views of buildings and green spaces.

areas via a rather significant green space that has as a back-drop the apartment buildings themselves. An added benefit is that these apartments serve to screen the parking from the green-space users and the through road.

CSD PATTERN

Site layouts are normally very confusing, as the buildings seem to be randomly strewn about the site with little or no effort to utilize building placement to create wayfinding clues for the visitor. Few sites possess a site plan theme that can convey an understanding of the layout without actually experiencing it. In other words, most lack an order or structure that instills a sense of place that makes a site memorable.

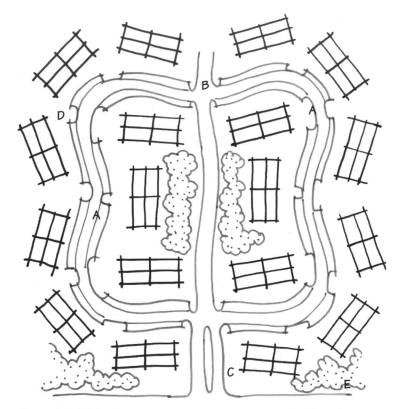

Sketch 6.20 **(A)** Parking areas are sequestered or separated from the through traffic. **(B)** Through traffic to remote or adjacent parcels without interfering with local traffic is provided, with direct access to rear of site. **(C)** View of the parking areas from the collector street is screened by the intervening buildings and green space. **(D)** Building and parking placement is very flexible, depending on site boundaries. **(E)** Streetscape view from off-site is of green space, not parking.

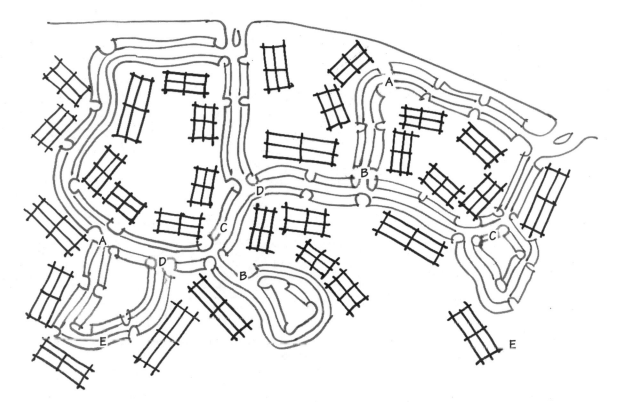

Sketch 6.21 **(A)** Random street pattern confuses both new residents and visitors. **(B)** No sense of center or focus to neighborhood is created by site layout. **(C)** No internal collector-street system to facilitate traffic. **(D)** Continuous parking creates dangerous backing pattern and congestion near entrances. **(E)** Scattered building locations make security and fire protection difficult.

TND ALTERNATIVE

Careful design of traffic and parking distribution can help create a sense of order and enable visitors and new residents to discern an underlying structure to the apartment complex, thereby making wayfinding easier while establishing a site plan theme. In addition, creating a theme imparts a stronger identity for the development, establishes a firmer sense of community, and enhances security and fire protection.

CSD PATTERN

Because of poor neighborhood layout, in many cases the parking spaces must be assigned to individual units to ensure that the residents can park within a reasonable distance of their unit. Poor building placement also results in ambiguous open-space areas that are not clearly perceived as being within the influence of a building or cluster of buildings. These unclaimed

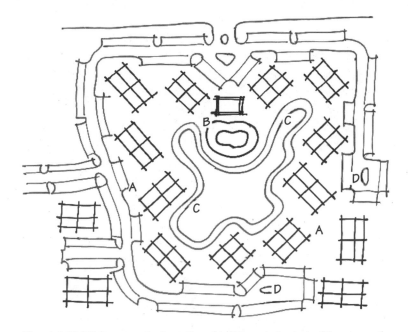

Sketch 6.22 **(A)** Structured orientation of buildings helps to instill a sense of order and neighborhood. **(B)** Community cneter and pool serve as a visual focal point and neighborhood activity center because of their prominent entrance location. **(C)** Central stormwater retention and walking path serve as neighborhood binding elements as well as site ameniities.

lands are a haven for miscreants. On a more personal level, most sites are not organized in a fashion conducive to social contact between the residents, which can lead to a sense of alienation and solitude, the antithesis of community.

TND ALTERNATIVE

An additional benefit of the aforementioned three organizing methods is that parking spaces need not be assigned by number, there being absolutely no question about which spaces are associated with which units: the structure of the layout defines the relationship. Likewise, careful building placement captures the surrounding ground area, thus enhancing the sense of ownership for that area by the residents. Creating subareas or clusters of buildings within the overall site plan is an effective method to reinforce this sense of responsibility. If a person has a feeling of ownership for an area, that person is more likely to be concerned with its use and take a more active role in monitoring it. The one thing a troublemaker dislikes most is a set of inquisitive eyes.

CSD PATTERN

Apartment sites, much like townhouses, are very inwardly oriented, almost seeming to shun the surrounding community rather than becoming a part of it. Typically, they have only one point of access, which concentrates traffic at that point and more often than not necessitates a traffic signal. In addition to this, other off-site street improvements may need to be made (e.g., acceleration and deceleration lanes, median breaks with left-turn lanes, or additional travel lanes across the entire frontage of the site).

When included as part of a planned urban development (PUD), apartments are most often situated up front, near the arterial road system. Marketing terms like *visibility, convenience,* and *easy access to interstates* may not necessarily mean that an apartment complex embraces the community.

Another location often used for apartments is directly behind a shopping center but separated from it by the shopping center's service lane; that void zone accommodates such things as occasional tractor trailers, Dumpsters, and piles of

Figure 6.16 Apartment buildings should be sited to contribute to the overall street edge.

Figure 6.17 Apartments often are sited just behind shopping centers, providing residents with a view of the service area.

wooden pallets or boxes. Screening this service bay is the obligatory privacy fence and, customarily, tall landscaping. Fences and bushes notwithstanding, residents still have to contend with the shopping center's rear wall, roof, ill-maintained fence, and aromas from Dumpsters on a hot summer day.

In this situation, apartments are used per the zoning code as a transition to lower-density land uses such as townhouses and single-family homes. While this is a long-standing approach, it shows that very little time was spent in the planning effort to integrate this transition housing into the fabric of the larger community. Locating apartments in pods with access to a street but no direct access to nearby commercial or office space requires vehicular access between two land uses that should have encouraged, not prevented, pedestrian access. Foot traffic is actually discouraged because the sidewalk is more ceremonial than inviting, and its proximity to speeding traffic and lack of enclosure offer a hostile pedestrian environment.

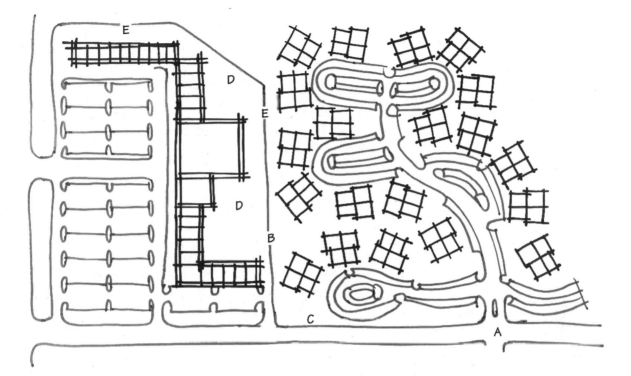

Sketch 6.23 **(A)** Single point of entry concentrates traffic, usually requiring signalization. **(B)** With no direct access to either adjacent commercial or residential areas, the apartment site is physically isolated and psychologically separated from its surroundings. **(C)** Lack of defined street edge undermines the sense of enclosure on collector street, weakening the community fabric. **(D)** Commercial service area requires elaborate screening and buffering, further creating a sense of separateness from the adjacent neighborhood. **(E)** The spaces between isolated use areas become unmonitored and dangerous.

TND ALTERNATIVE

In the past, marketing strategies dictated that most new apartment developments utilize a single point of access around which elaborate landscaping, attractive signage, and a prominent clubhouse were located to capture prospective tenants. This has led to very isolated developments that project an almost aloof disregard for the greater community. While in some cases topography and other existing conditions may require this orientation, as a rule, closer networking with the surrounding street system should be employed to help to blur the transitions between land uses—especially with other high-density residential neighborhoods such as townhouses or other apartments complexes. Most isolation problems occur when apartments are located in areas lacking the transitional residential elements. A step in the right direction would be to first locate apartments in the most appropriate settings, where access to other housing areas is not detrimental. A clear sense of entry can be established by using landscaping and signage elements at secondary entries while still providing alternative access points and stronger ties with the community at large.

Respect for scale, texture, and the attention to detail are essential elements for street-front design. By maintaining an established street edge in terms of setbacks and by transitioning the height of structures, the apartment complex will truly function as a contributing element of the community, not as an isolated enclave snubbing it.

If apartments must be located to the immediate rear of commercial sites, then reducing the normal space between the buildings, especially those oriented to the street, can alle-

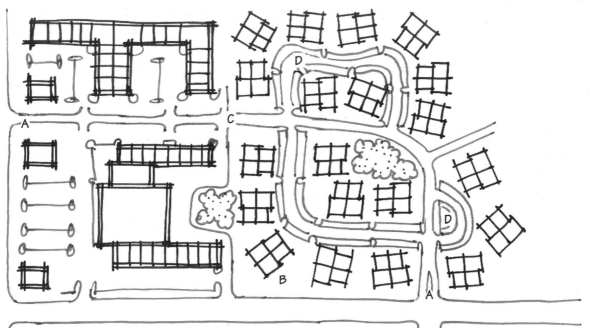

Sketch 6.24 **(A)** Primary access from the community collector street serves as the marketing entrance, while the secondary access points facilitate the traffic and pedestrian flows to other land uses. **(B)** Building location reinforces the local street edge and the sense of enclosure for both the collector street and the apartment site. **(C)** Direct access to the commercial area from the apartment site enhances the commercial activity while reducing the traffic on the community collector street and the primary intersection. **(D)** Apartment site layout utilizes elements of both the eyebrow and sequestered parking arrangements.

viate many of the conflicts. Minimizing setback requirements can create a street edge for commercial buildings, and the placement and reorganization of parking lots can help transition one use to the other. Another solution is to allow more direct vehicular access between uses not requiring local collector streets for all access. This can provide the opportunity to create more pleasant pedestrian spaces—those not requiring pedestrians to traverse an expansive commercial service area or parking lot. Transition spaces do not necessarily mean distinguishable edges that physically separate uses. The concept of community necessitates the networking of spaces to form functional relationships between uses, thus providing opportunity for maximum interaction between neighbors.

In Summary

One of the major problems with conventional suburban development is that it cloisters areas into single-use pods. This is nowhere more evident than in our living spaces. Euclidean zoning requires that each type of housing product, whether single-family detached, duplexes, townhouses, or apartments, be distinct and separate unto itself, where the automobile is the force that drives the design. The result is clusters of similar-income-range individuals and families who develop, intended or not, an us-versus-them mentality. This scenario ensures that affordable housing is placed at a higher density and that architectural design is more bland, ostensibly in order to keep developers' costs to a minimum. In many cases, these areas are seen as transitional rather than as a place to put down roots, which causes the social bonding between neighbors to suffer.

In true community planning, the focus is on interconnected neighborhoods where the distinction between homes and incomes is blurred by creating subtle transitions between them (as in allowing two different home types to share a common green space). More attention to the architectural detail on both types of homes reduces the apparent difference in income and helps allay the fear that lower property values are inevitable when proximity exists between two different uses. In fact, this neighborhood design technique can raise property values because of the overall design quality that can be achieved. One need only look at the increasing property values of the gentrified core neighborhoods in the first-tier suburbs to understand that many people want to live where a sense of place is evident and where they can put down roots. In true neighborhoods, families who move up to a bigger home may prefer to stay in "their" neighborhood, close to friends they have developed through schools, churches, and so on rather than facing the prospect of starting all over again somewhere else.

Where Would You Rather Shop?

At a Glance

❖ Understanding how retail centers have evolved and what they look like in conventional suburban developments

❖ Understanding the relationship between the different types of retail centers and the automobile

❖ Learning that there is a better design approach that favors users rather than their cars

❖ Applying the principles of traditional neighborhood development town centers to create walkable retail areas

Before the late 1940s, following the convention of the day, practically all commercial services were located in downtowns. Situated at the center of town, at a major crossroads, near a train station or a river fork, usually on the most level land around, one would find a relatively dense, compact cluster of buildings with shops and offices on the first floor and apartments or offices on the upper floors. With the exception of the five-and-ten store or the local department store, most goods and services were offered by individual merchants from their own storefront shops—a single service or line of merchandise per building.

The economic boom period following World War II was spawned by the reconstruction efforts directed toward war-torn Europe, which created unprecedented opportunities for growth and prosperity for the returning GIs. With the increased credit available and generous government housing programs, people began their escape from crowded apartments located between the downtowns and the associated industrial belts that surrounded them. In greater numbers than ever before, they escaped to newly developed suburbs in newly acquired automobiles.

Shopping Centers

What are now known as *shopping centers* sprang up along these routes into and out of town. Freestanding grocery stores and mail-order catalog stores were generally the first to exploit the potential of inexpensive sites at the edge of town that were large enough to accommodate both the building and the parking necessary to support it. This led to what has come to be known as the *miracle mile* of development—those commercial areas in what are now the older sections of town, with their chaotic variety of building shapes, sizes, and uses identified with all manner of signs, each larger and gaudier than the next. Usually only 100 to 150 feet deep, these sites consisted of simple, unornamented buildings with little or no storefront articulation. They were located at the back of the lot with undelineated direct pull-off parking from the highway—all in all a fairly sterile environment, but one that addressed the issue of convenience.

Over time, however, these miracle miles eventually evolved into the three basic types of shopping centers we're familiar with today: *neighborhood centers, community centers,* and *regional centers.* Each center is practically ordained to its location based on how far people are willing to travel for an increasingly larger selection of goods and on the standing population in the immediate area. In other words, it is easy to predict which type of center will eventually be built and, generally, where. People will typically travel 1.5 miles for food, 3 to 5 miles for apparel and household items, and 8 to 10 miles when price and selection are the primary considerations. Every locality possesses differing geographic and demographic anomalies that will affect the actual locations.

Neighborhood Centers

Neighborhood centers range in size from 30,000 to 150,000 square feet, depending on the size of the local population and the demand for services. They are designed to meet the day-to-day or immediate needs of a limited residential trade area of 2500 to 40,000 people. Offering goods and services such as

Sketch 7.1 Typical layout of early commercial areas. **(A)** Varied building locations create a look of chaos and clutter. **(B)** Individual sites and signs compete for motorists' attention. **(C)** Access between parcels is rare, if at all. **(D)** Building orientation isolates areas at the rear of the commercial sites.

Figure 7.1 The typical suburban retail corridor is grossly out of scale for pedestrians.

grocery markets and drugstores, dry cleaning and shoe repair, hair salons and dentists' offices, they are generally located at the intersection of a collector street and the entrance to a predominantly residential area, and they normally require from 3 to 10 acres of land area.

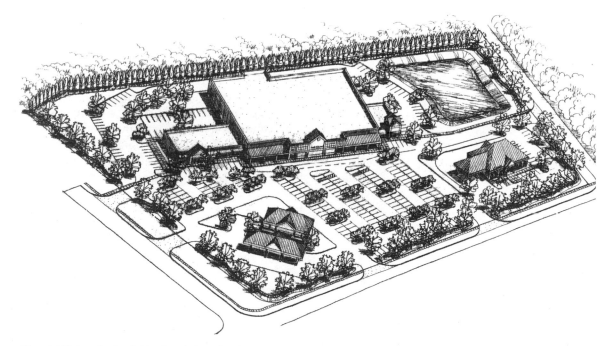

Sketch 7.2 A typical neighborhood shopping center.

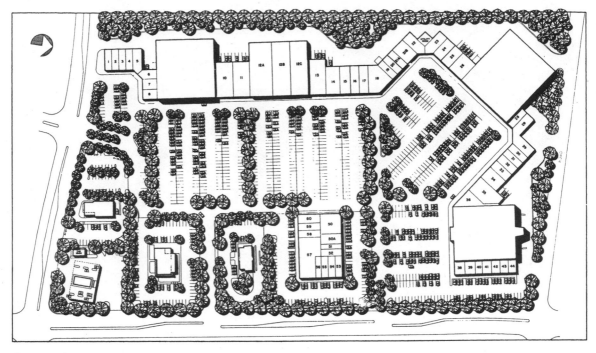

Sketch 7.3 A "community" center.

Community Centers

Community centers range in size from 100,000 to 350,000 square feet of gross leasable area, with the average size being at least 150,000 square feet. Offering all the services that the neighborhood ccntcr does as well as providing a discount department store, supermarket, and usually several more out-parcels than a neighborhood center, community centers serve a trade area of 40,000 to 150,000 people and are typically located at the signalized intersection of two collector streets (normally four lanes each). Except for grocery stores and discount department stores, the normal depth of the building used to be in the 80- to 120-foot range; however, with today's merchandising philosophy of having less storage space and more display space, lease space is generally in the 40- to 80-foot-deep range, with the typical storefront width being 20 to 30 feet. Community centers normally require from 10 to 30 acres of land area.

Regional Centers

Regional centers range in size from 400,000 to over 1 million square feet of gross leasable area, with a full complement of goods and services available (including full-line department stores as major anchors). Serving a trade area of over 150,000 people within a range of 10 to 15 miles, these sites have become the new "downtowns" of suburbia and normally require between 30 and 50+ acres to provide adequate parking. The larger of these have enclosed malls and are located at the intersection of a regional expressway system and a community arterial or collector street.

Common Elements of Shopping Centers

Shopping centers tend to have a unified architectural design treatment and typically are owned by either a corporation or a development group. All shopping centers possess on-site parking for customers and are designed to be accessed primarily by automobile. Service areas are separated from the public park-

Figure 7.2 A regional center.

Concentrations of civic, institutional, and commercial activity should be embedded in neighborhoods and districts, not isolated in remote, single-use complexes.

Charter of the Congress of New Urbanism

ing areas and therefore from the public's awareness. As a general rule in commercial development, building square footage consumes approximately 25 percent of the site area. Expressed differently, for every acre of land area roughly 10,000 square feet of commercial space can reasonably be expected.

Each shopping center possesses a structured tenant grouping to provide a balanced merchandise mix. The variety of shops are consciously chosen to complement one another and to minimize product overlap. To greater or lesser degrees, all shopping centers have pleasant surroundings, are generally safe in design, and contain some protection from the weather for customers. Shopping centers depend on automobile access for their success, but as our suburban areas grow more congested, people are wishing their neighborhood centers were accessible by foot, preferring to use their cars only for major shopping trips.

The problem with this is that the vast majority of shopping centers are almost completely separated from their constituent neighborhoods, making access by foot a dangerous undertaking. That is, vehicular and pedestrian access to these centers is limited to the collector streets that serve both areas, where traffic volumes and speeds are higher. These elements are not normally found in older commercial districts, which exhibit more varied architecture, less manipulation of the tenant mix, and fewer on-site parking spaces. However, they almost always provide on-street parking, something strictly forbidden in the shopping centers of conventional suburban development.

Most CSD retail centers provide a single land-use opportunity: retail. Rarely will one find related or supportive uses such as high-density residential or office space on-site. Instead, these are separated from one another and connected only by their common four- to six-lane collector street or across expansive parking lots. This separation of uses leads to inefficient space utilization by mandating a minimum number of parking spaces for each separate land use and thus requiring more land area than joint usage would necessitate.

Any new shopping center adds to the commercial stock of a region an amount of building area similar to that found in the commercial core of a small city. This is easier to understand if we think of each new center as the town center of a town or city equal to the size of the trading area of the center. New shopping centers do not create new business, they can only pull business from existing centers, usually those in disrepair or poorly located as a result of changing demographics.

Site Design: Points to Consider

Proper location is perhaps the single most important element that is most closely associated with the success or failure of a center. It must be easy, convenient, and quickly recognizable. However, the drawing power of a center is not due only to the distance to the next center but also to the convenience it offers its potential customers and the availability of desired merchandise. Conventional thinking has it that *neighborhood centers* must be located adja-cent to a major collector street. This may be true given the fact that major streets are the only practical means of accessing anything in our modern subur-ban areas. It is this mentality that has created sprawl in the first place. Because neighbor-hood centers serve a local clien-tele, it stands to reason that they would not necessarily have to be so located. For all intents and purposes, those who depend on these smaller centers for their immediate needs already know where they are located and what services are available.

The need is greater for *com-munity centers* to be sited adja-cent to major roadways, for they depend on a larger service area and thus require more conve-nient access directly to the site. Drawing from an even larger area, *regional centers* need to be located close to a regional ex-pressway system but not neces-sarily adjacent to it. If sited too close to off-ramps, merge lanes, and the like, access and maneu-verability can be compromised, leading to traffic congestion and driver frustration. A distance of between ½ and 1 mile from the

Sketch 7.4 An older, core commercial district. *(Drawing by Wesley Page)*

interchange would seem to be an appropriate distance to a primary entrance.

While it's easy to equate location with visibility, it would appear that too much emphasis has been put on visibility as a determinant of success, whereas prior knowledge of a center's location has not. You never see the Waldenbooks sign from the outside of the mall, but you are sure of its presence. Most shopping trips are destination-oriented. That is, one is usually going to a particular store or stores for a particular reason. Few people have ever bought a refrigerator while out shopping for a pair of shoes simply because they saw an advertisement in the window.

Conventional Suburban Configurations

The Strip Center

The *strip center,* the simplest and possibly the most prevalent, as the name implies is literally a straight line of shops set to the

Figure 7.3 Conventional suburban shopping: Is this what we really want?

rear of a parcel. Customer parking occurs between the building and the street, and the service area is located between the rear of the building and the rear property line. Smaller centers are typically no longer than 400 feet in order to keep all shops within an easy walking distance of one another; however, some early centers did not adhere to this standard, which resulted in some truly inhospitable spaces requiring extremely long walks. More often than not, this design led customers to simply move their cars from storefront to storefront to take advantage of the overabundant parking. This is the form of most neighborhood centers and many community centers today.

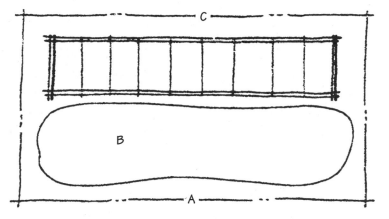

Sketch 7.5 The *strip* shopping center. **(A)** Straight-line orientation of building is typical. **(B)** Parking is always located between the center and the collector street. **(C)** Service area requires screening and buffering from the residential area that usually occurs behind the center.

Variations on a Theme

Variations on the strip are L-, U-, and T-shaped building patterns derived to more efficiently utilize the parcel shape and to maximize leasable space. These occupy sites that are usually larger than simple linear strips and more likely to be located at major intersections. Psychologically, these tend to make a large site appear smaller by encouraging the viewer's eye to follow the shape of the building from a point close to the access road to the rear of the site. A larger site so configured focuses attention on the building and not on the parking lot, thus rendering the center more approachable. This configuration also makes more of the storefronts visible to shoppers from the sidewalk—again, making the site appear smaller and encouraging more shopping.

The Cluster

The *cluster* is essentially a combination of the previous two types of centers arranged so that a purely pedestrian space results in the center. With the parking oriented to one side or completely encircling the buildings, the interior spaces begin to resemble a small village or the traditional downtowns of

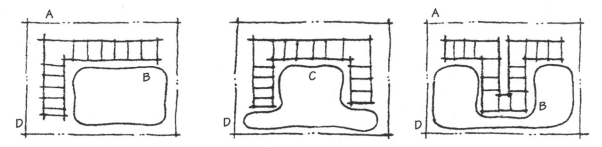

Sketch 7.6 Variants of the strip center—L-, U-, and T-shaped centers. **(A)** Typical for corner location. **(B)** View from one leg to another shortens the perceived distance between them. **(C)** Midblock location is typical for the U-shaped center. **(D)** Full-block location with two-corner exposure usually results in a large strip or T-shaped center.

small communities. This form has been adapted well to specialty centers that cater to tourists, who expect shopping to be an exciting event. Smaller shops offering a wide variety of small goods do well in these situations. However, the form does not adapt well for larger stores or anchors, which require larger service areas for regular tractor-trailer deliveries that mandate unimpeded visibility from adjacent collector streets. This form is rarely utilized in today's suburban landscape.

The Mall

The *mall* is simply the cluster configuration expanded and enclosed for weather protection. Initially, malls were designed in straight-line fashion, allowing an almost uninterrupted view within the length of the space. Now, mall designers follow design concepts gleaned from an earlier time. They utilize small pedestrian spaces (30 to 50 feet) between the storefronts and use angles and turns in the main corridor of the structure to reduce the visual distance and to focus attention on the brightly lighted window displays and kiosks. Malls are the predominant form of regional and superregional commercial

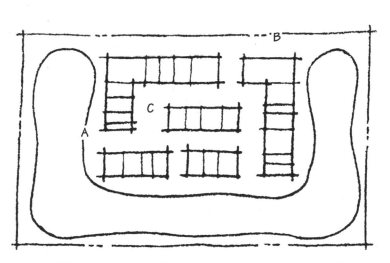

Sketch 7.7 The cluster center. **(A)** Unless shops are double-fronted, the exposure wall can be unattractive and uninviting. **(B)** Perceived lack of visibility may reduce the marketability of the rear space. **(C)** Service to interior spaces is difficult.

centers today. They have become the suburban downtowns, completely isolated and separated from the neighborhoods and communities that support them by their huge parking lots. Mall development has slowed in recent years due to over-building, reduced demand for commercial space, environmental concerns, and the advent of the big-box retail discount chain stores that offer everything from groceries to automotive parts under one roof at bargain prices.

Common Parking and Circulation Patterns

Most customer parking occurs within 300 feet of the building or storefront, and parking that is over 600 feet away will rarely be used; people tend not to venture this far away except at the busiest of times of the year. Parking should be orderly, logical, easily understood, and its pattern discernable to the entering customer. In most regional centers, parking is arranged in an angled, one-way system that confuses and frustrates the parking customer. In addition, this style of parking is not as efficient as two-way right-angled parking and therefore should be used only where site constraints demand it.

Parking should be designed in the smallest increment or compartment possible. That is, through access-lane location, landscaping, walkways, surface drainage retention areas, or whatever, the number of cars in a particular lot should be as small as is practical given the cost constraints of construction. In the case of regional centers, it is desirable to plan parking configurations for no more than 800 cars. Likewise,

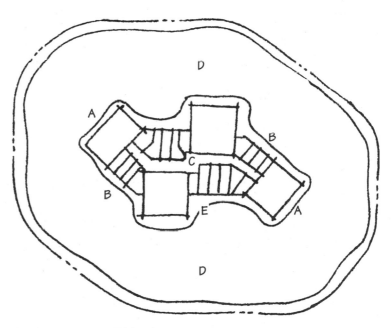

Sketch 7.8 The mall. **(A)** Access to the interior mall through the anchor stores is encouraged. Direct access to the mall interior usually is limited. **(B)** Few smaller shops possess exterior exposure to the parking area. High, blank-wall architecture is the norm. **(C)** Small shops survive on traffic generated by the anchor stores. **(D)** A vast parking area separates the mall from all other elements of the community. **(E)** Exposed service areas are a natural by-product of the mall configuration.

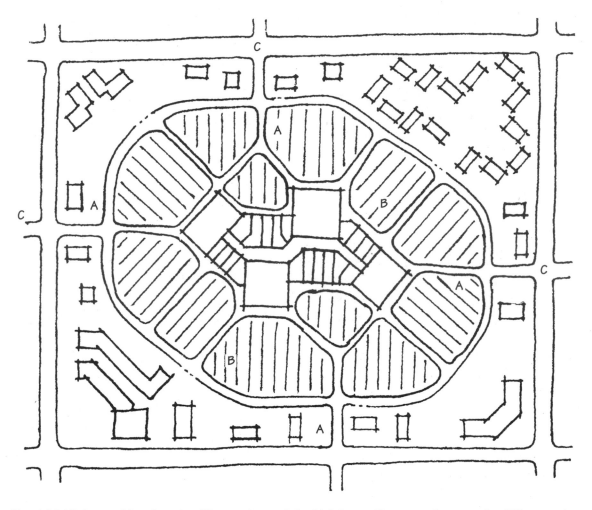

Sketch 7.9 **(A)** Access drives from the obligatory ring road should define parking areas of no more than 800 cars and should be heavily landscaped to create a sense of enclosure for the individual parking areas. **(B)** All parking should orient toward the building to psychologically shorten the distances, to ease pedestrian access, and to enhance surveillance opportunities. **(C)** Primary vehicle entry points to mall should be in the vicinity of the major anchor stores.

these should be defined by access lanes, landscaping, and so forth. This can enhance the wayfinding abilities of customers while visually making the entire lot more aesthetically pleasing.

All parking and travel lanes, landscaping, and walkways should orient toward the building. No pedestrian should be required to walk through successive parking bays to access the store. A person's path should be as clear of obstacles as possible. Circulation around regional centers is typically represented by a *ring road* located at some distance from the

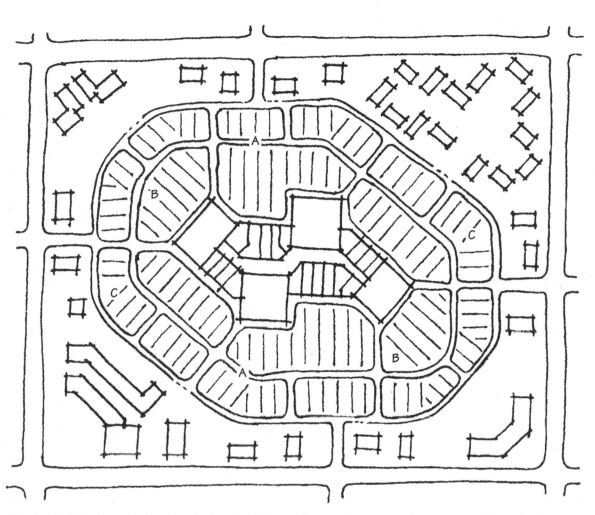

Sketch 7.10 **(A)** A ring road located at the functional 300-foot distance from the mall entrances would contain all the required parking for the vast majority of the time. **(B)** The internal ring road and its associated landscaping help reduce the size and scale of the parking lot. **(C)** The parcels created between the ring roads become excellent opportunities for infill development, particularly offices, as they provide daytime customers for the mall as well as nighttime and weekend parking.

building itself and travel lanes immediately adjacent to the building. Given the fact that most parking occurs within 300 feet of the building, a better location for these ring roads would seem to be at that distance, which would enhance access to those areas where parking will actually occur and would psychologically reduce the size and scale of the parking lot.

Parking requirements for commercial areas are biased toward the high side in most site plan ordinances. Rarely do they take into account the multiple stops that occur during one shopping trip, and thus no overlapping of parking requirements is even considered. Most regional commercial sites are now required to provide between 5 and 5.5 parking spaces per 1000 square feet of gross leasable space, or enough to satisfy parking needs for the holiday season. If we assume that most commercial space is open for 12 hours a day, seven days a week, then the parking areas of these commercial sites are potentially full only 0.25 percent of the time or less. Said another way, 99.75 percent of the time the lot is not full and is being underutilized. This expanse of unused asphalt is unattractive at best, appalling at worst. To design parking areas to be fully utilized for only a short period of time through the year is a waste of potential commercial space and the tax receipts that could result from a mixture of uses. It is also an affront to the environment, considering the heat gain to the ambient air from solar reflection and the increased surface drainage and pollution resulting from over-paving.

The large parking areas, required by ordinance, that surround all regional commercial sites have become the modern-day equivalent of moats, literally cutting off any normal pedestrian interaction between surrounding neighborhoods and their commercial center. Security has become a major issue with regard to the parking areas surrounding regional centers. These seas of parking leave one feeling exposed and vulnerable and have subsequently made shoppers easy targets for criminals. It is interesting to note that the threat of crime, whether real or imagined, contributed to the atrophy of the older, now stagnant shopping districts of our cities.

An Alternative Future

Of all that can be said about our suburban commercial districts, one item stands true: Americans are in a deep love-hate relationship with them. We simultaneously demand the convenience they offer and are dismayed by their appearance. Writing in 1962, Kevin Lynch perhaps said it best: "In its gaudy confusion, it seems to symbolize the worst of our material culture."[1] Typical commercial strip development is universally condemned by municipal authorities and residents alike to the point that many municipal comprehensive planning documents contain strident statements in an attempt to limit their application. And yet they persist, for they provide a service and function that we have all come to expect.

Figure 7.4 Shopping center parking lots are rarely, if ever, used to capacity and are a waste of prime real estate.

So we accept their inevitability and go about softening, screening, buffering, and separating them from our residential areas even more, using all manner of landscaping, fencing, and berming rather than exploring a different structure, a different way of designing these sites. These aesthetic Band-Aids are nothing more than surface remedies that do not go to the root of the problem.

Is there an alternative approach to commercial design? Can anything be done to stop this cycle of development that perpetuates itself simply because that's the way it's always been done? Definitely. But we must revisit and reassess the current commercial development patterns at five distinct levels to devise a more community-oriented, pedestrian-friendly, and less automobile-dependent solution for each. By examining these five levels of site design (individual sites, neighborhood centers, community centers, major intersections, and malls), solutions can be found and axioms established that work at the smallest scale and that can be built upon through each successive size and scale change to arrive at a potentially new form of suburban development—one for which community is more than a nice idea.

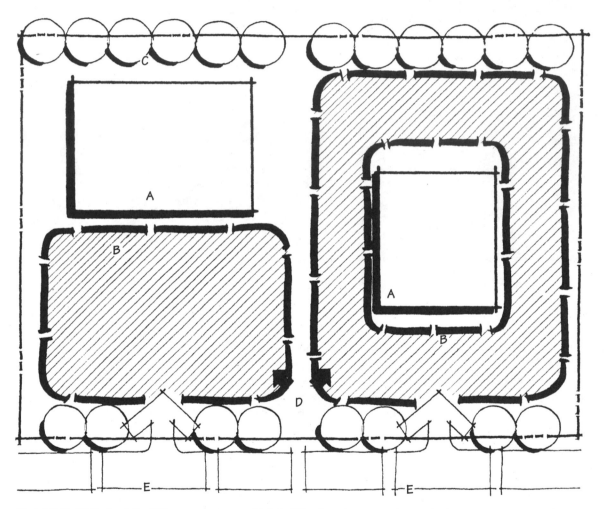

Sketch 7.11 **(A)** Setback flexibility encourages multiple building locations, creating confusion and chaotic conditions. **(B)** Setback requirement forces parking in front of building, reducing ability to connect to street, weakening pedestrian environment. **(C)** Rear building location requires extensive landscaping when adjacent to residential and eliminates potential for pedestrian access. **(D)** Parked cars dominate view. **(E)** Flexible curb-cut location can result in confusion and aggravate traffic. *(Courtesy of the Talbot Group)*

Figure 7.5 The suburban aesthetic.

Individual Sites

CSD PATTERN

Building placement on individual street-front lots, also known as *outparcels* or *pad sites,* when utilized in conjunction with shopping centers, is dictated by front, side, and rear setback lines. These setbacks, while mandating a minimum, generally allow the placement to occur anywhere behind or within these arbitrary lines, which usually results in the building being placed at the center or rear of the site. Zoning regulations then typically require a substantial landscape buffer if the site is adjacent to a residential neighborhood, effectively cutting off any direct connection between the two sites. The building is normally located between 30 and 35 feet from the right-of-way line, and the parking is located in the front of the building (and, in some cases, all around the building) in an effort to create as many spaces as possible. This approach ensures that the view from the adjacent street is always one of parked automobiles or, more often than not, a substantially empty parking lot. This multiple-placement option applied equally to every adjacent parcel results in a variable building line or

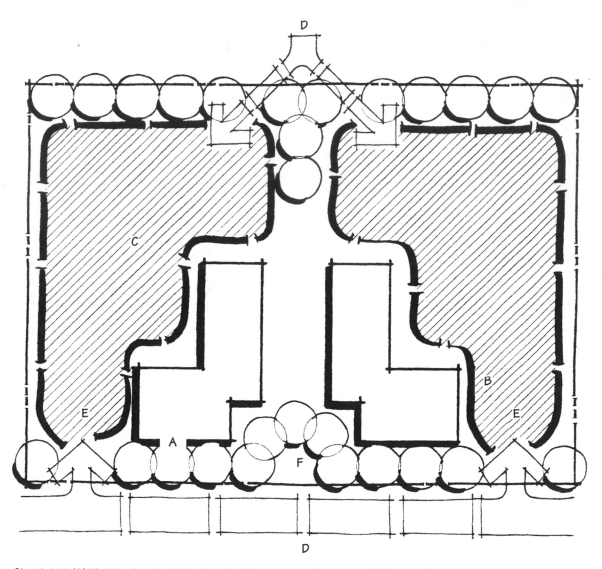

Sketch 7.12 **(A)** "Build-to" setback line sites building at street; increases visibility and fosters pedestrian environment. **(B)** Parking at or behind building line maintains street edge, draws attention to building. **(C)** Views of parked cars reduced by building location. **(D)** Neighborhood access encouraged by street-oriented building location. **(E)** Parking access separated to maximum extent and combined with adjacent parcel when applicable. **(F)** Usable exterior public space possible—artwork, fountain, bus stop, outdoor dining. *(Courtesy of the Talbot Group)*

Figure 7.6 A human-scale shopping center.

edge that guarantees one building will not relate to the next, further weakening their connection with the street and any continuity that might have occurred otherwise. This point is most important, for its continued implementation is weakening the streetscape environment, which goes to the very heart of the problem with the suburban aesthetics.

TND ALTERNATIVE

By requiring the buildings to be located at the setback line, many positive things can happen. It encourages the parking to be located at the side and rear of the building and reduces the impact of parked cars along the street. Locating the building closer to the street creates a potentially more human-scale streetscape while encouraging the development of exterior public spaces in the form of plazas, transit stops, outside eating areas, and so forth. It also reduces the need for freestanding signs, which can now be affixed to the building or designed as part of the structure itself. This practice alone can greatly improve the suburban visual environment.

In the case of areas where there is a potential for shallow commercial strips, this approach can aid in establishing an orderly arrangement of parking lot entrances, thus enhancing the safety of the street. An added advantage of the street-oriented approach is that it shifts the vehicular access between and across parcels to the rear of the site, reducing the points of conflict at the entrances and allowing a more structured access from the rear—be it a larger parking lot or a residential area.

It should be noted that in this example and in those that follow, both conventional and traditional neighborhood alternative scenarios are drawn at a similar scale and graphically depict the same buildings and parking areas. These basic design premises, while they may seem simplistic, are universal in that they can and should be applied to larger shopping centers or any other commercial areas.

Neighborhood Commercial Centers

CSD PATTERN

These 5- to 15-acre sites, located on virtually every major corner of our urban and suburban areas, symbolize both progress and sprawl. These centers typically include a major and minor anchor, a grocery store, a pharmacy, a spattering of smaller shops, and fast-food restaurants. They are most often built along the rear and/or side property lines. The void between the building and the street is then filled with a parking lot which, as in the case of the individual sites, destroys any viable pedestrian-friendly connection to the street and discourages pedestrian use of the sidewalks that access the commercial spaces from the neighborhoods. The fact that these areas are usually no more than one-third filled at any one time points to the need to reexamine our parking-to-building area requirements. It seems ludicrous to require such a high number of spaces that are fully utilized only three to four days a year at best. Typically, these structures are in a linear arrangement, stretching from one corner of the site to another, discouraging the casual, browsing form of shopping. In fact, their orientation seems to encourage shoppers to make multiple parking stops throughout the length of the center—in other words, driving from store to store instead of walking. An overabundance of parking, an overwhelming scale, and a lack of visual stimulation all combine to virtually

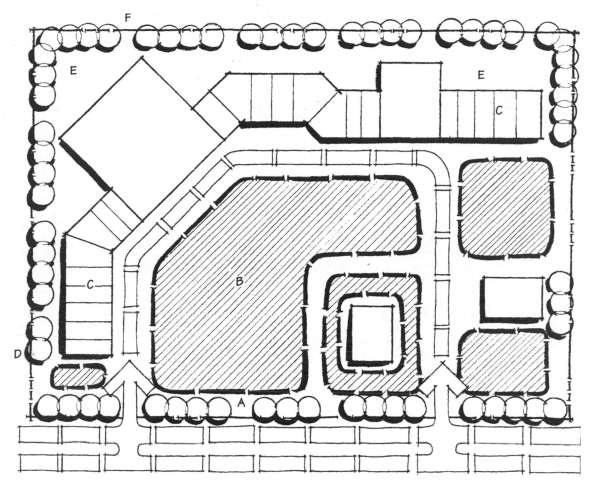

Sketch 7.13 **(A)** Lack of defined street edge discourages pedestrian access. **(B)** Primary view is of parking area, usually half empty. **(C)** Linear arrangement does not encourage multiple shopping stops. **(D)** Limited opportunity to connect to adjacent office/commercial. **(E)** Service area too expansive; underutilized, requires heavy landscape screening. **(F)** Layout eliminates any opportunity to connect to adjacent residential area. *(Courtesy of the Talbot Group)*

ensure that a shopper is never going to be very far from his or her means of private transportation. This arrangement literally requires the center to turn its back on whatever land use occurs behind it, usually residential.

This physical and psychological separation is fully achieved by locating an expansive and grossly underutilized service area that requires ever more landscaping Band-Aids to ameliorate its negative impact on the neighborhood. With this orientation, the adjacent residents are then required to access their shopping center via an off-site collector road system, mixing

Figure 7.7 A village commercial ambience.

local traffic with through traffic, thereby exacerbating traffic congestion.

TND ALTERNATIVE

Using the same concepts established in the individual sites section, a portion of the shops can be located closer to the street, creating that desirable street edge so painfully lacking in most neighborhood centers. The main parking area can then be centralized, allowing street-oriented shops to screen the vast majority of it from the roadway. This also encourages the scattering of smaller parking areas throughout the site, thus reducing their visual impact. By locating anchor stores along side property lines or back-to-back with adjacent commercial buildings, the service areas can be reduced in size, freeing space for either additional building or amenity space, and can be internalized to reduce the off-site visual impact. This puts the anchor stores adjacent to the bulk of the parking where there is a true need for it.

This arrangement also opens the site for the residents of adjacent housing to access the site via an internal road system, keeping separate local traffic from through traffic. In fact, additional, reduced-cost commercial frontage for smaller neighborhood-dependent shops is created while maintaining visibility to the anchor stores from both the residential side and the primary street. The resultant village-type commercial center, with its inward orientation and reduced spacing between buildings, encourages more shopping per trip, increases the efficiency of the neighborhood layout, and helps to make shopping an event to be enjoyed.

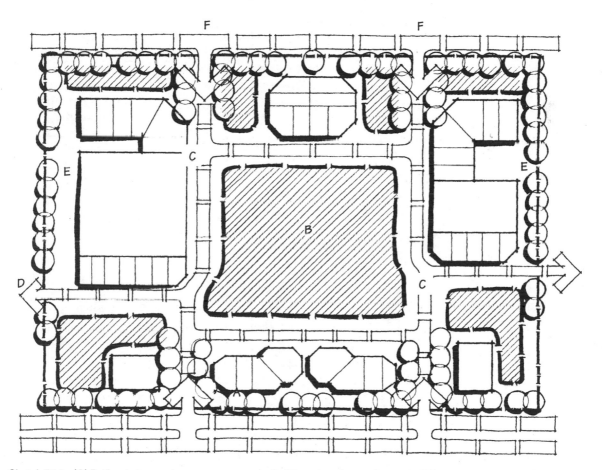

Sketch 7.14a **(A)** Defined street edge creates more desirable pedestrian environment. **(B)** Internal parking reduces negative impact from street. **(C)** Inward-focused arrangement creates a village feeling, encourages multiple shopping stops. **(D)** Strong connection to adjacent office/commercial areas. **(E)** Service areas reduced, oriented to adjacent office/commercial, less screening required. **(F)** Layout encourages use by adjacent residential, eliminating need to access via collector road system. *(Courtesy of the Talbot Group)*

Adapting the Layout

Being ubiquitous throughout suburbia, the neighborhood shopping center represents one of the best opportunities for adaptive reuse and integration into the fabric of the community. By simply extending streets from the surrounding residential areas into the commercial site, an entirely different relationship between the two use areas can develop. Doing so, they become interdependent and supportive of one another. It is relatively easy to redesign a portion of the structure and replace it with one that allows street extensions to occur. When coupled with a realistic recognition of actual (not peak) parking needs, the number of spaces required decreases, resulting in potentially more leasable space.

As Sketch 7.14b implies, a street orientation of shops that places parking at both the rear and side of the building and on the street results in transforming these waste spaces into productive places of neighborhood activity. In addition, strong street connections to the surrounding neighborhood reduce the amount of traffic on the local collector streets.

While this approach is certainly viable and preferable to the conventional situation, it is no replacement for designing these most basic of commercial areas as part of the neighborhood from the beginning.

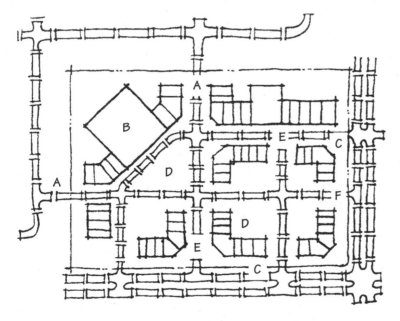

Sketch 7.14b Neighborhood centers—adaptive layout. **(A)** Street extensions into commercial site; encourages local access without impacting the collector streets. **(B)** Anchor store, usually a grocery, maintains adequate parking in front. **(C)** Street edge along local collector streets is reestablished.
(D) Bulk of shopping center parking is screened from local collector streets.
(E) Streetscape image extends into site. **(F)** Additional accessways distribute and dilute traffic impact.

Community Centers

CSD PATTERN

These 20- to 25-acre sites are just larger versions of the neighborhood centers with more of everything—more anchors, more outparcels, more parking, more problems. These are usually located at larger intersections and sometimes, as in the example, span the entire distance between the intersections. With a full complement of outparcels, curb cuts, and access lanes, chaos and confusion are the norm. Again,

Figure 7.8 A street orientation of shops that places parking at the side and rear of the buildings results in transforming the no-man's-land into productive neighborhood places of activity.

there is a weak street relationship, an overabundance of parking, and, because of their distance from the street and outparcel buildings, surprisingly little visibility for the anchor stores and primary shops. Being anywhere from 400 to 800 feet away from the primary thoroughfare seems to dispel the idea of visibility so staunchly advocated by the commercial real estate brokers. Of course, in this case there is also the expansive service area that must be sealed off from the adjacent residential neighborhoods and screened with more Band-Aids. The isolation this creates increases the perceived potential for crime and violence and becomes a major concern for both store owners and their employees.

Finally, while in some cases office centers are located adjacent or nearby, rarely are they designed to function together as a true node. More likely they are located just far enough away to require auto access between the two, resulting in more traffic and less pedestrian connectivity.

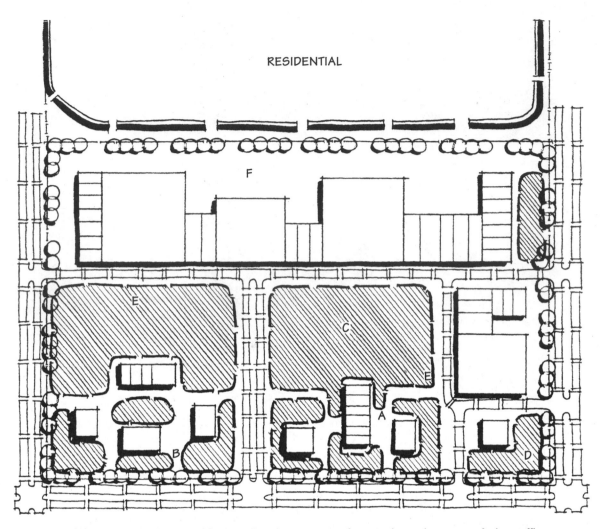

Sketch 7.15 **(A)** Multiple outparcels and freestanding shops compete for attention and create confusing traffic patterns. **(B)** Parking between building and street eliminates a viable pedestrian environment. **(C)** Outparcels reduce visibility of parking area and of storefronts as well. **(D)** Parking location weakens intersection visually. A missed opportunity for public space. **(E)** Expanse of parking and size of center discourage pedestrian access across site. **(F)** Expansive service area creates underutilized paved area that requires screening and security while eliminating direct pedestrian or vehicle access to center. *(Courtesy of the Talbot Group)*

TND ALTERNATIVE

The size and scale of community centers allow much more flexibility and creativity than is ever attempted in a conventional situation. With a little innovative site manipulation, the various elements can truly be pulled together to function as a node of community focus and not just as the community

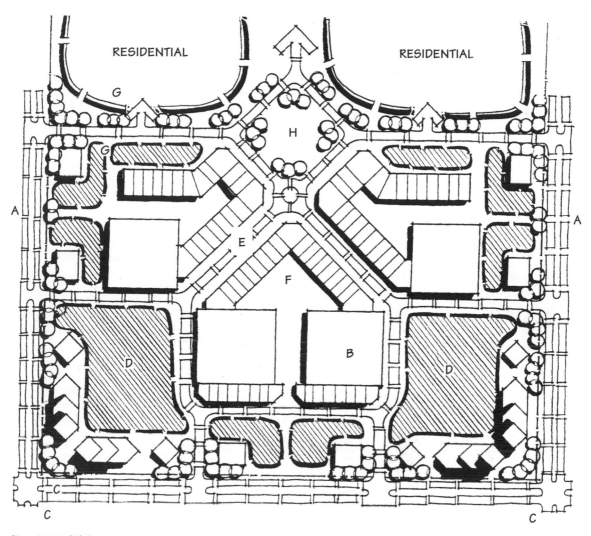

Sketch 7.16 **(A)** Separation of outparcels reduces confusion, and orientation reinforces streetscape. **(B)** Anchor stores' visibility remains the same, if not better. **(C)** Offices at intersection screen parking and foster public use of space. **(D)** Parking areas separated to reduce expansiveness and provide overlap opportunities. **(E)** Main Street with sidewalks and parallel parking re-creates hometown feeling, reinforces neighborhood identity, and encourages pedestrian activity. **(F)** Service areas consolidated, internalized, and controlled for security. **(G)** Access road serves both commercial and adjacent residential. **(H)** Village green as focal point/gathering area. *(Courtesy of the Talbot Group)*

shopping center. Again, using the premises established previously, the anchor stores could be relocated closer to the intersections, which would increase their visibility while reducing the visual impact of their parking lots. Providing office sites on street corners has the potential to greatly improve the aesthetics of the center by providing something other than the

Project Profile: Winter Springs, Florida

Location: Winter Springs, Florida

Client: The City of Winter Springs

Planning firm: Dover Kohl and Partners

Grants/funding received: $5 million from the
Florida State Trails and Greenways Program

Project size: 200 acres

Key Features:

- Tuskawilla Road, which runs parallel to state road 434, a recently widened four-lane arterial highway, will be designed as Main Street.

- Main Street will link a Market Square to the more quiet center, Magnolia Square.

- Mixed-use neighborhoods will connect to the squares and will include office, retail, and residential uses.

- The existing Cross Seminole Trail will be repositioned to offer alternate pedestrian and bicycle paths into the heart of the town center, with equestrian and hiking trails around the periphery.

- The trails will feature views of pristine wetland preserve areas.

- Wide sidewalks along tree-lined streets, elegant squares, and a rich mixture of urban architecture will reinforce the pedestrian scale of neighborhoods.

- A highly graphic, simple-to-use Town Center District Code was created to replace Winter Springs' existing land development regulations, to legalize mixed-use development as envisioned in the Master Plan, and to preapprove desirable development.

Project Approach:

The goal of the project was to create a clearly identifiable town center in the midst of an area consisting of individual planned unit developments (PUDs). The site for the proposed town center was approximately 200 acres of strategically located, mostly undeveloped land adjacent to a four-lane arterial highway. The proposed town center needed to be a physical place where many of the basic needs of citizens would be conveniently and tightly focused. Shopping, working, governance, entertainment, dwelling, and the arts needed to happen together in order to change the existing sprawl nature of the city to one that reflected its values and aspirations, its vision for the future.

typical franchise architecture so often seen in outparcel buildings. The higher form of architecture demanded by the office market at this location can give a greater significance to the streetscape and a stronger sense of place to an area typically weak in urban form. In addition, the increase in office space and the accompanying employees who work on-site create a built-in demand for commercial goods and services by those who heretofore have had to make a separate trip to satisfy those needs. The potential for reducing the number of lunchtime automobile trips in the immediate vicinity of the center is significant, since theoretically most of the desired shopping is available on-site. This site design also provides more opportunities to overlap parking areas, which in turn can reduce underutilized pavement.

To encourage stronger internal pedestrian and vehicular connections between adjacent parcels and the surrounding neighborhoods, the secondary shops that exist as a result of the spin-off business from the anchor stores can be configured much like an enclosed mall, producing a functional Main Street. This allows better vehicular and pedestrian access at lunchtime (for people who work nearby) and after work (for those on their way home). The small-scale shops and small offices that require less visibility from through traffic can be located at the rear of the site along a local neighborhood street. With homes fronting one side of the street and neighborhood commercial on the other, a true town commons can be created. One variable to this would be to add apartment flats above the first floor retail and office spaces. This allows both sides of the street to function on a 24-hour basis and increases the perception of security for both homes and retail stores. Adding a public green space or commons with a community focal point makes the space a true center by establishing an interface between two seemingly disparate uses. A nice by-product of this configuration is the ability to consolidate, internalize, and control access to the commercial service areas, making them both safer and less obtrusive in the landscape.

Major Intersections

CSD PATTERN

Major intersections are the prime community and subregional commercial locations that are found in every suburban growth area. Historically, they have evolved over a longer period of time than individual sites or neighborhood centers and therefore have had little benefit from long-range planning or a guided vision for the immediate area surrounding it. As Sketch 7.17 depicts, they are typically a combination of all the types we have discussed, more or less strewn about randomly. Not much can be said about these situations that hasn't been covered already, except that in most cases areawide circulation among the various commercial, office, and residential uses is channeled to and through one primary intersection. The resultant traffic is barely manageable at best and absolutely unbearable at peak demand. The ever increasing traffic counts require more and more intersection improvements, until what is realized is the all-too-familiar intersection consisting of at least eight lanes at each leg. This in effect separates one side of the road from the other to the extent that there is little, if any, normal pedestrian access possible from one to the other. Oh yes, the stop bars are there for automobiles, the striping, signage, and signals are there for the pedestrian—but *are* there any pedestrians? Rarely! The scale of these intersections is so vast that the introduction of a person actually walking across them seems odd and out of place. To see a person on foot here makes the passing motorist assume he or she is having car trouble and is obviously headed to one of the service stations located on each of the four corners. It's easy to understand how, in our attempt to solve traffic problems, we can actually destroy the underlying desirability of a place, thereby canceling out the need for the improvements.

The scattered and unfocused development along these major thoroughfares represents one of the inherent faults of the totally laissez-faire approach to physical planning by our municipal authorities. The missed opportunities at these critical points—opportunities to create a synergy, a focus, a true sense of place—are ones that will take a generation or more to correct.

TND ALTERNATIVE

Using similar patterns described for community centers and clustering them to focus on the four corners of the intersection, a unifying order and structure can be achieved while providing all the services and land uses that are apparently in demand. Elimination of individual curb cuts for freestanding buildings and outparcels along the primary thoroughfares can reduce the friction so hated by transportation engineers. Instead these outparcels can be clustered between median breaks and access granted using cross-access easements along

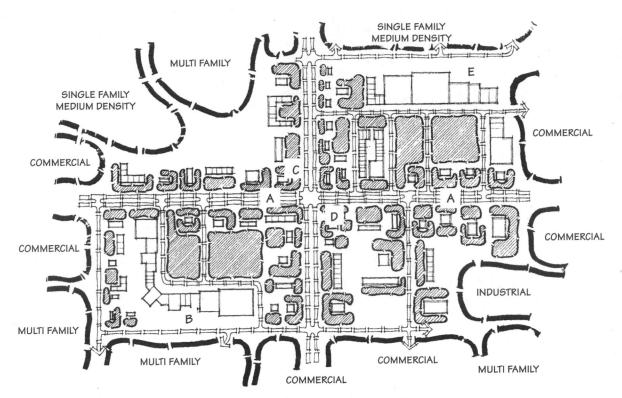

Sketch 7.17 **(A)** Multiple sites and curb cuts create confusion, visual clutter, traffic congestion, and weak streetscape. **(B)** Service areas exposed to residential discourage pedestrian access via main collector roads. **(C)** Most local and through traffic concentrates at one intersection. **(D)** No opportunity for urban amenity, community focal points. **(E)** Existing pattern encourages continuation of current development. *(Courtesy of the Talbot Group)*

the rear property line of each parcel. These critically located median breaks can be positioned to siphon off the local commercial traffic at eight points on the primary roads to feed the traffic into two circular collector loops that, in essence, circle the primary intersection. This separation of traffic allows a freer, less impeded movement of through traffic at the primary intersection and encourages commercial locations between the two loop roads. In addition, this technique can create an easier transition between the neighborhoods outside the loop road and the retail uses so that a community circulation system separates the commercial from the residential (as opposed to the barren service area that so typically performs this function). In effect, this becomes the neighborhood commercial street, directly accessible to the neighborhoods without requiring access via a major thoroughfare. Major anchor stores serviced by the inner circulation loop retain good visi-

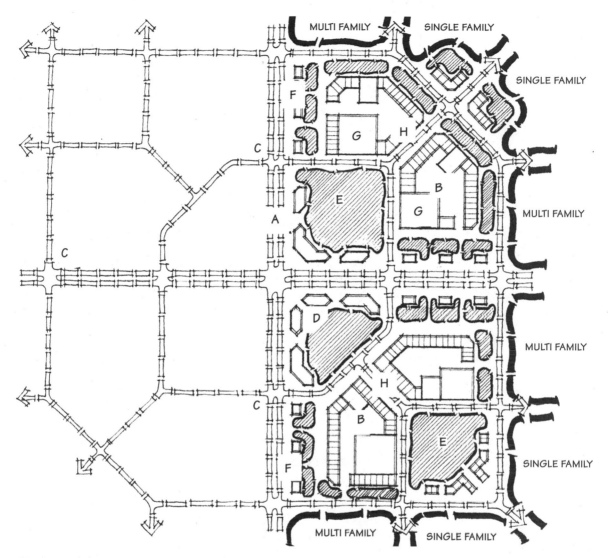

Sketch 7.18 **(A)** No curb cuts between median breaks; allows easy movement of through traffic. **(B)** Combined internalized service areas are more efficient and controllable and eliminate need for screening. **(C)** Multiple access points siphon local traffic from through traffic. **(D)** Multistory corporate offices at primary intersection; creates continuous street edge, enhancing pedestrian activity. **(E)** Primary parking areas screened from traffic provide overlap possibilities. **(F)** Outparcels clustered to support offices and shops while retaining visibility, shared entrances. **(G)** Anchor stores retain same or better visibility. **(H)** Neighborhood Main Street centrally located to support offices and residential. *(Courtesy of the Talbot Group)*

bility and access, while minor anchor stores, primarily supporting the neighborhood, can be accessed from the outer circulation loop with orientation toward the neighborhoods they serve.

With the commercial areas forming a doughnut shape around the primary intersection, this core area is then freed for the location of multistoried offices clustered adjacent to the intersection. Located in this manner to screen the parking areas and to enhance the pedestrian activity in the area, the result is an office and commercial district that is a true part of the community. In fact, it would form, and indeed function as, the heart of the community.

The alternative concepts discussed previously are certainly appropriate in this situation. Overlap parking between the office areas (daytime during-the-week users) and the commercial areas (nighttime during-the-week and weekend users) increases site efficiency. Screened, centralized service areas enhance safety and reduce the negative visual environment. Neighborhood Main Streets reinforce community identity while providing an alternative shopping experience. Obviously, this type of treatment could not and probably should not be applied at every intersection. Rather, a better application would be to consolidate a district's supporting commercial centers in fewer areas. For this reason, this focused approach is more effective when utilized sparingly—both because of the size of the area required to support it residentially and the desirability of creating a few truly distinct nodes that can be easily recognized as the center of a geographic region.

Malls

CSD PATTERN

These modern-day downtowns of suburban America are in many cases regional and superregional centers that can easily exceed 150 to 200 acres in size and be located in their own isolated extremely large superblock. Ideally, they are bordered by collector roads with relatively quick access to a limited-access highway. Originally they consisted of the mall site only, but now have evolved to the point of being surrounded by numerous transitional and support facilities. Such facilities may include neighborhood or community shopping centers and individual office sites as well as entire office developments, hotels, freestanding restaurants, automobile maintenance facilities, and medium- to high-density residential—all requiring separate, individual parking areas. These facilities tend to form a continuous protective zone around the centrally located mall structure, from which they are all completely separated by the giant parking lot.

Figure 7.9 Neighborhood main streets reinforce community identity while providing an alternative shopping experience.

The primary organizing element in this scenario is the ring road, which forms the outer limits of the mall site. Other than the occasional stormwater retention basin or landscaped parking lot island, nothing but asphalt occurs from this point to the mall itself, in some cases only a couple hundred feet, but more often than not, easily 600 to 800 feet or more. The purpose obviously is to provide adequate on-site circulation for the ancillary uses, but when riding this ring road in our quest to find the perfect parking space we resemble the little white ball on a roulette wheel, circling until we plunge inward to the center to find our resting spot.

This complex is linked to the area collector roads via several short entrance roads that serve as extensions of the local road system. This is typically the only halfhearted attempt to integrate these facilities with the surrounding community. In fact, most often, heavy landscape screening and buffering are mandated as a point-of-site plan approval to reduce the negative impact of such a monolithic and obviously out-of-scale structure.

Project Profile: Eastgate Mall, Chattanooga, Tennessee

Location: Chattanooga Tennessee

Client: The Chattanooga-Hamilton County Regional Planning Agency

Planning firm: Dover Kohl and Partners

Project type: Redevelopment of 1960s-vintage shopping mall

Key Features:

- A network of interconnected streets and blocks.
- Buildings fronting the streets and public spaces with parking in the rear.
- Buildings arranged to form a high-quality, well-defined streetscape, resulting in higher real estate values.
- Special sites for civic buildings.
- Mixed-use buildings.
- Pedestrian-friendly connections to adjacent areas.
- A greenway extending to a major trail.
- An adaptable layout for future transit opportunities.

Project Approach:

The goal of the project was to create a real town center for the Brainerd area of the city. This required that the mall property be substantially reconfigured by providing infill development within the surrounding surface parking areas and new development to reconnect the shopping center to the surrounding neighborhood and nearby office park. To facilitate this, the design team conducted a week-long charette inside the vacant mall with residents of the surrounding neighborhood, adjacent commercial property owners, city officials, retail experts, and traffic consultants. A market analysis and a multimodal transportation analysis were performed to determine the best tenant mix and transportation opportunities. Incremental phasing for the development of the project was essential to respond to anticipated market demand. The mall will be gradually replaced with a more traditional mixed-use environment found in traditional town centers.

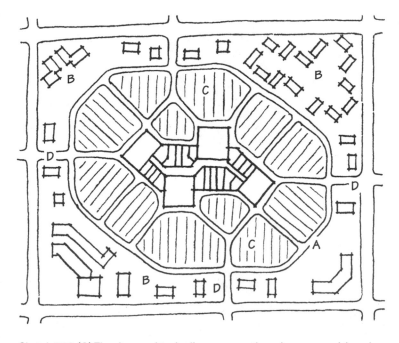

Sketch 7.19 **(A)** The ring road typically serves as the primary organizing element of the entire area. **(B)** A variety of related but unconnected uses such as restaurants, banks, offices, additional retail, and even residential surround the mall. **(C)** A massive parking lot usually separates the mall and its surrounding support structures. **(D)** Access to the surrounding road network is channelized and focused at only a few points, requiring signalization and exacerbating traffic flow.

The design intent of the relationship between the mall structure and its parking seems conflicted if we consider the true purpose of the structure itself. The mall is designed to pull people in primarily through prominently located and architecturally accented anchor stores. These command the premier positions with the most visibility and are located as far away from one another as the design will permit. The secondary entrances, those leading directly to the smaller mall shops, are likely to be understated to discourage access. However, these smaller shops form the filler between the anchors, and through interesting design, promotional activities, and seasonal displays they hope to catch your eye and make a sale. The dichotomy is that if access through the anchors is preferred, then why provide such an abundance of parking all around? Why not provide the majority of the required parking in the vicinity of the anchors only and utilize the other parking areas in more productive fashion: office, hotel, or even high-density housing in the form of apartments or housing for the elderly?

With the exception of the hotel and what little residential may be on-site, the vast majority of the uses would be the 8 A.M. to 5 P.M. offices and the 9 A.M. to 9 P.M. commercial spaces. This means that during a 24-hour period, much of this sea of asphalt would stand empty.

TND ALTERNATIVE

The automobile is the reason we have malls. Malls exist only because cars do, and cars are needed because most people don't live or work near a mall. To go from one place to another we need large, streamlined, superelevated, limited-access roads. These in turn allow people to live farther and farther out, which requires more roads and eventually results

Figures 7.10, 7.11 Where would you rather shop?

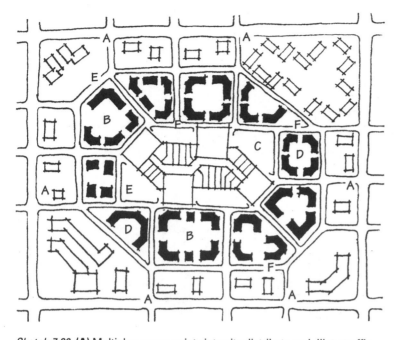

Sketch 7.20 **(A)** Multiple access points into site distribute and dilute traffic. **(B)** New development can easily occur between the ring road and the mall proper. Offices, street-oriented shops, and high-density residential are ideal complementary uses. **(C)** Realistic requirements reduce the need for an overabundance of parking spaces. **(D)** Parking at the rear of the new structures is screened from casual view from the new streets. **(E)** Surface and/or structured parking can be accommodated and afforded with the increased revenues resulting from the additional development. **(F)** Walkable streetscape reduces the perceived scale of the site and encourages pedestrian access.

in the need for yet another mall site. The cycle continues. Many feel that malls are the climax species of the commercial genre, the culmination of a merchandising concept begun in the first half of the twentieth century. But in order for malls to evolve to the next level, they must be redesigned to be more accommodating to the shopper rather than the automobile.

In applying traditional neighborhood design principles to malls, mall sites and their ancillary land uses should be developed as nodes and not as the isolated behemoths they are today. Entrance roads and ring roads should be configured as true extensions of the local street system, allowing direct access from the surrounding area and reducing traffic on the local collector streets.

As Sketch 7.20 suggests, we need to first identify how existing mall sites can be adapted to provide additional street-oriented uses (offices, commercial, residential, even warehouse/distribution operations) within the immediate area. Second, we need to design future mall sites with the idea that they will serve as the first phase or core of an eventual street-oriented mixed-use development.

If the ancillary support structures are developed using the design concepts stressed in previous portions of this chapter, what once were just mall sites could emerge as new suburban centers of shopping, social, and civic activities set in a radically different form from the isolated asphalt deserts we all know, but not so different from time-tested, tried-and-true solutions evident in memorable places the world over.

In Summary

With the problems that growth and development are creating—overtaxed infrastructure, lack of community attachment, polarization of various socioeconomic groups, and stresses on the environment—it is evident that conventional suburban development cannot sustain itself indefinitely. A new pattern must be identified to provide real alternatives that can sustain communities and deliver them intact to the next generation.

The commercial districts of our suburban areas must be rewoven into the fabric of the community by reestablishing a street orientation for these structures and by a realistic projection of parking requirements, subjugating the automobile and the parking lot to a secondary role. The box-in-a-lot mentality of site planning must be replaced by an approach that provides connections, both vehicular and pedestrian, to the neighborhoods served by these centers. Commercial activities should be embedded in our neighborhoods and districts to create true town centers.

Where Would You Rather Work?

At a Glance

❖ Understanding campus-style office parks as the most prevalent form of workplace in conventional suburban developments

❖ Exploring alternatives to single-use pod office parks by incorporating a mix of land uses within the framework of suburbia to create more traditional neighborhood options

❖ Establishing a variety of alternative design techniques that incorporate workplaces into the community, rather than thinking of them as separate and mutually exclusive

Where community residents choose to work is a choice that depends on any number of factors, including education, skill, training, and personal interest. Although there are countless places where people can work in the community, our primary focus here will be the suburban office park. While it is true that office parks account for only a portion of jobs, it is the office park that typifies suburban development, with commercial and retail businesses acting in a supporting role.

Office Parks

Most suburban office parks are one of three styles: (1) *campus,* (2) *freestanding independent structures,* or (3) *new suburban cores* (i.e., *urban villages*). With parcels ranging from 5 to 25 acres in size and possessing generous (50- to 100-foot) setbacks from adjacent roads and property lines, suburban office parks consume as much as *30 times* the land area per employee as offices located in a central business district (CBD). This is in large part due to the low-rise nature of the buildings as well as the on-site parking required for these typically remote sites. Successful office parks require several features to be located nearby: affordable housing, recreational and cultural facilities, possibly a college, university, or even a strong technical school, and support services (commercial, hotels, day care, restaurants, etc.). Initially, practically the only offices other than CBD freestanding independent structures were sited along the road out of town. These are now the exception, not the rule.

Campus-Style Development

Campus-style development is currently the predominant choice of most developers and tenants alike. This form is typified by low-rise, large-footprint structures spaciously separated from other office buildings by generous landscaping and equally generous parking lots. The more sophisticated developments maintain a design theme with regard to architectural style, signage, and landscaping, with covenants and restrictions to govern compliance. Covenants and restrictions address a wide range of criteria and are intended to ensure that a standard of excellence is established and maintained. Standards such as minimum building and parking setbacks from streets and property lines, landscaping guidelines, parking requirements, permitted and restricted uses, and acceptable building materials and site coverage are intended to supplement, not replace, local ordinances. Covenants and restrictions can help assuage the fears of local residents concerning the impact that the office park will have on surrounding neighborhoods, because people generally perceive that developments with restrictions are better designed and exhibit a higher level of continuity and context.

These additional restrictions may or may not ensure a better product, but the result is usually more landscaping, wider setbacks, and more open space between higher-intensity uses and lower-intensity ones. The result is often more land area accommodating the same amount of building square footage, which requires more streets to be built, larger parcels farther from existing development, increased commuter distances, and the elimination of any hope of mass transit access—while still not addressing the basic site design problems that prompted the need for the restrictions in the first place.

Edge Cities

A more recent phenomenon is *edge cities,* or *urban villages,* two names for essentially the same thing. Increasing land and

Where appropriate, new development contiguous to urban boundaries should be organized as neighborhoods and districts, and be integrated with the existing urban pattern. Noncontiguous development should be organized as towns and villages with their own urban edges, and planned for a jobs/housing balance, not as bedroom suburbs.

Charter of the Congress of New Urbanism

Figure 8.1 Freestanding independent structures, the "box in a lot."

development costs in these areas have resulted in the typical campus-style development going vertical, giving us a clustering of relatively tall office and apartment/condominium structures knitted together with a network of access roads, parking garages, and surface parking lots. Being neither urban nor suburban, these centers rival many core cities in terms of square footage and office workers.

In large part, they more or less evolved as opposed to being formally planned. Originally, most were minor crossroads on the outskirts of town. As residential development engulfed them and the time spent commuting to the urban core became untenable, land prices rose, making vertically oriented office, commercial, and residential development cost-effective. However, most were and are being developed using the campus-style design approach. This box-in-a-lot form of freestanding building situated in an expansive parking lot makes little or no attempt to address or respect the street much less other buildings adjacent to it, and yet architects try to outdo one another in garnering awards for these "innovative designs."

The trend for the last 40 years has been to build suburban office parks on the fringe of urbanized areas closer to the new residential neighborhoods. These suburban sites offered shorter commutes during a period when interstate freeways in those areas were either nonexistent or inadequate for the volume of traffic generated on a daily basis.

Subsequent to the development of the interstate highway system, the suburb-to-suburb commuter trips far outnumber the suburb-to-central-business-district trips of decades past. With entire regions of the suburban fringe opened for increased office park activity, particularly at the interstate interchange locations, the most visible parcels offered for both speculation office sites and corporate headquarters sites boast *location, access,* and *proximity* to all modes of transportation,

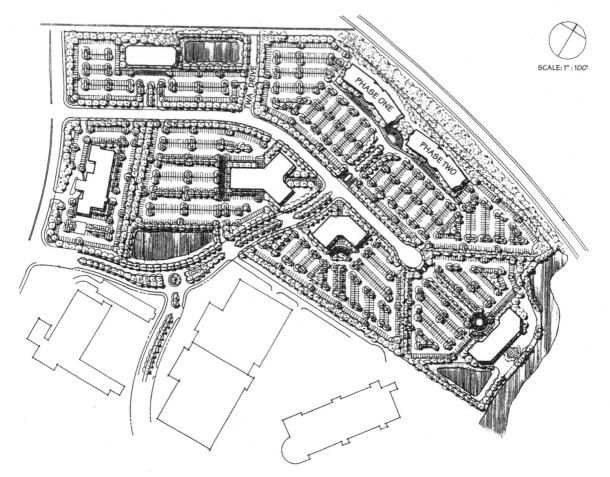

SCALE: 1" : 100'

Sketch 8.1 Typical office park.

these being extremely important to marketability. As an added bonus, the visibility afforded by this location is not only appealing to corporate clients and the architects of the buildings, the proximity allows employees to live closer to where they work and spend less time on the road.

Despite their seeming benefits, freeway orientation has led to the development of suburban office parks as separate enclaves from the neighborhoods around them. While boasting proximity, they are rarely tied directly to residential areas, forcing a reliance on the automobile for practically all access. Their low-density development design prohibits any real effort to serve the sites with mass transit unless a significantly sized mall is located nearby. Today, the increasing demand for sites farther and farther removed from the developed areas requires greater dependence on the automobile for access and increasingly longer reverse commutes for employees.

Development Patterns

CSD PATTERN

Too often, diversification of land uses is sacrificed to create a homogenous physical environment for all the parcels within the development. Parks are typically designed to provide a limited range of parcel sizes to prospective businesses in the interest of creating similarity of land uses and similarity of site design—so much so that one office park looks essentially like every other office park. In addition, this exclusion of certain uses limits *absorption* (site sales), inevitably increasing the time required to complete the park.

TND ALTERNATIVE

A number of land uses need to be incorporated within the framework of an office park. These should not just be located within the park boundaries but should be designed so that they are tied to it by more than common street access. Commercial, high-density residential, industrial, and yes, even single-family residential can all be considered acceptable/compatible uses within a well-designed park. The potential to live and work close by is becoming more appealing to a larger segment of society. Reduced traffic and commute times, more efficient land uses, greater security through the presence of people throughout the day, to say nothing of the reduced build-out time, are just a few of the benefits of this approach. Providing residential, office, and commercial uses within easy access of

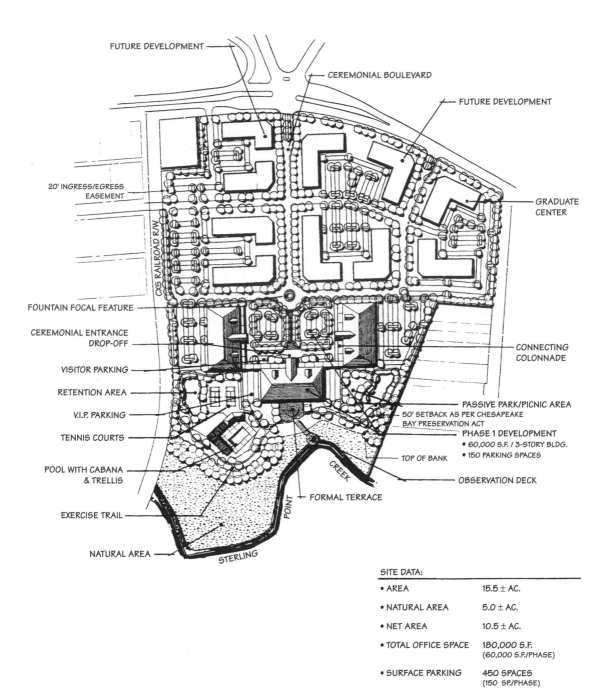

FUTURE DEVELOPMENT

CEREMONIAL BOULEVARD

FUTURE DEVELOPMENT

GRADUATE CENTER

20' INGRESS/EGRESS EASEMENT

CXS RAILROAD R/W

FOUNTAIN FOCAL FEATURE

CEREMONIAL ENTRANCE DROP-OFF

VISITOR PARKING

RETENTION AREA

V.I.P. PARKING

TENNIS COURTS

POOL WITH CABANA & TRELLIS

EXERCISE TRAIL

NATURAL AREA

STERLING

POINT

FORMAL TERRACE

CONNECTING COLONNADE

PASSIVE PARK/PICNIC AREA

50' SETBACK AS PER CHESAPEAKE BAY PRESERVATION ACT

PHASE 1 DEVELOPMENT
• 60,000 S.F. / 3-STORY BLDG.
• 150 PARKING SPACES

CREEK

TOP OF BANK

OBSERVATION DECK

SITE DATA:

• AREA	15.5 ± AC.
• NATURAL AREA	5.0 ± AC.
• NET AREA	10.5 ± AC.
• TOTAL OFFICE SPACE	180,000 S.F. (60,000 S.F./PHASE)
• SURFACE PARKING	450 SPACES (150 SP./PHASE)

Sketch 8.2

one another creates a strong symbiotic relationship between them. Offices need supplies and support services; employees need a place for lunch and quick shopping during their lunch hour and after work; residents need convenient access to professional services (doctors, lawyers, insurance agents, etc.). Commercial uses need a consistent daytime and evening population to survive. All uses depend on one another and are more successful because of their proximity to one another. In fact, if they are located, say, within one-quarter to one-half mile of one another, we might even see people using the sidewalks.

CSD PATTERN

Suburban office parks are nothing more than large subdivisions. Rights-of-way 50 to 60 feet wide create frontage for parcels for sale and development. This approach to land subdivision may be appropriate for residential use, but it leads to the typical box-in-a-lot site design for office parks. Buildings are placed in the center of a large parking lot, physically and psychologically separated from one another, with little or no inducement to encourage pedestrian access between them. Indeed, rarely is any direct vehicular access possible.

Some major corporate headquarters offer extreme examples of this. Located miles from other office centers and surrounded by acres of forest, in large part to satisfy the whims of the CEOs, they reinforce the philosophy of aloofness and disdain for our urban and suburban areas. It seems ludicrous to create such

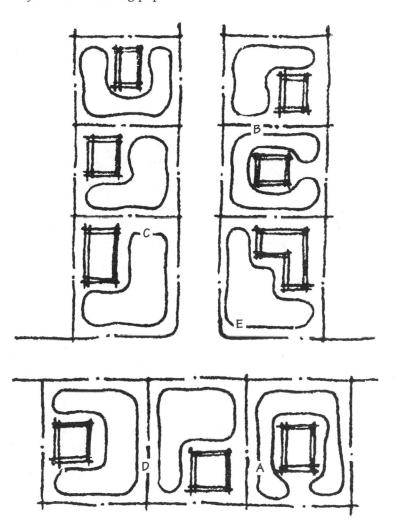

Sketch 8.3 **(A)** No sense of connection or continuity between parcels due to the varied placement of buildings. **(B)** Varied and uncoordinated setbacks create a ragged-edge quality to the streetscape. **(C)** Little, if any, physical connection between parking areas. **(D)** Distance between buildings and paved environment discourages pedestrian access and interaction. **(E)** Typical view from the street is primarily of pavement.

Sketch 8.4 **(A)** No clearly defined entrance announces the beginning of the development. **(B)** Random placement of buildings, varied building sizes, and arbitrary parcel sizes create a sense of chaos and disorder. **(C)** Uncelebrated center robs the development of a potential focal point or orientation element. **(D)** The lack of a definite street edge erodes overall continuity of the park. **(E)** Double and triple frontage lots reduce the efficiency of the park layout.

introverted office development so far removed from any other, having no contact with other offices or even with commercial centers for that matter. Many of these headquarters, under the guise of environmental sensitivity, require thousands of employees to drive extremely long distances through the countryside, only to arrive at a parking garage.

TND ALTERNATIVE

Buildings should be oriented toward the street and toward one another to create relationships between buildings and the street. Rather than creating stand-alone monuments to developers' or architects' egos, we should look for opportunities to tie structures together, to establish a context of design and a continuity of place. This will greatly enhance the off-site image of the park by drawing attention to the buildings—not to the parking lots, landscaping, and signage. Who knows, if we were to follow this approach, we might even achieve something resembling a streetscape in our suburban office parks.

In more intensely developed areas, building locations should anchor the street corners and provide access to the internal parking areas away from the corner, preferably combined with the entrance to another office site. This would enhance street aesthetics by reducing curb cuts while screening cars.

CSD PATTERN

Most developers overbuild their parking areas to make them more marketable. They feel that the availability of additional parking enhances their chances of leasing the property faster. The result is underutilized parking areas and overpaved sites, which increases surface runoff, degrading the environment and a creating a visually unappealing site. This is often aggravated by the local municipalities in that all required parking

Figure 8.2 Buildings should be oriented toward the street. *(Photo courtesy Hanbury Evans Newill Vlattas)*

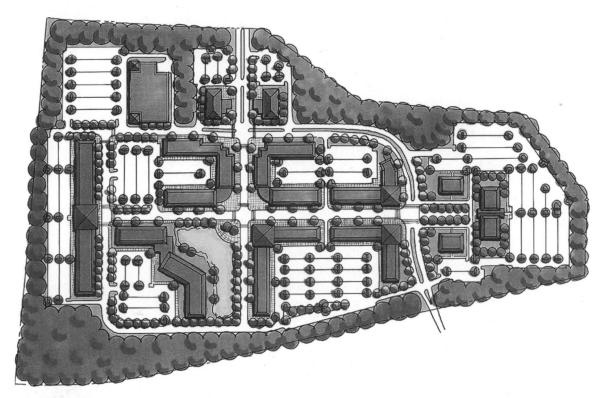

Sketch 8.5 Office uses should be part of a mixed-use town center, as this sketch depicts.

must be provided on-site with no allowances for on-street parking.

TND ALTERNATIVE

Municipalities should require parking only for leasable spaces within a building. So often, total building square footage is used to compute the number of parking spaces required. This includes all rest rooms, maintenance areas, lobby spaces, stairwells, and hallways—spaces not associated with leasable area. Not including these spaces in the calculation could reduce the required parking by anywhere from 10 to 30 percent. Municipalities should not allow more parking than is required unless a true need is established through a variance-approval process.

In addition, large collector roads usually provide the access for such parks and could be more efficient and productive if allowed to provide some on-street parking for the offices. This would work very well, especially if the buildings are sited toward the road and not the rear of the site. Most people are reluctant to walk more than 300 feet from car to office. On-street parking makes fiscal sense, too. Millions upon millions of tax dollars go toward the construction of major roadways with the express and exclusive use as a conduit from one place to another. These are usually filled only at peak hours and the rest of the time are underutilized. By encouraging some parking at key areas along these roads, taxpayers would receive more for their money and more land could be set aside for green-space preservation or developed as taxable property. When one considers that a parking space can cost anywhere from $1000 to $1500, it is a wonder that developers are willing to incur such additional expense.

CSD PATTERN

Collector streets inside and outside suburban office parks lack a sense of enclosure. The wide streets are not designed for pedestrians, even though sidewalks are mandated by municipal

Figure 8.3 People are uncomfortable when forced to walk adjacent to several lanes of moving traffic.

Project Profile: Seven Corners Gateway, Minnesota

Location: Saint Paul, Minnesota
Client: City of Saint Paul, Minnesota
Design firm: Town Planning Collaborative
Project type: Urban infill

Key Features:

- A neighborhood commercial district and to provide an attractive amenity to local residents, hospital employees, and businesses.

- Neighborhood preservation and redevelopment, adaptive reuse of older buildings, and new infill building opportunities in context of a larger citywide redevelopment program.

- The plan enhances one of the community's most fortunate assets, its traditional street and block pattern, by strengthening the existing street system and providing a human touch to the needs and comfort of pedestrian, bicycle, and transit travelers.

- New business ventures will be encouraged by the creation of a design district to be established for the three blocks of West Seventh Street that form the gateway from the city's downtown into the southwestern neighborhoods.

- Opportunities appeal to active seniors, new families, and single households who enjoy city life.

Project Approach:

The goal of this project is to bring new possibilities to an existing urban core neighborhood, with a focus toward building a vital, attractive, and desirable place to live, work, shop, and play for citizens. Kellogg Boulevard/Eagle Parkway is an urban seam between the Seven Corners Gateway District and downtown Saint Paul. While its primary purpose is moving high-volume traffic in and out of downtown Saint Paul, it also provides access to a number of destinations such as Children's/United Hospitals, West Seventh Street

business locations, historic Irvine Park neighborhood, the Mississippi River bluff, and downtown entertainment venues (RiverCentre, the Science Museum, Minnesota Wild Arena, etc.). The design team conducted an intensive four-day charette to examine means to better integrate the

needs of residential, commercial, entertainment, and medical stakeholders while investigating attendant issues such as parking, traffic, and urban design. The process included a citizen workshop, interviews with community leaders, design sessions, and an evening presentation.

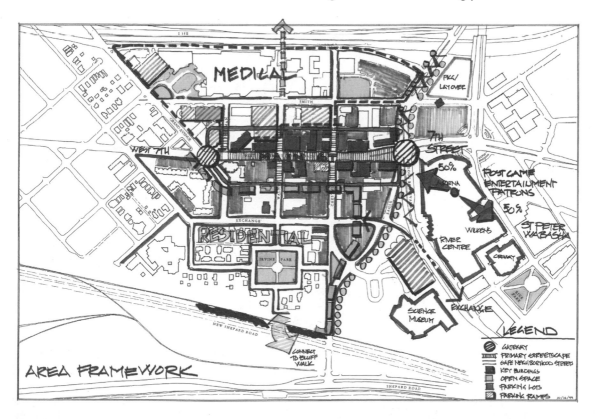

AREA FRAMEWORK

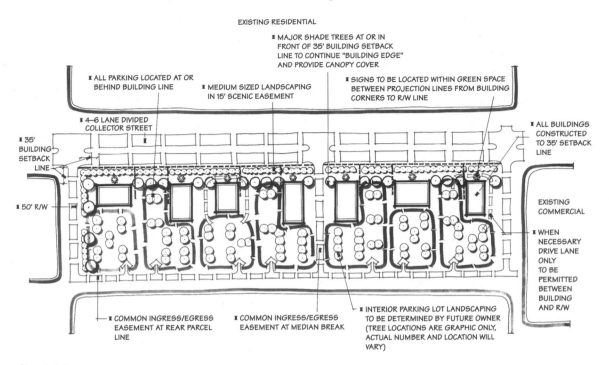

EXISTING RESIDENTIAL

☒ MAJOR SHADE TREES AT OR IN
FRONT OF 35' BUILDING SETBACK
LINE TO CONTINUE "BUILDING EDGE"
AND PROVIDE CANOPY COVER

☒ ALL PARKING LOCATED AT OR
BEHIND BUILDING LINE

☒ MEDIUM SIZED LANDSCAPING
IN 15' SCENIC EASEMENT

☒ SIGNS TO BE LOCATED WITHIN GREEN SPACE
BETWEEN PROJECTION LINES FROM BUILDING
CORNERS TO R/W LINE

☒ 4–6 LANE DIVIDED
COLLECTOR STREET

☒ ALL BUILDINGS
CONSTRUCTED
TO 35' SETBACK
LINE

☒ 35'
BUILDING
SETBACK
LINE

☒ 50' R/W

EXISTING
COMMERCIAL

☒ WHEN
NECESSARY
DRIVE LANE
ONLY
TO BE
PERMITTED
BETWEEN
BUILDING
AND R/W

☒ COMMON INGRESS/EGRESS
EASEMENT AT REAR PARCEL
LINE

☒ COMMON INGRESS/EGRESS
EASEMENT AT MEDIAN BREAK

☒ INTERIOR PARKING LOT LANDSCAPING
TO BE DETERMINED BY FUTURE OWNER
(TREE LOCATIONS ARE GRAPHIC ONLY,
ACTUAL NUMBER AND LOCATION WILL
VARY)

Sketch 8.6

code. In addition, having a large parking lot only a few feet away, the office building(s) located at the rear of the site, and street space that is too open leaves pedestrians feeling vulnerable. Generally, people feel uncomfortable in wide-open spaces, especially when forced to walk adjacent to several lanes of moving traffic. Even if there were someplace to walk, few would make the attempt. Pedestrians are seldom seen except standing at the occasional bus stop, which is often nothing more than a sign nailed to a telephone post.

TND ALTERNATIVE

By locating buildings closer to the street and placing parking lots at or behind the building setback line, a more hospitable pedestrian environment can be created. Buildings should be architecturally distinctive, with a rich palette of texture responding to the closer relationship to the street. People spaces should be well planned and landscaping should provide shade and color. Sidewalks should be separated from the street by a planting verge at least 8 feet wide, and shade trees should be planted at a minimum of 35 feet on center. Site furniture such as benches, bollards, litter receptacles, and the like should be spaced so that they will be used, not just serve as decorations.

CSD PATTERN

Often, the regional thoroughfare system is a deterrent to any reasonable jobs-housing balance in a particular area. With a high-volume, high-speed road system in place in most areas, remote living from our places of employment is not only possible, it is greatly encouraged. It is actually possible to live on the other side of town yet spend less time commuting to a suburban office park than someone living closer who is forced to use the local collector streets. Concentration of offices in just a few areas aggravates traffic regionally, requiring more and longer commuting trips. While low-density suburban office development may ease traffic within its own site, it has done so at the expense of the traffic off-site.

TND ALTERNATIVE

Municipal comprehensive plans should require that suburban office parks be more evenly dispersed throughout the region to provide reasonable office opportunities at the local scale. Local collector streets need to be tied to the local office clusters to provide direct access to them from the immediate neighborhoods that surround them. Besides, a trip to the office down a residentially scaled and commercially devoid local collector road can be a very pleasant experience. Given the choice, most people would opt for the local collector parkway. In the case of two-income families, this scenario allows and encourages at least one family member to work in the local office park and the other at a more remote site, with the latter dropping off the former at his or her place of employment.

CSD PATTERN

In the rare instances where other land uses occur near suburban office parks, there is usually no attempt to incorporate them into the larger development. Instead, great pains are taken to totally separate them from one another. Most municipalities have devised elaborate landscaping, fencing, and buffering ordinances to soften the edges between seemingly disparate uses. Zoning district lines are more than just so much ink on mylar—they are invaluable borders more important than property lines in establishing the checkerboard land-use patterns prevalent in our larger cities and suburbs. Rather than con-

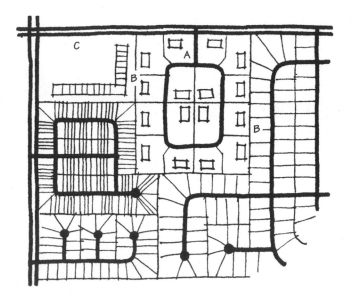

Sketch 8.7 **(A)** Singular point of access to office park and other proximate land uses requires collector road access, restricts cross-zoning movement, and exacerbates local traffic. **(B)** Supposedly incongruent land uses adjacent to one another require extensive setbacks, landscaping, fencing, and other buffers to force a separation between them. **(C)** Access to commercial area by local collector street only.

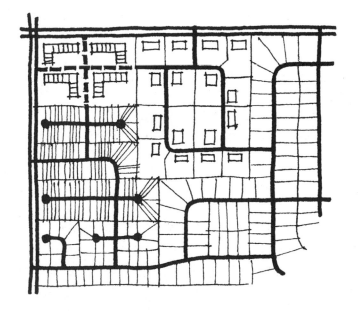

Sketch 8.8 Indirect movement through zoning areas and land uses is encouraged by street connections.

fronting the friction that exists between differing uses and arriving at a physical solution that addresses the concerns, they typically rely on the Band-Aids mentioned previously to smooth over the conflicts.

TND ALTERNATIVE

Generally, it is better design to transition one land use into another by using a sensitive system of streets, building locations, and parking arrangements to provide a smooth connection between land uses. All it takes is a little design effort to articulate the elements of open space, circulation, and structure, using the methods we've described to create a logical flow of uses throughout the width and breadth of developed and developing areas. The scenario established in Sketch 8.7 could be modified to incorporate more lines of movement between land uses, as depicted in Sketch 8.8. This is not an ideal situation, but it does depict how access could be adapted to create stronger cross-zoning ties. In Chapter 9 we will discover how this area could have been designed to truly integrate one land use with another.

In Summary

The areas in and around our suburban office parks should be examined for what they should and can be—mixed-use developments. In general, mixed-use

Figures 8.4, 8.5 **Where would you rather work?**

developments offer higher land values because various on-site activities take place for longer periods of time than with conventional single-use development. The hard transition lines so prevalent today can and should be eliminated. Otherwise, we will see more traffic congestion and longer commutes. We need to replace the kind of urban development that was unleashed with the availability of inexpensive fuel and the untethered highway construction of recent decades. We need to establish a variety of alternative design techniques that incorporate workplaces into community rather than thinking of them as separate and mutually exclusive. We need to think more of neighborhoods and less of subdivisions, more of interaction and less of screening, more of access and less of restriction—in short, more of community and less of sprawl.

CHAPTER 9

Where Would You Rather Relax?

At a Glance

❖ Understanding how parks and open spaces have been used in the past in order to better design them now

❖ Using them as integral parts of our neighborhoods and communities

❖ Learning to make them organizing elements rather than merely leftovers that meet a mandated minimum green-space requirement

❖ Establishing guidelines both for programming and locating them so that they serve the purpose for which they are intended

The importance of public open spaces throughout the course of history is indisputable. Whole volumes have been written documenting the various shapes and sizes of these common meeting grounds, from the Greek agora to Central Park in New York City. All previous cultures placed a high regard on these spaces and seemed to understand their significance to the well-being of their citizens. Indeed, through the nineteenth century in this country that significance was respected. More recently, however, the role of these spaces as a civilizing element seems to have been either forgotten or neglected.

Originally, public open spaces were the primary places for commercial activity, business, and politics, as well as a place to relax and enjoy friends and neighbors. They were the social heart of their communities and as such were usually the site of the more significant buildings—churches, guild halls, civic buildings, and prominent dwellings. They were either located within these spaces or formed an enclosure around the space. From a European perspective, the open space was the dominant element in this arrangement, and the buildings, playing a minor role, simply became the vertical elements of the space. These were essentially totally paved and resulted in a very flexible activities space because circulation and use areas were interchangeable. In America, open spaces were adapted to create a green enclosed by a street or road.

This was the predominant form of formal open space in America until Daniel Burnham and Frederick Law Olmsted collaborated on the 1893 World Columbian Exposition in Chicago. Following the premises of the popular City Beautiful movement of the day, they created a truly monumental city in classic style and organization, using sweeping vistas, wide, parklike boulevards, grand civic buildings, and green spaces as focal points. The City Beautiful movement had its beginnings with the rebuilding of Paris by Napoleon III and his lieutenant, Baron Haussmann; this was perhaps the first major effort of urban renewal.

This opening up of the city triggered a different perception of cities, wherein movement into and through them became much easier and allowed ample access to the open spaces beyond their borders. However, the advent of World War I put an end to any further serious attempts at incorporating open space into the fabric of the city. What emerged from this bleak period was a pragmatism, a practicality that would not allow attention to such "frivolous" matters as beauty, ambience, and grandeur. The age of innocence was gone. The grand pedestrian boulevards were transformed into urban expressways.

By the 1950s, following two world wars and an economic depression, the concept of city structure and open space had changed. Restrictive zoning was now the primary means of giving order to both the city and its burgeoning suburbs, and open space was merely the area lying between existing development and the leapfrog subdivisions popping up everywhere. The concepts of parks and recreation had been separated, and only active recreation forms that used ball fields and game courts were being given any serious attention; these were usually built in conjunction with the many junior high and high schools needed for the baby boomers.

In the rush to the suburbs we had sacrificed that unifying element of community that had served humankind so well for thousands of years, all in the name of progress. Open space had become merely the leftover space in subdivisions, areas that probably couldn't be developed anyway or were situated too far from existing utilities to be profitable as anything else. In the span of 30 to 35 years, community open space had gone from being on equal footing with the two elements we

A range of parks, from tot-lots and village greens to ballfields and community gardens, should be distributed within neighborhoods. Conservation areas and open lands should be used to define and connect different neighborhoods and districts.

Charter of the Congress of New Urbanism

discussed earlier, circulation and structure, to being subordinate to them. Note that during this same time period revolutions in traffic engineering have given us elevated freeways, grade-separated interchanges, and limited-access highways in addition to homogenized "franchise" architecture and the incredibly impersonal and aloof architecture of the Modernist movement. It might be said that these two revolutions in circulation and structure have done more to destroy the concept of community than any other elements.

Sports Place Versus People Space

It is true, however, that the last 10 to 15 years have brought a rediscovery, if you will, of center-city community spaces, especially in those cities fortunate enough to possess waterfronts. The unprecedented push to create or improve waterfront parks all across the nation points to the fact that people everywhere are starved for the type of interaction these modern-day agoras offer. The success of these urban parks (not recreation areas) gives hope that there is an innate desire on the part of people to congregate and enjoy one another's company in a public setting and that a similar desire can be manifested in a suburban setting, for it is these types of spaces that are so sorely lacking there. In fact, one might even say that it vindicates Burnham and Olmsted in their approach to urban open space.

Currently, open space takes two forms in suburbia: (1) activity areas for organized sports (softball, tennis, swimming, soccer, etc.) and (2) preservation areas (floodplain areas, wetlands, steep-slope areas, drainage channels, etc.). The former are flooded with Saturday morning soccer leagues and overweight softballers. The latter are usually so remote, inhospitable, or environmentally sensitive that they are totally unusable.

Rarely is there a place in suburban development where one can go simply to be outside, enjoy nature, and perhaps have a picnic. And that's the problem—too much emphasis has been placed on the active recreation areas used by only a limited range of people during a limited amount of time. The rest of the time these places go unused. This is not only insensitive to a broad range of people, it is inefficient use of commonly held land and tax dollars.

However, as the population ages and we hang up our cleats and begrudgingly bequeath our ball gloves to the next generation, it is almost certain that open space will take on an

Figure 9.1 Preservation areas are one form of open space in suburbia.

additional role, one much closer to what Burnham and Olmsted had in mind. Therefore, a different approach to the way we view recreation and open space will be needed to ensure that we adequately address the wishes, desires, and needs of the future. To do this, we must reassess our thinking with regard to recreation and open space in terms of programming, location, and design.

Programming Aspects

Everyone should have equal access to parks. All ages and segments of society should be served in as many ways as possible on all sites. Old, young, male, female, rich, poor, active, and passive should all have something that appeals to them in every park setting. Too often, the emphasis is strictly on the number of ball fields or tennis courts that can fit into a specific area to serve a limited clientele. When areas evolve into a softball complex or skateboard center, one segment of users attains dominance, which results in other potential users abandoning the site. In addition, this results in specialized locations for specific uses, which means that everyone must access them by vehicle.

The difference between leisure and recreation must be better understood. Leisure is time- and experienced-based, whereas recreation is activity- and space-based. One is aesthetically oriented, the other functionally oriented. We must escape the mentality that equates the two and assumes that the quantity of fields or courts is a measure of satisfactory leisure pursuits. At present, the emphasis is clearly on recreation or functionally oriented activities, and the aesthetically oriented are usually relegated to the rare and difficult-to-access preservation areas. Consequently, the varying needs of the citizenry are not being met in equal proportion.

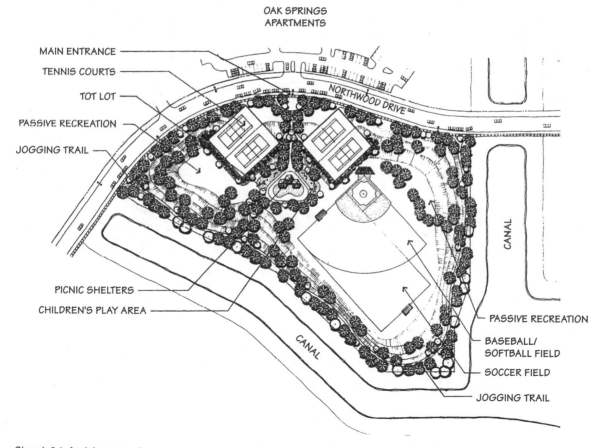

Sketch 9.1 Activity areas for organized sports are the other form of open space in suburbia.

Contrary to popular thinking, most people today have less leisure time than did previous generations. Economic issues, the increasing trend toward the dissolution of the traditional family, and the related demands on family members' time are in large part the cause. As a result, both park use and time spent in parks is lower. It is just not convenient to use the 20-acre, district-sized, and larger parks. For whatever reason—effort, time, convenience, or even fear—these parks are not generally used as much as neighborhood parks. More emphasis needs to be given to smaller, more usable neighborhood parks, which are easier to access, contain more familiar faces, and can be more easily monitored because of size and perceived sense of ownership.

With increasing budgetary constraints impacting practically all municipalities, parks, recreation, and open-space allocations are a fraction of what they need to be. However, rather than relying on higher taxes to provide the necessary services, innovative ways of privatizing them must be explored. Neighborhood parks are an especially good opportunity. Most neighborhoods would gladly assume the maintenance responsibilities of their smaller,

Figure 9.2 In many suburban municipalities the bigger the neighborhood park the better. The problem is, they are so big, only a few residents live within convenient walking distance, and most parents won't allow their small children to go there alone.

more intimate parks if given the choice of that or increased taxes. In addition, this truly fosters a sense of ownership and responsibility on the part of the residents, which more likely than not would result in a lower vandalism rate.

Good community design utilizes open space and green areas as definition elements—edges, so to speak, of areas or districts that provide a sense of movement and transition between them. This not only provides a sense of rhythm and delineation, it enhances the feeling of being in a separate locality, a distinct corner of the world, as it were. We should capitalize on opportunities such as this by borrowing green space from golf courses, school grounds, environmental preserves, farmlands, remnant woodlands, even cemeteries. Using these visually open spaces is an inexpensive but effective method to foster the feeling of openness in a community.

Of all the things that open space should provide or do for the community, it should pervade its very fabric just as other structural systems like roads and utilities do. It should be continuous, accessible, and visible.

Development Patterns

CSD PATTERN

Municipal codes often require that a percentage of open space be set aside as public green space in every residential subdivision, but more often than not little guidance is given the developer regarding the proper placement of it. Developers are given a lot of leeway about what counts toward meeting this requirement, too. For instance, stormwater detention ponds are allowed to be counted even though they would be necessary anyway. This allows the developer to place the ponds so that they are a commonly shared amenity. However, in many cases they are put in out-of-the-way places and fenced off to limit the developer's liability if someone is injured or drowns. In other instances, lakes are totally surrounded by homes with privacy fences, so only a privileged few have waterfront property and lake access.

Playgrounds are very often put in out-of-the-way places, with the most extensive types being constructed at the larger city-owned parks. These are often very nicely done and have restrooms and picnic areas close by. However, one needs to drive to these sites to be able to use them because they are often remote. When they are built within walking distance of homes, they are often placed behind the homes. And because

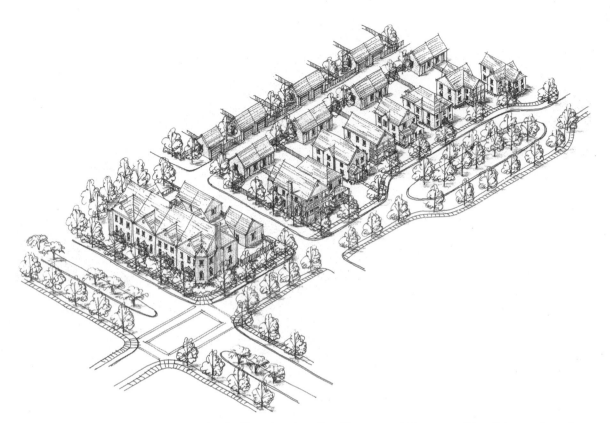

Sketch 9.2 Neighborhood parks should be distributed so that all residents are within easy walking distance of a park.

privacy fences are standard procedure for most suburbanites, the playground is often inaccessible to children from their own backyards. Parents may not bother putting in gates to allow their children easy access to the park.

TND ALTERNATIVE

A park should be within walking distance of every resident. Ideally, neighborhoods should be designed with a park or a series of miniparks distributed throughout and linked together by walking paths. When this is not possible, a good rule of thumb is to locate it in a highly visible and easily accessible location within the limits of the neighborhood so that residents develop a sense of pride and ownership of it. This is the best way to ensure that the park will be cared for and maintained properly. In all cases, parks should be in a convenient, centralized location and be bordered on at least two sides by public streets. This allows homes to be fronted on the park, helping to monitor activities occurring there. It also looks good to prospective home buyers.

CSD PATTERN

In suburbia, park spaces are often recreation-oriented. Softball complexes, basketball courts, soccer fields, and little league fields abound because we are more activity-oriented than leisure-oriented. We push our children into sports, ostensibly to keep them out of trouble. We wear ourselves out every Saturday going from one sporting event to another. On the other hand, our elected officials actively pursue semiprofessional and professional sports teams. They authorize funding for sports complexes to lure teams and the tax revenue they will generate. They also build large recreation centers for the public with Olympic-sized pools, gymnasiums, weight rooms, and racquetball courts, with space and program specialists for all kinds of classes from basket weaving to karate. There's nothing wrong with any of this. Municipalities should offer a wide range of opportunities for its citizens, but these are often being done to the exclusion of providing civic open space.

TND ALTERNATIVE

Parks and open spaces should be prominently placed so that we are aware of them throughout the day in our normal routine. We should be as equally if not more exposed to them as we are to the onerous examples of commercial space that girdle our highways and thoroughfares. The pleasure to be gained from viewing parks and open spaces even while traveling at 45 to 50 miles per hour far exceeds the amount of information or convenience to be gained by an equal amount of commercial space and signage.

CSD PATTERN

Most people do not live where major recreational activities occur. Large-scale acquisitions of land for district parks on the

Streets and (public) squares should be safe, comfortable, and interesting to the pedestrian. Properly configured, they encourage walking and enable neighbors to know each other and protect their communities.

Charter of the Congress of New Urbanism

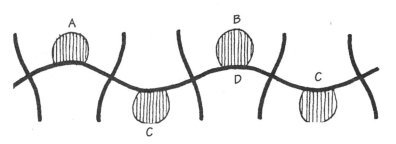

Sketch 9.3 **(A)** Potential locations of major parks or green spaces. **(B)** Ideal location is on major thoroughfares and preferably on the outside curve to serve as a focal point. **(C)** Parks should be regularly spaced to create a sense of rhythm to the collector street by interrupting other continuous development. **(D)** These locations serve the local neighborhoods while providing an aesthetic view along the collector streets.

Sketch 9.4 Parks and open spaces should be prominently placed for maximum visibility.

fringe of developing suburban areas will never host the number of visitors that most are designed to accommodate. With low-density zoning currently serving as the de facto growth control measure in most areas, it is almost assured that relatively few people will ever come into casual contact with these sites, and it's practically guaranteed that no form of convenient access, much less mass transit, will ever be available. Instead, opportunities closer to the bulk of the population should be the focus.

TND ALTERNATIVE

Parks, by their location, should encourage spontaneous use by visitors. If people are required to make advanced preparations before going to a park, a great deal of the enjoyment is lost. Parks should be located to maximize interaction with and access to other destinations. District parks can become excellent transition spaces between different land uses, benefiting both. For example, a location between a residential area and an office zone provides value to the offices, a convenient lunch place for employees, unimpeded evening uses by the local residents, and ample parking area at the offices for peak weekend use.

CSD PATTERN

As with many parks, schools and school yards have been designed to literally wall themselves off from the surrounding neighborhoods to control access. Often they are located on a high-volume, high-speed collector street for convenient access, but this ensures that everyone must arrive by car or school bus; walking to school would be too dangerous. The typical suburban school costs millions of dollars to construct and is equipped with ball fields, running tracks, playgrounds, basketball courts, tennis courts, and an ample amount of open space. But these facilities are off-limits except during school hours, and then

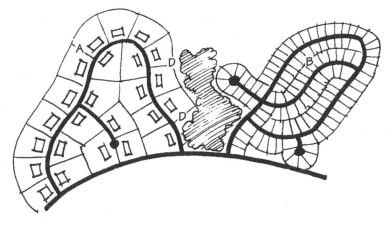

Sketch 9.5 **(A)** Office development. **(B)** Residential neighborhood. **(C)** Park location serves as an excellent separation and buffering element between differing uses, offering lunchtime activities for the office workers and evening use by the residents. **(D)** Existing parking at the office sites becomes overflow parking during peak weekend residential use.

only to students and staff. What happens after school? What happens during the summer? What happens during the holidays? You guessed it: not much. The facilities sit idle for the most part except for the school principal and secretaries. The entire complex is cooled or heated for only a handful of people. This seems to defeat the entire purpose of the relationship our public spaces should have with the community. Only

Figure 9.3 Suburban schools are often fenced off from their adjacent neighborhoods, requiring access by vehicle only.

in the convoluted suburban planning model does this disconnect make sense.

TND ALTERNATIVE

School sites are tremendous assets to the community and could be vastly more utilized than they are. They could operate longer during the day and become the location of numerous community functions, hosting activities such as neighborhood meetings, distance learning, community-based tutoring, sports camps, and cooking classes; in essence, they could be recreation centers within the neighborhood in the evenings and summers, eliminating the need for everyone to drive to the major recreation center across town. This would help to

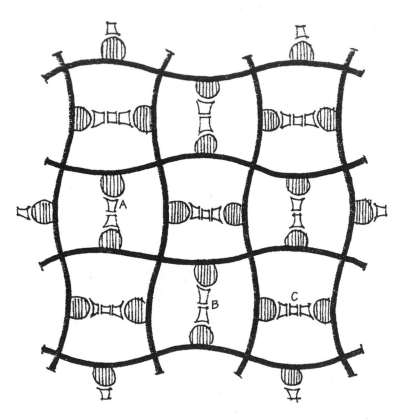

Sketch 9.6a **(A)** Linkages between park sites expand the exposure to parks and enhance the usability of sites. **(B)** Connections between park sites may be natural, undevelopable green areas or may even take the form of landscaped boulevards. **(C)** Vehicular access through parks should be allowed and encouraged (up to a point) to enhance exposure to and convenient use of the areas.

expand social bonds within the neighborhood by allowing residents to meet and interact who otherwise might not. This is not to say that the same staff should oversee all these programs; principals and secretaries have enough to do with their school-related activities.

CSD PATTERN

The suburban planning model often has no mechanism for linking open spaces together. Open space is more often than not simply leftover space, so it tends to be isolated in pods within residential subdivisions. Individual neighborhoods may contain a tot lot, a community building with a swimming pool, or a walking path, but they are essentially isolated from the broader community. District parks, though often very well done, are frequently located in isolated spots requiring access by car. Farmland, remnant woodland, and naturally occurring water bodies are most often in a holding pattern until the owner decides to sell or until municipal services are extended and land values rise. Areas rich in natural resources

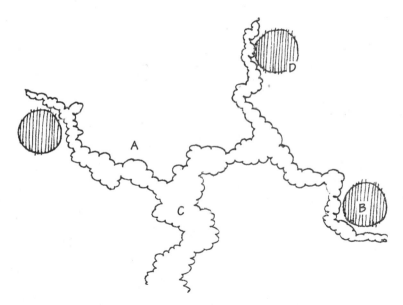

Sketch 9.6b **(A)** Naturally occurring green space not considered developable for residential or commercial use. **(B)** Potential community park site locations. **(C)** Natural drainage ways, creeks, and changes in grade can provide a ready-made link between recreation areas if they are situated adjacent to them. **(D)** Considered separately, each site and the natural area have limited recreation value and drawing power; considered as a unit, an accessible regional park begins to emerge.

such as coastal communities with numerous lakes, rivers, and estuaries are subject to environmental regulations to ensure that much of this land will remain undisturbed. If there is an open-space plan in a municipality's comprehensive planning document, it often contains only recommendations, not a real plan for action.

TND ALTERNATIVE

Linkages between existing parks need to be identified and actively pursued. These are some of the best opportunities to expand use of existing open space while increasing access for more residents. Most usable land in suburban areas has been designated for "more productive" uses than open space, with the exception of environmentally sensitive areas that serve as green-space buffers. Although the recreation potential of these areas is relatively insignificant, nevertheless they do form the framework of what can be a truly integrated, linked, open-space system. Working with developers to coordinate the location of any required park space is simple if only municipal planners will only take a broader view of the process.

More parks should be located to reinforce existing and proposed public buildings. Public buildings and their related green spaces should be located in more prominent locations in order to become community focal points and activity centers. A new library or recreation center should be a symbol of pride and community belonging and thus be given an exalted position in the landscape. Too often, these are located either on land already owned by the municipality or on land that

Figure 9.4 A park should have a focal point.

has been cheaply acquired. Fiscal restraint is certainly in order, but not at the expense of these extremely significant and rarely built structures. We shouldn't miss such opportunities to reinforce community pride. So often, the highly visible sites are preordained for commercial use; however, in some cases a compromise could and should be in order. Important civic structures and their supporting open spaces can be designed into and as part of an overall commercial area. Just a little more attention to site design will produce spaces that help support one another. There are literally tens of thousands of examples of how this can be sensitively accomplished. They are found in small-town America.

Common Design Aspects

Not nearly enough emphasis is being given to the visual and aesthetic considerations of parks. So often they assume the form of very utilitarian spaces offering only ball fields, rest rooms, fenced tennis courts, and unscreened parking areas. More landscape design needs to be incorporated to make these spaces inviting, appealing, and hospitable. Again, the emphasis should be on quality, not necessarily quantity.

All park and recreation design should be approached using the same design elements utilized for larger-scale community design—namely, paths, edges, districts, nodes, and landmarks. They are the basic building blocks of any land planning and should be followed. An aesthetic functionalism should be perceived on the part of the user. The experience of a park should occur in a natural, orderly flow, with one use area blending harmoniously into the next.

As in all design, a park should have a focal point, a theme, a center, a heart, a reason for its existence; it must be desirable above anything else. Be it a view of the ocean, an ancient stand of trees, or merely a meticulously kept azalea garden, all parks must have an underlying purpose to give them a significance that will be apparent to all who use them.

Parks that possess activity areas should be designed with both the player/performer and the spectator in mind. Albert Rutledge, in his book *A Visual Approach to Park Design* likens a park to a theater and each of its activity areas to a potential stage.[1] Formal as well as subtle positions for each must be provided, one for display, one for viewing. In addition, where size permits, viewing the activities from afar is also desirable as it permits one to enjoy the activity without becoming a part of it.

Project Profile: Cherry Hill Village, Canton, Michigan

Location: Canton Township, Michigan
Client: Biltmore Properties Corporation
Architect: Looney Ricks Kiss Architects
Project size: 378 acres
Project type: Village Plan

Key Features:

- A new village square, situated directly opposite the historic schoolhouse, terminating the view at the major village street intersection.

- The square is intended to be the node where community activities occur, to focus the configuration of commercial uses, and to establish important sites, terminating views for new civic buildings to be constructed by the Township.

- A network of open spaces creates a village-scale system of parks, greens, squares, pedestrian courtyards, and vest-pocket parks.

- At village gateway locations, open space is provided in forms more compatible with the rural/agricultural character at the edge of the village.

- As distance increases from the core, the pattern transitions to larger home sites ranging from small-lot single-family cottages to four-unit manor houses developed in response to the survey and local market analysis.

- A *pattern book* governs key elements of design and detail.

Project Approach:

The goal of the project was to integrate significant new development into the existing historic fabric of Canton Township. This development had to be compatible with the vision established by the Township's master plan to adequately meet future residents' needs for housing, shopping, employment, recreation, and community amenities. In order to accomplish this goal, a computer-based *Community Image Survey* was created. The survey allowed participants to compare and select alternative design concepts for streetscapes, homes, parks, and commercial areas. The survey equipment was installed at designated sites around the Township and formed the basis for the subsequent charette where Township officials, the developer, residents, and the architect discussed ideas and alternatives. This process provided immediate feedback to the designers while giving mutual authorship to all who participated. The resulting plan enhances the existing village core as the hub of civic, social, commercial, and special activities and provides a compact mix of new housing types located within easy walking distance of it.

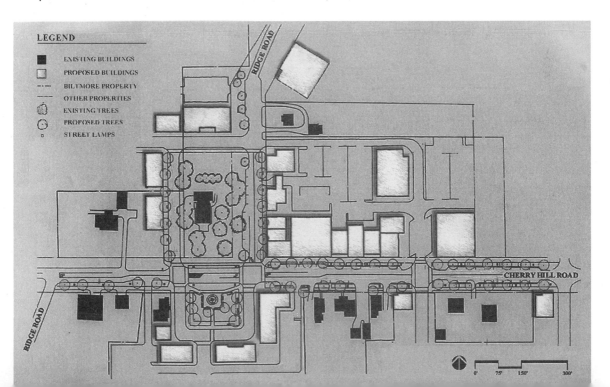

LEGEND
- ◼ EXISTING BUILDINGS
- ☐ PROPOSED BUILDINGS
- --- BILTMORE PROPERTY
- ── OTHER PROPERTIES
- ◯ EXISTING TREES
- ◯ PROPOSED TREES
- ▫ STREET LAMPS

Figure 9.5 A park should reflect the character of the neighborhood that surrounds it.

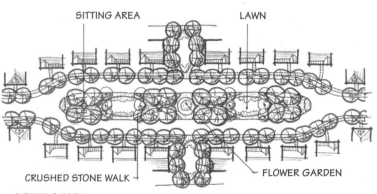

SITTING AREA   LAWN

CRUSHED STONE WALK →   ← FLOWER GARDEN

STREET PARK

Sketch 9.7 A park should satisfy both function and aesthetic.

Too much space between activities has a dissipating effect overall and dilutes the sense of activity. To better utilize the space available, it is wise to bring similar activities together wherever possible. This allows various activities to occur simultaneously, creating a sense of activity and excitement, a hot spot, if you will. Care should be taken, though, so that one activity does not dominate another.

Parks are used by people, and therefore the scale of the space should always relate to human dimensions. Seat heights, walkway widths, seating arrangements, and plaza areas must all feel comfortable to the people using them and, as well, relate to the scale of the entire space. Seating orientation is particularly important in creating a pleasurable space for conversation and privacy. To maximize the ability of people to associate in small groups, benches should be coupled or otherwise oriented to encourage a face-to-face arrangement. This does not mean they must be squarely in front of one another, but somehow the benches and their associated space should form a nook or recess off a walkway.

Park design should always respond to user needs, not necessarily to what the designer thinks is important to include in the plan. There isn't a better recipe for disaster than to provide something that people don't want or need. According to Rutledge, there are eight design goals that every park must satisfy in order to be successful:

1. *Everything must have a purpose.* A professor once told me that a designer can do anything that he or she desires

Figure 9.6 A park design must be for people. *(Photo courtesy Looney Ricks Kiss Architects)*

Figure 9.7 A park should establish a substantial experience, as this fountain plaza does in Celebration, Florida. *(Photo courtesy of Hanbury Evans Newill Vlattas)*

as long as it can be justified and defended. There is no room for superfluous uses. All must address an identified need.

2. *Design must be for people.*   Too much reliance on standards for maintenance equipment, parking requirements, numbers and types of play equipment, and so forth tends to depersonalize and homogenize the space.

3. *Both function and aesthetic must be satisfied.*   Neither should take precedence over the other. A balance is in order. Efficiency and desirability are simultaneously achievable.

4. *Establish a substantial experience.*   Nothing should be randomly placed. Using the elements of design, various feelings or moods should be evoked. The park should become a composition in itself.

5. *Establish an appropriate experience.*   In a word, instill *context* (there's that word again). The design should fit the site; it should blend with and reinforce its surroundings.

6. *Satisfy the technical requirements.* Standard playing field and court sizes should be utilized. Proper orientation and number of activities are required for success.
7. *Meet needs for the lowest possible cost.* Cost-benefit analysis should determine priorities. Attention to site constraints allows more efficient design.
8. *Provide for ease of supervision.* Logical and orderly arrangement of activities linked with an easily understood circulation system reduces conflict.

In Summary

Parks and public open spaces need to be thought of in terms of being an integral part of the community. In fact, they should be considered the primary organizing elements of our communities. In past societies they were, and the formula served humankind well for over 8000 years. In the continuum of human existence, our social and physical planning experiments over the last 75 to 100 years are but a moment in time and will be recorded as simply another swing of the pendulum.

The ancients knew and understood the importance and benefit that a well-ordered and functional arrangement of circulation, structure, and open space provided to civilization. They give testimony to an almost infinite number of ways that these three elements can be combined while still adhering to certain basic design tenets that create a community with common goals, aspirations, and beliefs. They understood that open space is not negative space or a void, but rather that it is tangible, can be formed to create certain feelings, and is elemental to the existence of community.

Figures 9.8–9.11 **What kind of park would you prefer to have in your neighborhood?**

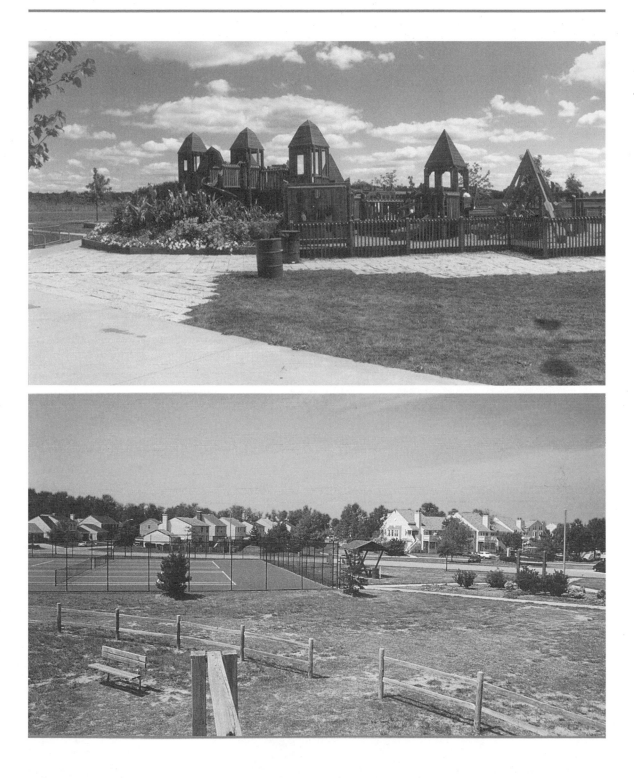

Learning How to Put It All Together

At a Glance

❖ Understanding that the typical leapfrog development of conventional suburbia has options

❖ Placing an emphasis on the pedestrian experience rather than the vehicular experience

❖ Learning techniques to create neighborhoods that contain a mixture of uses rather than clusters of single-use pods

❖ Applying the concepts found in traditional neighborhoods built prior to World War II in order to bring scale and sense of place to today's communities

In Chapters 6 through 9 we have asked you to make a lot of choices about where you would rather live, work, shop, and relax. We have asked you to compare images and consider choices. We have contrasted the principles of conventional suburban development with those of traditional neighborhood development in order to explore the types of communities created by each. The point of this exercise has been to articulate a vision that directs us as neighbors toward the kind of communities that can stand the test of time. It is obvious that many of the places a majority of us call home have not been patterned after the principles that have been laid out in this book. And although the majority of Americans now live in cities or suburban areas, if given a choice most of us would probably opt for a smaller, more intimate setting, a *hometown* wherein we are known and where we know our neighbors. In the modern suburban setting, we are acquainted with a great many people: the teenager at the grocery store checkout, the cleaning person at the office, the person who takes your quarter at the tollbooth. We recognize many people, but do we know them? Not really, nor they us—not like the people in a small New England village, a midsized, midwestern prairie town, or even a slow, sleepy southern railroad company town. In these, the scale of the community has not grown to the point of overwhelming the individual. In these places, the car is a convenience, not a requirement. In fact, it is still possible to walk from one end of town to the other in a reasonable time frame. A Burlington, Vermont, an Annapolis, Maryland, a Williamsburg, Virginia, or an Aspen, Colorado, could never be built using today's standard zoning codes. The places that come to mind when thinking of a walkable, memorable community are practically unknown in and around our suburban centers.

Putting it all together implies a certain directed assuredness, a cognitive, knowledgeable approach in planning the built environment; it implies making something whole or complete. In this context it appears that our growth areas have not benefited from such a proactive approach; instead, they've been left to grow like so much mold in a petri dish, consuming its host environment. Most areas surrounding our urban centers have no clear goal of development, no vision of what they could and should become; they are simply designated as an agricultural or very low density single-family *holding district* awaiting its time for rezoning to its highest and best use.

Don't misunderstand, the free market is by far the wisest and most effective way to develop property. We certainly don't advocate a central planning authority that attempts to dictate market desires; but it does appear that more expansive thinking on the part of municipal planners and the citizens themselves is needed to articulate development potentialities that place a higher value on human habitability than on ease of automobile access. That's not to say that they can't coexist, for they certainly can; it just takes a lot more effort.

In order to articulate this vision for the *whole* community, we would like to bring together in one place everything that we have discussed thus far. We want to show how the tools of community design and the principles of traditional neighborhood development can effect real change in our existing suburban areas as well as establish a benchmark for growth in the less populated small towns of the American landscape. The *why* of this task is obvious: We must address the growing concern that, for all its standards and conveniences, the way we have approached community design for the past 50 years has produced chaos. How, then, can we change our approach to community planning to allow for sustained growth without creating a mass of indistinguishable cul-de-sacs and franchised architecture? Let's see.

Development Patterns

As in Chapters 6 through 9, we intend to compare sprawl-type conventional suburban development with traditional neighborhood development. This will allow us to establish a scenario easily identifiable in a majority of communities and then provide an alternative that will articulate the vision and principles needed for practicing community by design. Again, we use the terms *conventional suburban development* (CSD) and *traditional neighborhood development* (TND) to embody the two ideas.

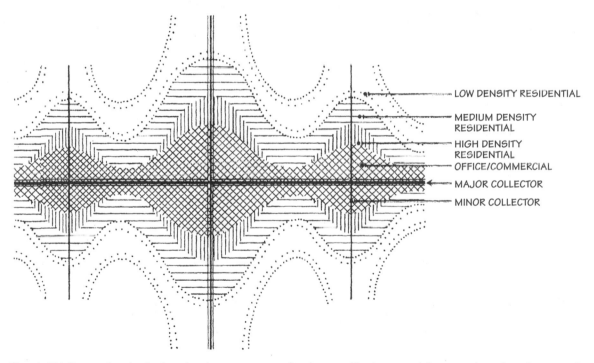

LOW DENSITY RESIDENTIAL

MEDIUM DENSITY RESIDENTIAL

HIGH DENSITY RESIDENTIAL

OFFICE/COMMERCIAL

MAJOR COLLECTOR

MINOR COLLECTOR

Sketch 10.1 Conventional suburban development pattern. Continuous office/commercial occurs along the primary corridors. Primary intersections encourage major concentrations of commercial. Successive bands of multifamily, medium-density, and low-density residential evolve behind the primary corridor. To access commercial concentrations, all residential traffic must utilize the collector streets, as no other alternate route exists. Increasing traffic requires constant upgrading of collector streets, which in turn attracts more traffic. Continued sprawl along the collector streets is the ultimate result of this approach.

Conventional Suburban Development

History tells us how development patterns will evolve if left to their own devices. The CSD pattern initially begins with leapfrog low-density residential occurring in primarily agricultural districts. As more and more subdivisions are completed, traffic on the local farm-to-market two-lane rural roads becomes increasingly congested, resulting in road improvements by the municipality to ease congestion. These improvements in turn make the area more desirable for higher-density residential, which continues to occur until the traffic counts warrant rezoning a parcel for a shopping center at one or two of the intersecting farm-to-market roads. This pattern continues until the principal road in the area is bordered by almost continuous commercial and office development, with successive bands of multifamily, medium-, and low-density residential away from the roadway. The vast majority of the traffic from these developments is channeled directly to the major collector road, formerly the farm-to-market road, with little if any parallel access to it. That is, there is usually no viable alternative access between two points save for the collector road that connects them, and we all know what can happen when a single traffic signal malfunctions at rush hour.

With this reliance on such a hierarchical street pattern and the accumulation of even more traffic on fewer and fewer roads, it's only natural that commercial development creeps farther into the rural transitional areas, lured there by the promise of increasing traffic counts.

Traditional Neighborhood Development Alternative

Our communities need to be designed for the pedestrian experience, at 3 to 4 miles per hour, as well as that of the commuter, at 35 to 45 miles per hour. It can be done by establishing a two-tiered circulation system that separates local traffic from through traffic and by *requiring* (not just encouraging) a mixture of land uses at major intersections.

Beginning with the solutions discussed in Chapter 7 and building on them to include high-, medium-, and low-density residential in close proximity to each other and to the commercial and office areas, we can begin to establish a new planning paradigm to replace that found in suburban growth areas today. This new paradigm could be easily adopted as a preferred method of development in the comprehensive planning documents of practically all municipalities. By graphically identifying preferred locations around major intersections and

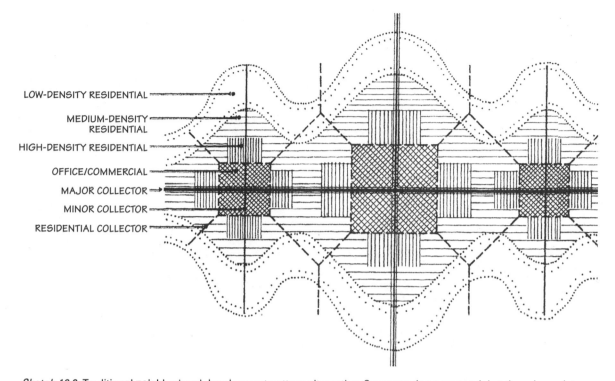

LOW-DENSITY RESIDENTIAL

MEDIUM-DENSITY RESIDENTIAL

HIGH-DENSITY RESIDENTIAL

OFFICE/COMMERCIAL

MAJOR COLLECTOR

MINOR COLLECTOR

RESIDENTIAL COLLECTOR

Sketch 10.2 Traditional neighborhood development pattern alternative. Concentrating commercial at the primary intersections and limiting its expansion capability creates a confined commercial district. Multifamily areas hold the commercial in place and provide high-density housing within easy walking distance. Residential collector street channels local traffic to the office/commercial areas without conflicting with the through traffic on the primary collector streets. Secondary loop street around the office/commercial allows convenient local traffic movement without mixing with the through traffic at the primary intersection. With the commercial and high-density residential focused at the primary intersections, the intervening lower-density residential and/or green spaces create a sense of rhythm between the nodes and help to establish a separate identity for each.

not necessarily limiting their applicability, the time, energy, and expense of many rezoning battles could be eliminated or reduced.

If community vision were articulated in this manner, developers and citizens alike would possess a much clearer picture of the goals of development. The result: a richer mixture of uses; an emphasis on streets and the pedestrian experience; in short, the creation of small-scale, easily identifiable communities within the context of the larger municipality, not just another planned unit development or large-scale subdivision. The beauty of this concept is that it could easily occur relatively quickly, as it requires no wholesale revision of existing zoning or subdivision ordinances.

Project Profile: Harbor Town, Memphis, Tennessee

Location: Mud Island, Memphis, Tennessee

Client/developer: Henry Turley, Jr.

Architect: J. Carson Looney, AIA, Looney Ricks Kiss Architects, Inc.

Site planner: RTKL Associates

Project size: 135 acres

Project type: Mixed-use urban village

Key Features:

- The project consists of 745 units (5.5 units per acre).
- It includes a Montessori school.
- There is a 50-slip marina.
- Mixed-use town center contains shops, services, and a 6500-square-foot corner grocery store.
- A yacht club and office building (53,000 square feet) are incorporated.
- The project includes high-end condominiums.
- Streets and blocks frame views of the Mississippi River and the Memphis skyline.
- Radial boulevards orient the neighborhood to the river.
- Wetlands preservation area running through the center of the site is designed to look like a stream and ponds to create a natural edge between neighborhoods.
- Multifamily apartments are located at each end of the neighborhood and sited along the streets and sidewalks, creating a porch- and balcony-lined streetscape that is compatible with the adjacent single-family homes. Parking is located at the rear of the buildings in interior courts and is screened.

Project Approach:

The goal of the Harbor Town project was to seamlessly integrate widely diverse housing types, styles, and price ranges into a traditional neighborhood development reminiscent of the Memphis neighborhoods of the 1920s, where homes would be located within walking distance of shops and services. Neighborhoods are designed to provide a mix of lot sizes, unit types, and price ranges (from $800-per-month apartments to $800,000 riverfront homes). Neighborhoods provide a variety of lot widths (25 to 50 feet wide) in order to capture a variety of market requirements. Alleys provide automobile access to the rear of larger homesites, and a combination of recessed garages and side-loaded driveways allow automobiles to be away from the front of smaller homes. The original master plan has a strong axial design, fronting interior neighborhood homes onto a series of parks and squares, and this ensures premiums for homes that lack river views. To ensure design quality throughout different phases of development, a set of visual design guidelines were implemented to set basic standards for scale and proportion, facades, and key details.

**Development patterns
should not blur or eradicate
the edges of the metropolis.
Infill development within
existing urban areas conserves
environmental resources,
economic investment, and
social fabric while reclaiming
marginal and abandoned areas.
Metropolitan regions should
develop strategies to encourage
such infill development over
peripheral expansion.**

*Charter of the Congress
of New Urbanism*

A REGIONAL APPLICATION FOR THE TND APPROACH

While we recognize that it is not the role of municipal planners to plan individual properties, and it shouldn't be, it is their role to determine the areas of future growth and its intensity, timing, and sequence. Many comprehensive plans prepared by municipalities fail to provide a clear vision of a region and its ultimate physical organization. Too often, these plans are little more than a patchwork quilt of various zoning districts superimposed over a property line or tax map, offering few if any definitive conclusions and leaving one rather baffled about the vision for an area's development.

This intentional vagueness in comprehensive planning is a fallacy. If specific target plans are not developed for each geographically identifiable zone within a jurisdiction, then true planning has not taken place—only policy formulation. In addition, if these target plans are not reinforced with specific graphic design guidelines that depict a preferred method or structure of development, then the same kinds of conventional scenarios with all of their accompanying pitfalls will result.

Only through a process of physical analysis that identifies the attributes, opportunities, constraints, and character of a region can a true potential image for an area emerge. The natural boundaries of an area should be acknowledged and accentuated to reinforce its unique identity and to ascertain the logical future development nodes and their degree of importance for the area.

These nodes, or town centers, are the key elements that give a region an identity and are precisely what's lacking in suburbia. However, they could be built by private development if landowners, property developers, engineers, and architects were provided the development goals and incentives for action. As for the smaller cities discussed earlier, these town centers should contain all aspects of a community: schools, libraries, government offices, cultural facilities, churches, commercial offices, retail, residential, and recreation. While all these features currently exist in suburban districts, they are usually distributed across such a wide area that they possess no sense of focus or connection. However, with the establishment of a strong conceptual framework of design that ensures a thematic continuity of structures, these centers would be instantly valuable and desirable as a location and could easily be sized to accommodate the anticipated population as determined by regional analysis.

Rethinking our established circulation patterns is another factor that can greatly enhance movement of people and vehicles in and around these nodal centers. As we have seen, most suburban development occurs on a project-by-project basis, employing a minimum number of access points to the local collector streets, with few if any street ties to adjacent properties. Usually, commercial zoning and development end up filling the gaps between residential entry points and the primary intersections. The result is heavy traffic on all of the local collector streets, for they are carrying 100 percent of the off-site residential trips simply because there is no other alternative.

By applying the circulation patterns evident at the city or regional scale, along with the separation of local and through

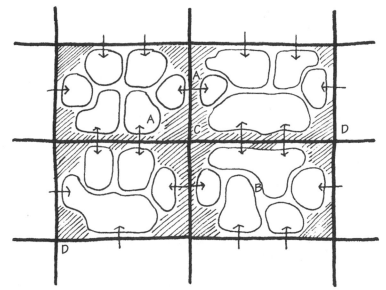

Sketch 10.3 **(A)** Individual residential sites are developed at different times and usually possess their own identity entrance. **(B)** Normally, only indirect street ties between residential areas occur. **(C)** Commercial development occurs at the major intersections and creeps into those areas between and in front of the residential areas. **(D)** Practically all off-site traffic is directed to the local collector streets.

traffic as discussed earlier, to this smaller nodal scale, traffic problems can certainly be eased. Minibeltways around major intersections not only provide alternate access to major thoroughfares, but also create additional valuable property for office, commercial, and medium- to high-density residential uses. This system can result in local collector streets that contain fewer travel lanes carrying less traffic, while a network of residential parkways containing no commercial uses provides an alternative means of access to both residential and commercial areas. Considering the cost of road construction and land acquisition to accommodate larger and larger collector street rights-of-way, fewer tax dollars would need to be expended in this manner. With this system, the residential collector system costs can and should be borne by the individual developers. All that is required for this to happen is for the municipality to adopt guidelines of development that state this desire with regard to new residential construction.

If we can apply the beltway concept found around most urban centers to this smaller scale, can other city design fea-

Project Profile: Greater Lake Okeechobee, Florida

Location: Central Florida

Client: Greater Lake Okeechobee Tourism
   Alliance

Planning firm: Dover Kohl and Partners

Project size: 2600 square miles

Project type: Regional vision plan

Key Features:

- The plan identifies a new market position for the region, focusing on eco-tourism and sustainability.

- The plan identifies specific opportunities to create tourist-supportive facilities and attractions that celebrate the area's environment and culture (trails and trailheads, marinas, locks and lighthouses, shade, cabins, restaurants atop the levee, mule train, crop art, museums, retreat lodges, camping, scenic hotels, equestrian centers, etc.).

- An emphasis is placed on revitalizing historic towns and on ways to make them memorable.

- The relationship between existing towns and nature will be strengthened.

- Each town should have a detailed design plan shunning conventional suburban sprawl and following a pattern of traditional neighborhood development.

- Each town should have a signature entry portal that makes it distinct and memorable.

Project Approach:

The goal of this project was to create a regional vision that makes clear distinctions between town and country and include a plan for a connected infrastructure for hikers, cyclists, and equestrians that spanned numerous municipal jurisdictions. The planning team and regional planning officials from the Treasure Coast Regional Planning Council toured the region and interviewed key stakeholders. They also conducted a three-part, traveling charette to obtain public opinion from the various localities around the lake. The team studied historic maps, technical data, and town plans for Clewiston and Canal Point, both by architect and town planner John Nolen. They created a plan and images that advanced a unified vision for the ecologically sensitive region around the lake, attempting to provide a framework that reconciles development with conservation.

tures also be applied to make suburban centers functional and appealing? Examination shows that several, and perhaps many, commonalities of cities could serve a useful purpose in redesigning suburban centers:

- Radiating streets emanating from the city center literally pull the hinterlands inward and serve to anchor the city to its surroundings. Suburban centers are usually approached via one or two collector streets.

- Grand boulevards offer the dual function of directing traffic flow and providing an active living environment for the residents. Grand parking lots are the suburban equivalent.

- A gridded system of streets provides multiple travel options at the heart of most urban areas. In suburbia, hierarchical street systems direct all traffic to a few specific points.

- A strong street orientation of the buildings creates a reassuring and continuous edge for pedestrian and motorist alike. Visually uncontained spaces, deep building setbacks filled with asphalt parking areas, and large, low-level monolithic structures make suburban centers inhospitable.

- A mixture of uses in close proximity to one another, in most cases over one another, creates a vibrant energy lacking in all but a few suburban mixed-use developments. The separating of land uses into various zones of similarity, which requires automobile access between them and robs the street of pedestrian use, is the normal situation in suburbia today.

Many of the activities of daily living should occur within walking distance, allowing independence of those who do not drive, especially the elderly and the young. Interconnected networks of streets should be designed to encourage walking, reduce the number and length of automobile trips, and conserve energy.

Charter of the Congress of New Urbanism

While these are just a few salient points that highlight the difference between proven traditional neighborhood design principles and those that have been used during the last 40 or 50 years, it is obvious that conscious, objective planning is either not occurring or is ineffective in creating environments that are scaled for the individual and responsive to the human experience. Instead, today's communities of quality are being built at the direction of enlightened developers or progressive corporations in spite of the restrictions placed on them by zoning, subdivision, and site plan ordinances. By amassing large landholdings, they can literally create their own communities with the appropriate land-use mixes, the proper emphasis on construction detailing, and an unswerving focus inspired by a vision.

What are these singularly focused individuals and groups doing that our municipal planners either can't do or are not allowed to do? Is it simply a matter of differences in scale, or is it a lack of understanding on the part of our hired, appointed, and elected officials regarding the true nature of community? A rhetorical question to be sure, and the answer will not be found here. What we will do is attempt to annotate some of the universal design principles that are being applied in nonconventional projects and that seem to be working.

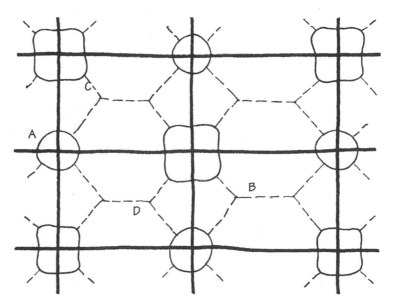

Sketch 10.4 **(A)** If minibeltways are provided around the primary intersections, local traffic can be siphoned off the major collector intersections, freeing them for through traffic. **(B)** Residential collector system allows access to the primary intersections and the commercial concentrations without utilizing the major collectors. **(C)** Additional local traffic entering the minibeltway from the residential collector enhances land values for commercial in the area. **(D)** With the residential collector in place, fewer travel lanes are needed in the major collectors, thus reducing construction costs.

Site Design Principles

First we need to reject euclidean zoning as the only approach to community design. This wholesale separation of uses has probably created more problems than it attempted to solve. In its beginning there was a logical, defendable reason for its use: Smokestack industries were lying adjacent to single-family housing districts and tightly packed sweatshop factories were becoming fire hazards. Now this form of zoning merely separates one socioeconomic stratum from another and all housing from its dependent commercial areas. As Sketch 10.5 depicts, it is possible and feasible to include a variety of housing types as well as office and commercial facilities in close proximity to one another and served by an interconnected road system to encourage interaction and access. With this basic concept it's possible to completely separate through traffic from local traffic without the need for limited-access highways and grade-separated interchanges. Sketch 10.6 shows a practical example of this design concept.

Planners and citizens need to be informed of the concept of a town center versus a shopping center as the focus for community commercial, office, and social activities. A shopping cen-

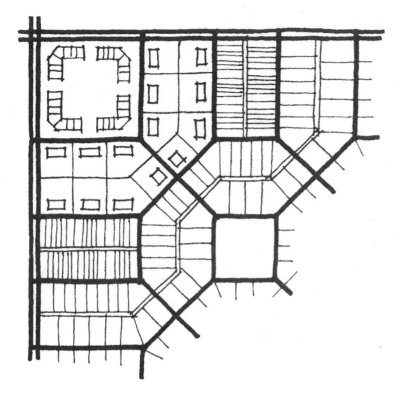

Sketch 10.5 Commercial, offices, apartments, townhouses, and medium- and low-density housing can all occur in a confined area and be served by a continuous, interconnected street network. A logical, orderly progression of land uses can coexist without the normal zoning Band-Aids of setbacks, landscaping, and fences. Instead, streets and alleys serve as the transitional elements.

ter implies typical retail uses—grocery store, pizza parlor, dry cleaner's, and an outparcel or two containing a fast-food franchise and a self-serve gas station. A town center, on the other hand, brings to mind a complex mix of divergent uses—office, retail, civic, cultural, housing, even light industry—in a defined, centralized area, visually and physically connected to its supportive areas. A town center implies a certain excitement, enchantment, and electricity generated from chance meetings and unexpected occurrences that result from such an urban bazaar. Sketch 10.7, a variation of Sketch 10.6, expresses how adaptable this form is to an entire quadrant of an intersection. If this idea is replicated in the remaining quadrants, the image of a small town emerges. Granted, this is an idealized form; nevertheless it represents a structure that begins to establish a town center concept of development as opposed to the typical isolated commercial strip subdivision.

We also need to eliminate the typical commercial strip as an acceptable land use within the boundaries of the community. While there may be a need for this kind of commercial activity, there is also a growing recognition that the form of the structure, not the use, is the negative factor. We need a greater emphasis on design and an understanding that visibility is not the requirement that most commercial real estate agents profess. Any enclosed mall is a good example of this fact. An acceptable combination of off-site-oriented and internally oriented commercial can be achieved in a neighborhood setting. While this may not fit the ideal of the previous examples, it does reflect a realistic transition to that ideal, an adaptation to circumstances, as it were. This gives us encour-

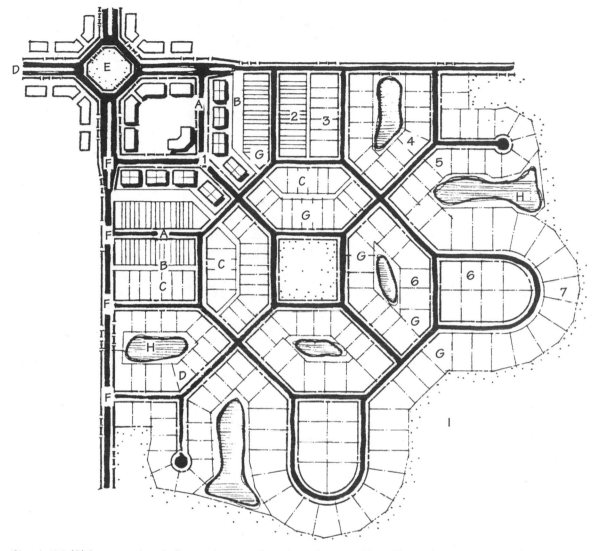

Sketch 10.6 **(A)** Apartment/condo flats and street-oriented townhouses with parking and garages to rear of unit enhance streetscape. **(B)** Rear parking provides secure resident parking and on-street visitor parking. **(C)** Street-oriented 3500- to 6000-square-foot single-family lots with alleyway and rear-garage resident parking continue the streetscape. **(D)** Single-family lots, 7500+ square feet, are smallest to be allowed front-loaded garages to reduce cluttered driveway parking. **(E)** Traffic circle or diamond creates community focal point and reinforces pedestrian environment while providing opportunity for statuary, other artwork, or landscape elements. **(F)** Multiple access points from through road allow direct access to the various housing types, enhancing marketability. **(G)** Gradual transition of housing options from apartment/condo to 20,000+-square-foot lots without restrictive zoning lines helps establish a less stratified neighborhood. **(H)** Stormwater retention areas are located to enhance lot values, expand open space, and provide interconnected stormwater management systems with multiple outfall options. **(I)** Recreational/visual amenities such as golf courses, regional lake system, and equestrian/jogging trails serve as the edge delineator of the village, prohibiting unchecked expansion. *(Courtesy of the Talbot Group)*

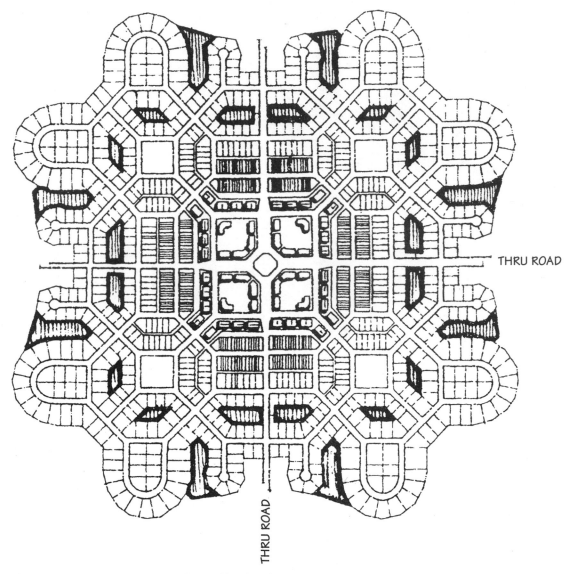

THRU ROAD

THRU ROAD

Sketch 10.7 Stylized village plan with transitional zoning.

agement that, on awkward, landlocked, and passed-over parcels, more innovative forms of planning can still be applied to create better environments than the typical or expected.

A more formal arrangement in the siting and layout of streets and the organization of spaces needs to be used. At higher densities and more intense uses, curved streets begin

Figure 10.1 A rediscovery of the alley as a civilizing community element needs to take place.

to lose their effectiveness and efficiency. They are literally more at home in low- to middensity residential areas. Curvilinear streets denote a sense of privacy and separation, whereas a grid system implies openness, accessibility, and connectedness. No longer are *symmetry* and *balance* dirty words in planning parlance. On the contrary, the public and planners alike seem to be rediscovering the implied structure, order, and perceptibility that this form of neighborhood design imparts. In addition, a grid system is more easily understood and more predictable than a curvilinear pattern, which by its very nature is confusing, confounding, and unpredictable.

More streets need to be considered usable and frontable. Unlike a hierarchical system that places housing on only the smallest streets and relegates the larger collector streets to access and circulation, there is a growing tendency to utilize a greater portion of all roadways and streets for a variety of productive and directly accessible land uses. This leads to less street being required to serve a given land area and number of units. Lower initial development costs and reduced maintenance costs for the municipality result in more affordable housing. A pleasant by-product is a sense of ownership of and responsibility for the attendant streets on the part of the homeowners.

A rediscovery of the alley as a civilizing community element has to take place. The reintroduction of the alley is allowing an alternative to the garage-door-dominant streetscape typical of suburban areas. This technique is being effectively used in townhouse developments and smaller, higher-density, single-family areas, which results in a reduction in the amount of paving in the front of the dwelling, a firmer streetscape edge, more visitor parking, less street congestion, and generally a more aesthetically pleasing visual environment.

Deliberate attempts have to be made to reduce the negative impacts of the omnipresent automobile in new developments. With the mushrooming of car ownership in the last 15 to 20 years, it is no longer possible to simply treat with disdain their presence in our midst. We must actively pursue more sensitive and innovative methods of accommodating them. All elements of community design, from landscape screening to highway geometrics, need to be reexamined regarding their primary and secondary roles in serving the community. If, in their strict adherence to typical standards, they are found to undermine the concept of community, then we must modify them.

We need to place less emphasis on the separation of pedestrians and vehicles. It is widely accepted that the 1970s planning concept to encourage linear greenbelts throughout residential areas resulted in some very dull and boring streetscapes and, in many cases, some very real safety concerns for the residents adjacent to them. In contrast, today the street is to be celebrated and enjoyed as a place for community interaction, with the rear yard to be enjoyed by close friends and family, away from the casual view of the passing public.

A greater emphasis must be placed on and concern given for the fabric of the street; that is, structures should face and address the street to possess a true street address. Whether they are housing, commercial, or office, buildings must be thought of as being part of a continuous street edge, a vertical wall that contains the street and encloses the space. Too many gaps or breaks in this wall weaken the ability of the remaining structures to create a desirable sense of place. Only in this manner does a street take on a true character, a unique spatial quality of livability; otherwise, it becomes just another lifeless collector street.

Figure 10.2 Greater emphasis must be placed on and concern given for the fabric of the street.

Our parks and open spaces should be designed as the front lawn of the community, places to be designed for and enjoyed by people of all ages. They should offer more than just ball fields, play areas, and parking lots. They should be spaces truly designed for a purpose, not just leftover parcels that couldn't be served by gravity sewer lines. These prominently displayed, proactively designed community spaces serve to both separate and connect. They should complete or frame views, act as dignified or classical parks to complement civic architecture, function as community celebration areas, or merely be quiet oases where one can be alone in a crowd.

Landscaping should be understood as something more than just so much greenery to be used to dress up a place. Size, habit, texture, color, massing possibilities, design suitability, and aesthetic quality are a few of the factors that should be applied to trees as they relate to community structure and the articulation of open space. Trees should be used to delineate space effectively, to direct attention to some focal point, and as buffer enhancements and transitional elements in addition

Figure 10.3 Landscaping should be understood as something more than just so much greenery to be used to dress up a place.

Civic buildings and public gathering spaces require important sites to reinforce community identity and the culture of democracy. They deserve distinctive form, because their role is different from that of other buildings and places that constitute the fabric of the city.

Charter of the Congress of New Urbanism

to their obvious use of providing shade. Plant material from the ground up is truly the glue that holds it all together.

Gradual transitions of land uses and densities are necessary to create the perception of a center or focus for the community. One use should blend into another in an orderly, organized progression that builds to a crescendo: *the 100 percent place.* Unlike current planning, which relies on sudden, harsh, and abrupt changes in zoning and land use requiring all manner of landscape screening and buffering devices to divide separate land uses, true communities should be designed to allow a variety of housing types and commercial structures within the context of a continuous street network and culminating in the center of the community.

Building an Architecture of Place

To build an "architecture of place," we need to increase the general understanding of the impact of scale and texture of a building on its streetscape. Each building plays an important role in creating interesting and enjoyable spaces. Monolithic walls and slick, glass-skinned structures take on a sculptural quality when seen from a distant expressway at 65 miles per hour. However, from the adjacent sidewalk these same structures appear cold, aloof, and fortresslike—strangely alien constructs apparently designed for beings larger than ourselves. Buildings that celebrate textural changes by showing detail, that utilize more common and familiar materials, and that go to great lengths to establish a sense of depth (by the effective use of seam patterns, reveals, cornices, bases, and finials) create human-scaled structures that can easily be perceived and comprehended.

There is a new respect for contextualism in civic architecture, commercial structures, and residential dwellings. Community design needs to champion this recognition by reinforcing the principle that community consists of all the structures that occur within its bounds and that interest and variety are possible while adhering to a theme and a predominant building style. Overwhelming, out-of-place, or outlandish architecture serve to rend the community, not to reinforce it.

Figure 10.4 Inhuman-scaled architecture.

Increasingly, people are beginning to believe that, contrary to what the planning profession has preached for the last 40 to 50 years, offering different uses within the same building,

Figure 10.5 Human-scaled architecture. *(Photo courtesy Hanbury Evans Newill Vlattas)*

one over the other, is not a negative, but in practically all cases creates a more interesting and healthy economic environment. While we're all familiar with the giant, glowing megastructures occurring in most urban places in America, the point here is that developers and land planners are increasingly desirous of more intimately scaled, low- to midrise structures providing small offices and apartment/condominiums as opposed to street-oriented commercial. While this form is common in the small towns that came of age in the nineteenth century, it appears to be fairly radical for suburbia.

A greater attempt needs to be made to anchor new development to its site surroundings by use of local lore, indigenous architecture, and native building materials to emulate surrounding development patterns and nomenclature. Attention to these details vis-à-vis the local color can easily determine the success or failure of a development, as it is extremely important to reinforce the image of the existing community, not conflict with it.

Figure 10.6 Civic architecture should respect the context of its community. *(Photo courtesy Hanbury Evans Newill Vlattas)*

In Summary

The current approach to planning our suburban areas is failing. It has begun to create more problems than it has solved. A half century ago our planners rejected many of the practical and proven methods of community design that had worked for humankind for millennia. In our rush to adapt to the new transportation age, we literally threw out the baby with the bathwater.

What has resulted is a landscape of sprawl and chaos. We have allowed our transportation requirements to define the structure of our towns and neighborhoods, situating the various community elements along these arteries like so many separate and distinct monocultures of activity. We have relegated the noble profession of city planning to mere site plan review, in which the primary concern and result is one of screening, buffering, or otherwise hiding one use area from another. With such a focus on detail, little true planning appears to be taking place—merely processing.

While it is true that municipal planners are charged with identifying long-range trends and projections with regard to

Figure 10.7 This Nantucket street is a blend of both retail and residential uses, one over the other. *(Photo taken by Jean and Michael Sleeman)*

population and the physical infrastructure required to support it, there exists a wide chasm between visionary thinking (long-range comprehensive planning) and mundane realism (site plan review). Somewhere between these two extremes resides the concept of community. Within this realm, change can be most readily effected—by establishing defined goals and parameters to determine how the developing areas will function and how the various elements will fit together to create something more than just so many separate shopping centers and office parks strewn about an intersection. This book attempts to identify some potential solutions to common problems evident in this range and, hopefully, to affect the thinking of all the players involved in community building. The principles found here are not the complete answer; on the contrary, they are a meager beginning to help solve the problem so pervasive in our suburban growth areas. These ideas and concepts are intended to promote a vision and, in most cases, to provide techniques for addressing the problems that result from conventional suburban development.

A reexamination of what constitutes *community* is in order as we reassess the form it should take for the future. We must reacquaint ourselves with the physical attributes of a community and, in organizing them, truly *design* our communities. We must plan in a manner that can be easily understood, not only by elected officials and municipal staff but everyone else as well. Municipal planners are more involved with policy formation and goal setting, leaving it to others to actually come up with the ideas of what communities should look like. In order for planners to be more effective in the future, they must go beyond policy and goal issues and take the process to the next step: *design conceptualization*. They need not prepare specific plans for specific areas, but they must give graphic expression to the preferred reality as generally stated in the goals, objectives, and policy. Unless every planning document contains preferred methods and standards of development that clearly convey a desired future, the future will be merely an up-to-date version of the present chaos and sprawl.

We must recognize that a community is more than the sum of its parts. When properly conceived, it provides for all the needs of its inhabitants within a geographically identifiable area and instills in them a sense of identity and belonging. A community must impart to all who are exposed to it a particular image of itself, a unique and individual character recognizable by others. Its various elements must complement and support one another by functioning interactively. In short, a community should bind its people in a common identity, not separate or divide them. Achieving this desirable goal requires a change in approach to community design. Real solutions must be developed, and a new vision of suburbia must be mandated.

Notes

Introduction

1. By permission, from the Charter of the Congress of New Urbanism.

Chapter 1

1. John R. Stilgoe. *Common Landscape of America 1580 to 1845*. New Haven, CT: Yale University Press, 1982.

2. Ibid.

3. Keller Easterling. *American Town Plans: A Comparative Time Line*. Princeton, NJ: Princeton Architectural Press, 1993.

4. By permission, from *Merriam-Webster's Collegiate Dictionary,* tenth edition. Copyright 1993 by Merriam-Webster Inc., publisher of the Merriam-Webster dictionaries.

5. E. Barbara Phillips and Richard T. LeGates. *City Lights: An Introduction to Urban Studies*. New York: Oxford University Press, 1981.

6. By permission, from *Merriam-Webster's Collegiate Dictionary,* tenth edition. Copyright 1993 by Merriam-Webster Inc., publisher of the Merriam-Webster dictionaries.

7. George B. Tobey. *A History of Landscape Architecture: The Relationship of People to the Environment,* originally published by the American Elsevier Publishing Company, Inc., now distributed by Books on Demand, a division of University Microfilms International, Ann Arbor, MI, 1973.

8. Kevin Lynch. *The Image of the City.* Cambridge, MA: M.I.T. Press, 1960.

Chapter 2

1. U.S. Army Corps of Engineers.

2. Proverbs 16:18.

Chapter 5

1. Institute of Traffic Engineers. *Traditional Neighborhood Development Street Design Guidelines.* Washington, DC: ITE, 1999.

2. William H. Whyte. *The Social Life of Small Urban Spaces.* Originally published by the Conservation Foundation and now distributed by Books on Demand, a division of University Microfilms International, Ann Arbor, MI.

3. Jane Jacobs. *The Life and Death of Great American Cities.* New York: Random House, 1961.

Chapter 6

1. By permission, from the Charter of the Congress of New Urbanism.

Chapter 7

1. Kevin Lynch. *Site Planning,* second edition. Cambridge, MA: M.I.T. Press, 1962.

Chapter 9

1. Albert Rutledge. *A Visual Approach to Park Design.* New York: Garland Publishing, Inc., 1981.

Bibliography

Arendt, Randall. *Crossroads, Hamlet, Village, Town: Design Characteristics of Traditional Neighborhoods, Old and New.* Washington, DC: American Planning Association, 1999.

Arendt, Randall. *Rural by Design: Maintaining Small Town Character.* Washington, DC: Planners Press, 1994.

Attoe, Wayne, and Donn Logan. *American Urban Architecture, Catalysts in the Design of Cities.* Berkeley, CA: University of California Press, 1989.

Beckley, Robert M. "Urban Design." In *Introduction to Urban Planning.* Edited by Anthony J. Catanese and James C. Snyder. New York: McGraw-Hill, 1979.

Bishop, Kirk W. *Designing Urban Corridors.* Washington, DC: American Planning Association, 1989.

Boden, Margaret A. *The Creative Mind: Myths and Mechanisms.* New York: HarperCollins, 1991.

Business and Industrial Park Development Handbook. Washington, DC: Urban Land Institute, 1988.

Cervero, Robert. *Suburban Gridlock*. New Brunswick, NY: Center for Urban Policy Research, 1986.

Coleman, Richard C. "Sub-Urban Design: Re-creation of a Town Center in the Face of Suburban Growth." In *Urban Design and Preservation Quarterly,* winter 1990.

Cost Effective Site Planning. Washington, DC: National Association of Home Builders, 1976.

Cullen, Gordan. *The Concise Townscape*. New York: Van Nostrand Reinhold, 1961.

DeChiara, Joseph, and Lee Koppelman. *Site Planning Standards*. New York: McGraw-Hill, 1978.

DeChiara, Joseph, and Lee Koppleman. *Urban Planning and Design Criteria*. New York: Van Nostrand Reinhold, 1982.

Duany, Andres, Elizabeth Plater-Zyberk, and Jeff Speck. *Suburban Nation: The Rise of Sprawl and the Decline of the American Dream*. San Francisco: North Point Press, 2000.

Duany Plater-Zyberk and Company. *The Lexicon of the New Urbanism*. Miami, FL: DPZ, 1999.

Duany Plater-Zyberk and Company. *Towns and Town Making Principles*. New York: Rizzoli, 1991.

Easterling, Keller. *American Town Plans: A Comparative Time Line*. Princeton, NJ: Princeton Architectural Press, 1993.

Glaser, Nathan, and Mark Lilla. *The Public Face of Architecture, Civic Culture and Public Spaces*. New York: The Free Press, a Division of Macmillan, Inc., 1987.

Gold, Seymour M. *Recreation Planning and Design*. New York: McGraw-Hill, 1980.

Graves, Maitland. *The Art of Color and Design,* second edition. New York: McGraw-Hill, 1951.

Heckscher, August. *Open Spaces, The Life of American Cities*. The Twentieth Century Fund, Inc. New York: Harper & Row, 1971.

Hedman, Richard, and Andrew Jaszewske. *Fundamentals of Urban Design*. Washington, DC: APA Press, 1984.

Howard, Ebenezer. *Garden Cities of Tomorrow*. Cambridge, MA: The M.I.T. Press, 1973.

Howard, Ebenezer. *Garden Cities of Tomorrow*. England: Faber and Faber Ltd., 1965.

Institute of Traffic Engineers. *Traditional Neighborhood Development: Street Design Guidelines*. Washington, DC: Transportation Planning Council Committee SP-8, 1999.

Jacobs, Jane. *The Death and Life of Great American Cities*. New York: Random House, 1961.

Katz, Peter. *The New Urbanism: Toward an Architecture of Community*. New York: McGraw-Hill, 1994.

Kunstler, James Howard. *The Geography of Nowhere: The Rise and Decline of America's Man-Made Landscape*. New York: Simon and Schuster, 1994.

Langdon, Philip. *A Better Place to Live: Reshaping the American Suburb*. New York: Harper Perennial, 1995.

Laseau, Paul. *Graphic Problem Solving for Architects and Designers*. Second edition. New York: Van Nostrand Reinhold, 1986.

Lynch, Kevin. *The Image of the City*. Cambridge, MA: The M.I.T. Press, 1960.

Lynch, Kevin. *Site Planning,* second edition. Cambridge, MA: The M.I.T. Press, 1962.

McMahon, John. *Property Development, Effective Decision Making in Uncertain Times*. New York: McGraw-Hill, 1976.

Merriam-Webster's Collegiate Dictionary, tenth edition. Springfield, MA: Merriam-Webster, 1993.

Newman, Oscar. *Defensible Space*. New York: Collier Books, 1973.

Parking Requirements for Shopping Centers: Summary Recommendations and Research Study Report. Washington, DC: Urban Land Institute, 1982.

Philips, E. Barbara, and Richard T. LeGates. *City Lights, An Introduction to Urban Studies*. London, New York: Oxford University Press, 1981.

Planning for Better Housing. Washington, DC: The National Association of Home Builders, 1980.

Planning for Housing, Development Alternatives for Better Environments. Washington, DC: Special Committee on Land Development, National Association of Home Builders, 1980.

Residential Development Handbook. Washington, DC: Residential Council, Urban Land Institute, 1978.

Residential Streets. Washington, DC: Urban Land Institute, American Society of Civil Engineers, National Association of Home Builders, 1974.

Rubenstein, Harvey M. *A Guide to Site and Environmental Planning.* New York: John Wiley & Sons, Inc., 1969.

Rutledge, Albert J. *Anatomy of a Park: The Essentials of Recreation Planning and Design.* New York: McGraw-Hill, 1971.

Rutledge, Albert J. *A Visual Approach to Park Design.* New York: Garland STPM Press, 1981.

Sherderjian, Denise. *Uncommon Genius: How Great Ideas Are Born.* New York: Viking Books, 1990.

Shopping Center Development Handbook. Washington, DC: Commercial and Office Development Council, Urban Land Institute, 1977.

Skokowski, Henry, and Mark Brodeur. "Maintaining the Pedestrian Quality of Small Town Downtowns." In *Urban Design and Preservation Quarterly,* winter 1990.

Stilgoe, John R. *Common Landscape of America: 1580–1845.* New Haven, CT: Yale University Press, 1982.

Tobey, George B. *A History of Landscape Architecture: The Relationship of People to the Environment.* New York: American Elsevier Publishing Company, Inc., 1973. Now distributed by Books on Demand (Ann Arbor, MI), a division of University Microfilms International.

Todd, Kim W. *Site, Space, and Structure.* New York: Van Nostrand Reinhold, 1985.

Tucker, William. "Revolt in Queens." In *The American Spectator,* February 1993.

Untermann, Richard, and Anne Vernez Moudon. "Designing Pedestrian Friendly Commercial Streets." In *Urban Design and Preservation Quarterly,* fall 1990.

Untermann, Richard, and Robert Small. *Site Planning for Cluster Housing.* New York: Van Nostrand Reinhold, 1977.

Unwin, Raymond. *Town Planning in Practice: An Introduction to the Art of Designing Cities and Suburbs.* Princeton, NJ: Princeton Architectural Press, 1994.

VanDyke, Scott. *From Line to Design, Design Graphics Communication,* second edition. PDA Publishers Corporation, 1985.

Wang, Thomas C. *Plan and Section Drawing*. New York: Van Nostrand Reinhold, 1979.

Wentling, John W., and Lloyd W. Bookout. *Density by Design*. Washington, DC: Urban Land Institute, 1988.

White, William H. *City, Rediscovering the Center*. New York: Doubleday, a Division of Bantam Doubleday Dell Publishing Group, Inc., 1988.

Whyte, William H. *The Social Life of Small Urban Spaces*. Ann Arbor, MI: The Conservation Foundation, 1980.

Witherspoon, Robert E., Jon P. Abbett, and Robert M. Gladstone. *Mixed Use Developments: New Ways of Land Use*. Washington, DC: Urban Land Institute, 1976.

Glossary

Absorption The rate at which the components of a project (home, retail space, office space, etc.) are leased or sold.

Band-Aid landscaping Landscape screens or planting buffers used to cover up or mitigate poor planning.

Benchmark A stationary object located by the survey and used as a reference point in the field.

BMP An acronym for *best management practice*. Used in reference to any kind of stormwater management facility (e.g., a retention or detention pond). The term literally means using the best stormwater solution for a given situation.

Boulevard A wide, tree-lined street, sometimes referred to as a *parkway* because of its heavy landscaping.

Brownfield site A piece of land that has been previously developed for another use, typically an urban site, and available for redevelopment.

Charette A brief, intense design workshop in which community design teams work together with municipal staff, city council members, the landowner, the developer, and all interested citizens in order to produce a plan that addresses the needs of the community.

Climax species The ultimate stage of commercial development.

Concept ideation The attempt to relate the goals of the design program to the needs of the market and the constraints of the site.

Conditional zoning A variance in a zoning constraint to allow a use that would otherwise be restricted in exchange for some guarantee or proffer made by a developer to the municipality. For example, higher density may be allowed on a parcel in exchange for open-space development.

Construction documents The plans, details, and elevations or blueprints used for construction.

Conterminous United States The 48 states that share a common boundary.

Demographics The vital statistics and characteristics of human population.

Detention ponds An engineered drainage facility designed to collect stormwater for complete gradual discharge.

Ditch lines Drainage ditches.

Diversity A mixture of uses that provides something for everybody, resulting in activity and vitality.

Dominant element An object that because of some overpowering characteristic (size, color, etc.) commands attention and provides a reference point.

Easement Access rights to a portion of property for which the owner gives up rights of development so that another party (usually government or a utility company) may use it for a specific purpose (e.g., a power line).

Ecosystem The dynamic whole produced by the inhabitants of a living habitat.

Enclosure The sensation created by objects in close proximity to one another.

Euclidean zoning Regulations that compartmentalize land uses into single-use pods. The name is adopted from a landmark U.S. Supreme Court decision in 1926 that confirmed the constitutionality of land-use regulations implemented by the Village of Euclid, Ohio.

Final subdivision plan An accurate scale representation of a proposed land use.

First-tier suburbs The earliest suburbs of an urban-core-style city.

Floodplain The land area adjacent to a body of water or watercourse that is subject to inundation.

Franchise architecture Building forms of similar characteristic, color, and material that are typical of chain stores and fast-food establishments.

Friction Anything that slows down the flow of automobile traffic, requiring vehicle stops and starts (intersections, curb cuts, median breaks, mailboxes, etc.).

Greenfield sites A term that refers to undeveloped land such as agricultural fields or wooded lots. Building housing subdivisions, shopping centers, and office parks on greenfield sites is the prevalent form of land development in suburbia.

Hardsheet The mathematically correct drawing that establishes a project concept in the three-dimensional plane.

Hardship A burden created when general zoning restrictions prohibit owners from using their property in the way they wish.

Infrastructure Streets, storm sewers, pumping stations, sanitary sewer lines, water lines, and so forth that provide the basic framework for daily life.

Ingress/egress Entrance and exit points.

Invert The top of a drainage pipe below grade.

Landschaft A medieval term designating a cluster of dwellings and other buildings immediately surrounded by farm fields, with forest or marsh at the extreme perimeter. The connotation of *landschaft* to its inhabitants was one of both obligation and responsibility to one another and to the land.

Light-duty road A byway used for limited access to some remote area—for example, a road used to access a fire tower.

Open space The non-built environment that provides green relief.

Orthophoto Quadrangle A computer-generated photo produced by the U.S. Geological Survey.

Overlay district A zoning mechanism that defines an area of special use. Overlay districts are often applied over an existing zoning category to provide additional provisions for the use of land within their boundaries (e.g., historic districts).

Parcel A portion of a subdivision (a tract or lot).

Physical survey The field location of physical elements and legal boundaries performed by a qualified land surveyor.

Plan A method of action, a way of doing a thing.

Planned unit development (PUD) A zoning category that allows a mix of land uses, often at a greater density than would be allowed under any other zoning category.

Plat A recordable document that gives form, detail, and substance to a plan.

Plot A two-dimensional hand-drawn or computer-produced graphic.

Primary highway The principal roadway dedicated to vehicular traffic.

Proffer A guarantee made by a developer/owner to provide some kind of service or amenity in exchange for municipal approval of his or her plan. For example, the developer volunteers to pay for extending municipal infrastructure to a site if project approval is granted by the planning commission.

Program The goals/expectations for a project. The desired behaviors or activities that will occur within the subject site, place, or locale.

Quadrangle window The area captured in the USGS map sheet.

Retention An engineered facility for the collection and storage of stormwater.

Review board Some group whose task it is to review proposed land use (planning commission, city council, etc.).

Right-of-way The easement dedicated to municipal use on either side of a publicly owned street.

Rim The pavement or at-grade elevation of a manhole cover or drain inlet.

Ring road The road that forms the outer limits of a shopping mall.

Scenic easement A portion of land on one or both sides of a street that is dedicated to open space or landscaping.

Secondary highway A alternative road to a primary highway (e.g., the two-lane business route at an interstate exit).

Setback That required distance measured from the public right-of-way in which no private construction may encroach without prior approval from the municipality.

Site coverage The percentage of a site that is covered by the built environment.

Stakeholders Those who may be affected by or who have a direct interest in a potential land development project.

Stereo pairs Two overlapping high-resolution stereoscopic photographs.

Stereoscopic photographs Photographs that appear three-dimensional, revealing topographic characteristics when viewed with a stereoscope.

Subdivision plat Recording document that establishes property ownership, utility easements, and public rights-of-way.

Suburban sprawl Uncontrolled development; unplanned creep into the hinterlands.

Superelevation The cross-slope of a high-speed road that allows a vehicle to safely hug the road in a curve.

Takedown A portion of a subdivided parcel of land that is bought at a given time.

Urban growth boundary An arbitrarily drawn line on a map duly voted on by the elected officials of a city that represents the limits to which that city or its suburbs will grow. No city utilities will be extended beyond the line and no land development will be approved.

Vertical curve The parabolic curve that allows safe and efficient vehicular travel on roads with vertical grade change.

Watershed The land area drained by a stream or river.

Index

About the Authors

KENNETH B. HALL, JR., ASLA, is a landscape architect with the award-winning firm Hanbury Evans Newill Vlattas & Company in Norfolk, Virginia, where he specializes in community planning. He holds a B.S. in history from the University of Montevallo and a master's in landscape architecture from Virginia Tech. He has published a variety of articles focusing on issues related to community design and is a member of the American Society of Landscape Architects and the Congress for New Urbanism.

GERALD A. PORTERFIELD is the president of the Porterfield Design Center in Chesapeake, Virginia. He holds a B.S. in landscape architecture from West Virginia University and is a member of the Urban Land Institute, the American Society of Landscape Architects, the Congress for New Urbanism, and the American Planning Association. He is also a frequent speaker on land development issues.